GW00871173

AAT

FOUNDATION TEXT

Foundation Unit 20

Working with Information Technology

July 2001 edition

This Interactive Text for Unit 20 *Working with Information Technology* is designed to be easy on the eye and easy to use.

- Clear language and presentation

- Many illustrations

- Practical examples - with data supplied on CD-ROM for use with Sage Line 50 or Sage Instant Accounting, Microsoft Word and Microsoft Excel

The text fully reflects the standards for Unit 20. It is up to date with developments in subject matter as at 1 June 2001.

BPP Publishing
June 2001

Second edition June 2001

ISBN 0 7517 6520 1 (Previous edition 0 7517 6209 1)

British Library Cataloguing-in-Publication Data
A catalogue record for this book
is available from the British Library

Published by

BPP Publishing Limited
Aldine House, Aldine Place
London W12 8AW

www.bpp.com

Printed in Great Britain by Ashford Colour Press

We are grateful to the Lead Body for Accounting for permission to reproduce
extracts from the Standards of Competence for Accounting, and to the AAT for
permission to reproduce extracts from the mapping and Guidance Notes.

Page

INTRODUCTION

PART A: DATA PROCESSING

PART B: USING ACCOUNTING SOFTWARE

PART C: INFORMATION TECHNOLOGY AND SECURITY

PART D: ASSIGNMENTS

PART E: SOLUTIONS

BPP PUBLISHING

Contents

PART F: APPENDICES

ORDER FORM

REVIEW FORM & FREE PRIZE DRAW

HOW TO USE THIS INTERACTIVE TEXT

Aims of this Interactive Text

> **To provide the knowledge and practice to help you succeed in the devolved assessment for Foundation Unit 20 *Working with Information Technology*.**

To pass the devolved assessment you need a thorough understanding in all areas covered by the standards of competence.

The case study

The case study is about a newly-established company of contract cleaners, Blitz Limited. The company has been operating for just over one month when the assignments in the book begin.

The data for each assignment is held in a separate Sage back-up file on the CD-ROM that accompanies this book. The files allow you to attempt 'later' assignments (eg Assignment 4) without having to do earlier assignments (eg Assignments 1, 2 and 3) first.

The book and CD contains 6 assignments for credit and cash transactions and a variety of simple word processing and spreadsheet exercises. Guidance is given on how to carry out the tasks in each assignment using Sage or Microsoft Word or Microsoft Excel.

How much prior knowledge is needed?

Some basic knowledge of accounting is presumed. You should have an understanding of the logic behind the processing of accounting transactions. This book (ant the Unit 20 syllabus) does not explain ledgers, accounts, invoices, credit notes and so on. It assumes some prior knowledge of what these are and what information they should contain.

Explanations are given for each assignment about how the computerised accounting system is being used, and why. It is important to understand what the computerised processing being performed means in accounting terms.

Using the Sage data with your Sage software

Sage software is produced by the Sage Group plc, the leading producer of accounting software in the UK. The **CD** packaged with this book contains **data** only – you need **access to either Sage Line 50 version 6 or 7, or Sage Instant Accounting version 6** to use this data.

See **Chapter 2 (sections 7 and 8)** and **Appendix 3** for information regarding how to use the data held on the CD.

If you have any queries about setting up Sage software please contact Sage Software Limited – see your Sage documentation for contact details.

FOUNDATION QUALIFICATION STRUCTURE

The competence-based Education and Training Scheme of the Association of Accounting Technicians is based on an analysis of the work of accounting staff in a wide range of industries and types of organisation. The Standards of Competence for Accounting which students are expected to meet are based on this analysis.

The Standards identify the key purpose of the accounting occupation, which is to operate, maintain and improve systems to record, plan, monitor and report on the financial activities of an organisation, and a number of key roles of the occupation. Each key role is subdivided into units of competence, which are further divided into elements of competences. By successfully completing assessments in specified units of competence, students can gain qualifications at NVQ/SVQ levels 2, 3 and 4, which correspond to the AAT Foundation, Intermediate and Technician stages of competence respectively.

Whether you are competent in a Unit is demonstrated by means of:

- *Either* a Central Assessment (set and marked by AAT assessors)

- *Or* a Devolved Assessment (where competence is judged by an Approved Assessment Centre to whom responsibility for this is devolved)

- Or *both* Central *and* Devolved Assessment

Below we set out the overall structure of the Foundation (NVQ/SVQ Level 2) stage, indicating how competence in each Unit is assessed. In the next section there is more detail about the Devolved Assessment for Unit 20.

All units are assessed by Devolved Assessment, and Unit 3 is also assessed by Central Assessment.

NVQ/SVQ Level 2 - Foundation (All units are mandatory)

Unit of competence

Elements of competence

Unit 1 Recording income and receipts	1.1 Process documents relating to goods and services supplied
	1.2 Receive and record receipts

Unit 2 Making and recording payments	2.1 Process documents relating to goods and services received
	2.2 Prepare authorised payments
	2.3 Make and record payments

Unit 3 Preparing ledger balances and an initial trial balance	3.1 Balance bank transactions
	3.2 Prepare ledger balances and control accounts
	3.3 Draft an initial trial balance

Unit 4 Supplying information for management control	4.1 Code and extract information
	4.2 Provide comparisons on costs and income

Unit 20 Working with information technology	20.1 Input, store and output data
	20.2 Minimise risks to data held on a computer system

Unit 22 Monitor and maintain a healthy safe and secure workplace (ASC)	22.1 Monitor and maintain health and safety within the workplace
	22.2 Monitor and maintain the security of the workplace

Unit 23 Achieving personal effectiveness	23.1 Plan and organise own work
	23.2 Establish and maintain working relationships
	23.3 Maintain accounting files and records

BPP PUBLISHING

UNIT 20 STANDARDS OF COMPETENCE

The structure of the Standards for Unit 20

The Unit commences with a statement of the **knowledge and understanding** which underpin competence in the Unit's elements.

The Unit of Competence is then divided into **elements of competence** describing activities which the individual should be able to perform.

Each element includes:

(a) **A** set of **performance criteria.** This defines what constitutes competent performance.

(b) A **range statement.** This defines the situations, contexts, methods etc in which competence should be displayed.

(c) **Evidence requirements.** These state that competence must be demonstrated consistently, over an appropriate time scale with evidence of performance being provided from the appropriate sources.

(d) **Sources of evidence.** These are suggestions of ways in which you can find evidence to demonstrate that competence. These fall under the headings: 'observed performance; work produced by the candidate; authenticated testimonies from relevant witnesses; personal account of competence; other sources of evidence.'

The elements of competence for Unit 20 *Using Information Technology* are set out below. Knowledge and understanding required for the unit as a whole are listed first, followed by the performance criteria and range statements for each element.

Unit 20: Using Information Technology

What is the unit about?

This unit is about using information technology as part of the accounting technician's role. The first element involves inputting data into the computer system using accountancy packages, in line with the organisational requirements. The element also requires the individual to generate unique codes as necessary, identify and correct errors in inputting and make use of search facilities. The individual is also expected to output data as both a hard copy and on disk, and to send it electronically via fax and e-mail.

Knowledge and understanding

General Information Technology

- The relationship between different software packages: accountancy packages; spreadsheets; databases; word processors (Element 20.1)

- The purpose and application of different software packages: accountancy packages; spreadsheets; databases; word processors (Element 20.1)

- Types of data held on a computer system (Elements 20.1 & 20.2)

- How to save, transfer and print documents (Element 20.1)

- Relevant security and legal regulations: data protection legislation; copyright; VDU legislation; health and safety; retention of documents (Elements 20.1 & 20.2)

- The purpose of passwords (Element 20.2)

- Different types of risks: viruses; confidentiality; hardware; software (Element 20.2)

- Causes of difficulties: necessary files which have been damaged or deleted; printer problems; hardware problems (Element 20.2)

The Organisation

- House style for the presentation of documents (Element 20.1)

- Location of information sources (Element 20.1)

- Organisational security policies (Elements 20.1 & 20.2)

- The organisation's computer software, systems and networking (Elements 20.1 & 20.2)

- Organisation procedures for changing passwords and making back ups (Element 20.2)

- Location of hardware, software and back up copies (Element 20.2)

Element 20.1 Input, Store and Output Data

Performance criteria

1 Data to be input into the computer system is clarified with, and authorised by, the appropriate person

2 Data is input and stored in the appropriate location

3 New unique codes are generated as necessary

4 All vital fields are completed

5 Errors in inputting and coding are identified and corrected

6 Data required from the computer system is clarified with the appropriate person

7 Effective use is made of available search facilities

8 Confidentiality of data is maintained at all times

9 Data is output as required in line with agreed deadlines

Range statement

1 Input: manual source documents; computerised source documents

2 Output: print; e-mail; fax; disk; to other systems

Evidence Requirements

- Competence must be demonstrated consistently with evidence of performance being provided of data being input and stored, and then output as a hard copy and on disk, and sent electronically

Sources of Evidence (these are examples of sources of evidence, but candidates and assessors may be able to identify other, appropriate sources)

- Observed performance, eg

    - Inputting information into a computer system

    - Generating new unique codes

    - Correcting errors in inputting and coding

    - Using search facilities

- Work produced by candidate, eg

    - Bar chart

    - Pie chart

    - Histogram

    - Invoice

    - Remittance advice

    - Pay run

    - Statement of accounts

    - Infringement report

    - Flexitime report

    - E-mails or faxes which have been sent

- Authenticated testimonies from relevant witnesses

- Personal accounts of competence, eg

    - Report of performance

- Other sources of evidence to prove competence or knowledge and understanding where it is not apparent from performance, eg

    - Reports

    - Performance in simulation

    - Answers to questions

Element 20.2 Minimise Risks to Data held on a Computer

Performance criteria

1   Work carried out on a computer is saved on a regular basis

2   Back ups of work are made in accordance with organisational procedures

3   Passwords are used where limitations on access to data are required

4   Passwords are kept secret and are discreetly changed at appropriate times

5   The computer is closed down in a way so as not to cause loss of information or damage to the computer system or storage media

6   Immediate assistance is sought in the case of difficulties

7   Hardware and software are securely located

8   Potential risks to data from different sources are identified and the appropriate person is promptly notified

Range Statement

1   Appropriate times: on a regular basis; if disclosure is suspected

2   Difficulties: failure of equipment

3   Potential risks: viruses; confidentiality; hardware; software

4   Sources of data: internal; external

Evidence Requirements

•   Competence must be demonstrated consistently with evidence of performance being provided of potential risks to data from both internal and eternal sources being identified and minimised

Sources of Evidence (these are examples of sources of evidence, but candidates and assessors may be able to identify other, appropriate sources)

•   Observed performance, eg

   - Saving data

   - Backing up work

   - Closing down the computer

   - Seeking assistance

   - Relocating hardware or software

•   Work produced by candidate, eg

   - Report on potential risks

   - Back ups of data

•   Authenticated testimonies from relevant witnesses

•   Personal accounts of competence, eg

   - Report of performance

•   Other sources of evidence to prove competence or knowledge and understanding where it is not apparent from performance, eg

   - Reports

   - Answers to questions

ASSESSMENT STRATEGY

This unit is assessed by **devolved assessment**.

Devolved Assessment

Devolved assessment is a means of collecting evidence of your ability to carry out practical activities and to **operate effectively in the conditions of the workplace** to the standards required. Evidence may be collected at your place of work or at an Approved Assessment Centre by means of simulations of workplace activity, or by a combination of these methods.

If the Approved Assessment Centre is a **workplace** you may be observed carrying out accounting activities as part of your normal work routine. You should collect documentary evidence of the work you have done, or contributed, in an **accounting portfolio**. Evidence collected in a portfolio can be assessed in addition to observed performance or where it is not possible to assess by observation.

Where the Approved Assessment Centre is a **college or training organisation**, devolved assessment will be by means of a combination of the following.

(a)   Documentary evidence of activities carried out at the workplace, collected by you in an **accounting portfolio**

(b)   Realistic **simulations** of workplace activities; these simulations may take the form of case studies and in-tray exercises and involve the use of primary documents and reference sources

(c)   **Projects and assignments** designed to assess the Standards of Competence

If you are unable to provide workplace evidence, you will be able to complete the assessment requirements by the alternative methods listed above.

Part A
Data
processing

BPP
PUBLISHING

1 Introduction to data processing

This chapter contains

1   Hardware

2   Software

3   Input of data

4   Keyboard, mouse and screen

5   Data retrieval

6   Output

7   Distribution

Learning objectives

On completion of this chapter you will be able to:

- Describe the principle hardware and software elements that make up a typical business computer system

- Understand the principles of data input, retrieval, output and distribution

Knowledge and understanding

1   The relationship between different software packages.

2   The purpose and application of different software packages.

3   Types of data held on a computer system.

4   How to save, transfer and print documents.

5   The organisation's computer software, systems and networking.

BPP PUBLISHING

1 HARDWARE

1.1 It is common for a data processing system in business to be a computerised system. Accounting systems in particular are normally computerised, and anyone training to be an accountant should be able to work with them.

1.2 Computer systems consist of two integrated elements - **hardware** and **software**. We will look first at hardware.

1.3 **Hardware** means the physical components (or equipment) which comprise a computer system. This consists of a central processor, devices for data input, storage (filing data) and output or data display, and the wiring, cables and telecommunications links that connect the hardware components to each other.

Central processor

1.4 Every system, from the smallest to the largest, has a central processor. In a typical desk-top PC (personal computer) the central processor consists of several 'boards' of microchips, housed in a plastic box or container that also houses one or two disk drives, and perhaps a CD-ROM or DVD-ROM drive. The diagram below shows a typical configuration.

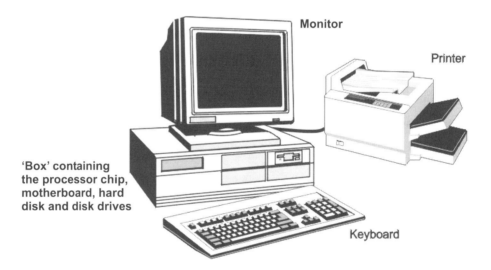

1.5 PCs can be used on their own as **'stand-alone'** computers, or they can be linked to other computers in a **network**, often via a **server** (a more powerful PC), or used as **terminals** for a mainframe computer system.

1.6 In a **network**, several users can share the same files, printers and other facilities and devices. Accounting systems are particularly well-suited to a network system, allowing several accounting to access the same data files.

1.7 **Mainframe** computers are very powerful processors, normally used only by very large organisations such as banks. Older models are enormous and need to be located in a separate, environmentally-controlled-room. Newer mainframes are much smaller and more robust. The only hardware that users of a mainframe computer will normally see is their 'terminal' (keyboard and screen), and perhaps a printer.

Input, storage and output devices

1.8 Equipment is needed to **input** data to the computer for processing, to **store** data on **file** and for the **retrieval** of data or to produce **output** from the system. These are input, storage and output devices.

1.9 Input devices commonly used in office systems are the **keyboard** and the **mouse**. These are used in conjunction with a monitor or VDU screen, which displays the data that is being (or has been) entered for processing.

1.10 The box containing the central processor usually includes one or more 'hard disks' which hold both software and data.

1.11 Data can also be stored on external storage devices. The most common of these is the 3½ inch floppy disk. Other storage devices include magnetic tapes or cassettes, compact discs (CD), digital versatile disks (DVD) and zip disks (a special disk similar to a floppy disk in appearance but with greater storage capacity.

1.12 Computer storage devices, just like audio and video tapes and disks, hold data but need a 'player' - special equipment - to use them. Disks, for example, have to be inserted in a disk drive that can read data from the disk into the central processor or copy data from the central processor to disk. In PC-based systems with one floppy disk drive, the drive is usually called the 'A drive. The hard disk in the central processor is usually the 'C drive'. Similarly, tapes need a tape unit or tape streamer, CDs require a CD drive, and DVDs need a DVD drive. (DVD drives can 'play' CDs, but CD drives can't 'play' DVDs.)

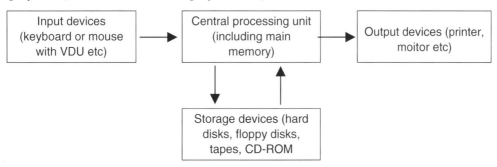

2 SOFTWARE

2.1 **Software** is the general name for all types of computer program. Two main types of software are operating system software and applications software.

2.2 **Operating system software** consists of programs that control the operation of the computer hardware and, quite simply, make the computer operate. PCs use different operating systems from larger computers. PCs generally use a version of Microsoft Windows, such as 95, 98 or Millennium Edition (ME).

2.3 **Applications software** is any program that is written to perform a particular data processing job.

 (a) Examples of **applications packages** are a sales order processing system and a payroll system. Packages might be modules that can either be linked together as part of a larger system, or used on their own. For example, packages for sales order processing, the sales ledger, the purchase ledger, the nominal ledger, stock control and payroll can be linked to form a complete, **integrated** accounting system.

(b) **General purpose packages** are programs that have a broad purpose, but can be adapted to specific requirements of the user. They include word processing packages, spreadsheet packages and database packages.

Word processing packages

2.4 A **word processing (WP) package** has the general purpose of allowing the user to prepare documents. Specific applications of a WP package are writing letters, and producing reports or documents. Examples of WP packages are Microsoft Word and WordPerfect. There are opportunities to use word processing packages later in this book.

Databases

2.5 A **database package** is software that allows the user to create a file of data. The file (a 'database') can then be used for retrieving specific data at any time, according to the user's requirements. Examples of database packages include Microsoft Access and Corel Paradox.

2.6 The term 'database' is also used more generally to mean any major file of data, such as a customer database (for example a file of customer records) a supplier database, a stock control database and an employee/payroll database.

Spreadsheets

2.7 Many accountants use **spreadsheet packages**. A computer spreadsheet can be compared to a large piece of squared paper, whose individual squares ('cells') can be filled with numbers, labels and formulae, to produce a table.

2.8 The user constructs the table he or she wants on the spreadsheet template. Typical uses of spreadsheets are for preparing forecasts and budgets, since these, after all, are simply tables of figures with labels (column headings and row descriptions).

2.9 Examples of spreadsheet packages are Lotus 1-2-3 and **Microsoft Excel**. The use of spreadsheets is covered in depth at the AAT Intermediate stage, but you will have a chance to get some hands-on experience later in this book.

3 INPUT OF DATA

3.1 Data is **input to a computer system for processing**. When data is input, any of the following could happen.

(a) The data might be **processed immediately**, and the results either output from the system or transferred to a file perhaps to a floppy disk or to the hard disk.

(b) The data might be held in a file, for **processing at a future time**.

(c) The data might be used to '**update' or amend other data already held on the file**. For example, an item of data could be input to record the payment of an invoice by a customer, T Smith. This data would update the account for T Smith in the sales ledger file.

    (d)   Input could simply be a **'file enquiry'**, to retrieve an item of data already held on file for displaying on a VDU screen or printing out in 'hard copy' form.

3.2   Data for input to a computer system can sometimes be 'captured' and input **directly at the point where the transaction occurs**. For example, laser readers or bar-code wands are used at many supermarkets.

3.3   In other situations data may be written on paper and the document used when keying the data into the computer system. Here are two examples.

    (a)   A customer order is recorded on a sales order form. This is then used as the source document for input of the sales order transaction details into the sales order processing and accounts systems.

    (b)   A goods received note and the supplier's purchase invoice are used for input to a stock control and purchase ledger system.

3.4   In many computer processing applications, it is usual to collect several source documents of a single type and input the data for all of them at the same time as a 'batch' of transactions.

3.5   EXAMPLE: BATCH PROCESSING

Aston Barton Limited is a Midlands-based company that manufactures carpets for selling to department stores and wholesalers. In a typical week, the company receives ten payments by cheque from customers, and the average cheque amount is £8,000.

It is good financial practice to bank a cheque on the day that it is received. However, the accounts department can wait to input details of the receipts into the accounts system. It might be decided, for example, to process receipts once a week, and input the transaction details in a single batch (of about ten payment transactions each time).

Records and fields

3.6   The data that is input for a particular transaction is sometimes called a **transaction record** or **input record**. Similarly, all the data held on file for a customer, supplier, employee or stock item is called a **customer record, supplier record, employee record** or **stock record**.

3.7   The data in a record is divided into separate items, called **fields**. For example, when data is input to open a new customer account on the sales ledger, the input record will include fields for:

- Customer name
- Customer reference code
- Customer address
- Telephone number
- Contact name
- Credit limit

Data validation

3.8   A program might refuse to accept input data that it knows is invalid. Checks can be carried out **by the program** on any data field or combination of data fields. For example, if a record contains an 8 digit field for the date (such as 31122000 = 31 December 2000) the program might refuse to accept:

- Any letter instead of a figure in the date field
- Any number over 31 for the first two digits combined
- Any number over 12 for the third and fourth digits combined

3.9   Program checks on the validity of input data fields are known as '**data validation**'.

Codes

3.10   Codes are widely used in computer systems, because they **save time** (**and storage space** on file). When sitting the system up, a list of codes and their meaning has to be input, and held on file. Having inserted the non-coded name once, however, the code can be used instead of the full name for all subsequent input of data.

3.11 EXAMPLE: CODES

An accounts system might use codes to identify suppliers and customers, with, say, a 5-letter code for each supplier and a 10-digit code for each customer. The code ROBER could be used to represent a supplier, Robertson Castings Ltd of Great Mill Estate, Skelmersdale Road, Bolton, Lancashire.

To process any transaction involving this supplier, the computer user could simply specify the code ROBER in the supplier reference code field, and the computer system will identify the supplier's name and address (and file record). Typically, as soon as the code is entered, the name (or name and address) will be displayed on the computer user's VDU screen.

Unique reference codes

3.12   In some cases, there must be a **unique** identification code or reference code for each record on file. In a sales ledger system, for example, there must be a unique code to identify each customer. Two different customers **must never have the same code**.

3.13   Similarly, there must be unique reference codes in a purchase ledger system for suppliers, in a stock control system for stock items, and in a payroll system for employees. The field in a record which contains a unique reference code is called the '**key field**'.

3.14   Some codes do not have to be unique. Two or more records on file can have the same code in a particular field. For example, in a payroll system, several employees can have the same tax code, and the same code for their department of employment.

Authorisation

3.15 Only transactions that have been authorised by a person with the required level of authority should be input. Computerised systems have some controls built-in for this purpose, for example only certain log-in names may be able to process journal entries. If you are given an input form or a verbal instruction to process a transaction you should always check that your organisation's authorisation policies have been met.

Deadlines

3.16 Many computer systems support office routines that are carried out regularly, day by day, week by week and month by month. It is often extremely important, particularly in accountancy, that work should be completed by certain deadlines, or as soon as possible after a 'cut-off' date.

3.17 EXAMPLE: DEADLINES

In an accounting system, **end-of-month routines** are carried out as soon as all the relevant data has been input to the system. It can be important to make sure that all this data is input within just a day or so after the month end. Working to deadlines, for both input and output, is therefore a feature of many computer-based systems.

4 KEYBOARD, MOUSE AND SCREEN

4.1 Much input of data for accounting applications is done with a keyboard or mouse, in conjunction with a monitor. To work with computers, you must be familiar with how a keyboard and mouse should be used.

VDU screen or monitor

4.2 The screen facilitates communication between the computer program and the user.

4.3 The screen displays messages or information, and often asks the user to give an instruction or to input data into a field that is indicated by a pointer or **cursor**. The cursor is highlighted on the screen, perhaps in a distinctive colour or as a flashing marker.

4.4 Various kinds of screen message can be displayed.

(a) A screen can give '**prompts**', instructing the user what to do next. The screen can also prompt the user to select from a choice of things to do next, by displaying a selection of different options.

(b) A screen can prompt the user to enter data for a particular field in a record, by displaying the fields on screen and positioning the cursor in the field which should be entered next.

(c) The screen displays the data that the user keys in. The user can check that it is correct before 'entering' it into the system. Incorrect data can then be amended or abandoned before it is entered.

BPP PUBLISHING

Menus

4.5   Many applications packages provide prompts to the user by displaying a list of options for selection in a 'menu'. The user selects an option from the menu, and the screen then shows another display for further processing.

4.6   Some systems use a hierarchy of menus, starting with a main menu at the top of the hierarchy and working down to sub-menus and sub-sub-menus. The program begins by prompting the user to make a selection from the main menu, and then lists a sub-menu for further selection.

4.7   EXAMPLE: HIERARCHY OF MENUS

Windows uses a hierarchy of menus starting from the 'start' button, as shown in the diagram below.

Tabs

4.8   Some systems (eg Sage Line 50) use not only menus but also screens that are laid out like index cards, one underneath another, with a series of **tabs** at the top giving the title of each 'card'. In the following example the tab showing the main **Details** of a supplier's account has been selected.

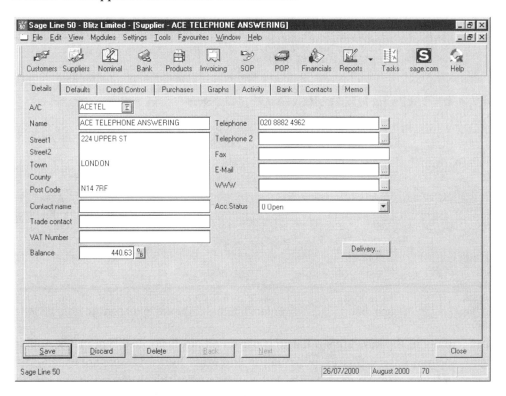

4.9   The user can click on any other tab to get a different information about this supplier. Below, the user has clicked on the tab that says **Activity.**

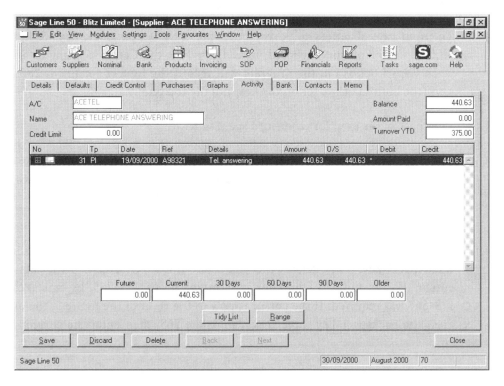

BPP
PUBLISHING

Keyboard

4.10   A typical computer keyboard is shown below.

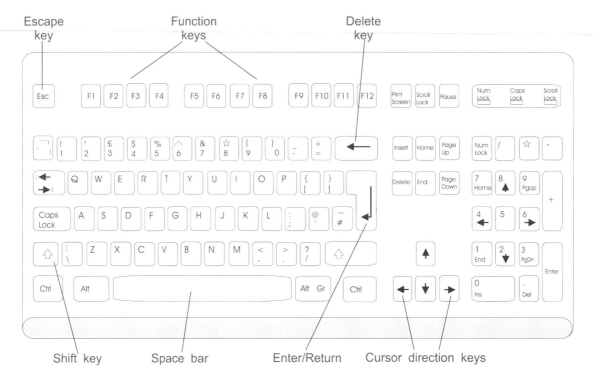

4.11   Many of the keys are similar to those on an old-fashioned typewriter, and are used to enter letters, figures, punctuation and other items. Letters are usually displayed in lower case. To get a capital letter press one of the **shift** keys at the same time as the letter key. Similarly, to enter the top character where two are shown on the same key, for example to get a £ sign from the £/3 key, press the shift key at the same time as the £/3 key.

4.12   To input capital letters for everything, press the **Caps Lock** key. A light will probably show on the keyboard, to indicate that the Caps Lock key is on. Even when Caps Lock is on, the program will record the **figures** for the 1, 2, 3 ... to 0 keys (the bottom character on the key, not the top one).

4.13   The space bar is used for entering a space in text.

4.14   The direction arrow keys ↑ ← ↓ and → can be used to move the **cursor** on the VDU screen in the direction indicated by the arrow. They are sometimes called the cursor up, cursor left, cursor down and cursor right keys. The cursor is a small flashing oblong or vertical line that indicates your current position on the screen.

4.15   The key with the longer arrowed line pointing left, below the F12 key, is a 'backspace' key. This deletes the character shown on screen to the **left of the cursor**. For example, a computer user might input 1234765, by mistake, when 1234567 was required. If the cursor is now to the right of the figure 5, the user can press the backspace key three times, to delete 765, then enter the correct figures 567.

4.16   The **Enter key,** also called the **Return key**, has various uses. For convenience there are two enter keys – one on the right of the 'main' key area and another next to the numeric keypad.

(a) Until the Enter key is pressed (or in some cases the Tab key), the data has not been fully entered into the system.

In the Sage accounting package that you will be using with this book the **Tab** key is used for this function.

(b) The Enter key can be used to **select an option**, for example to select an option from a menu. The direction arrow keys can be used to move the cursor to the menu item required, and the option is then selected by pressing Enter.

(c) When writing a letter, say, or a report, the Enter key can be pressed to move down from one line of text to the next, and 'return' to the left hand side of the next line. The Enter key is also called the Return key for this reason, especially in word processing systems.

4.17 There are five keys associated with **looking through a list of items** on screen; for example, to **search** through a list of customer names and reference codes. Such a list could be very long, and much too long to fit on the screen at the same time, or to search through line by line using the cursor direction keys ↓ and ↑.

4.18 The computer user can search through the list by 'scrolling' down or up to find the record that he or she is looking for.

(a) The **Page Down** key takes the screen down the list.

(b) The **Page Up** key takes the screen back up the list.

(c) The **End** key takes the screen to the bottom items on the list.

(d) The **Home** key is for returning back to the top of the list.

(e) The **Scroll Lock** key is to stop the scrolling up or down, and 'lock' the display on screen at any point in the middle of the list.

4.19 There are 12 **function keys** F1 to F12 at the top of the keyboard. These can be used to give instructions to the computer. The nature of the instruction associated with each key varies from program to program.

4.20 The numeric keys are duplicated on the right hand side in a number pad. These keys are for use with packages where most input is in figures rather than letters. Access to the use of these keys can be obtained by pressing the **Num Lock** key near the top right-hand side of the keyboard.

Mouse

4.21 Most software packages allow the user to enter instructions with a **mouse** as an alternative to using the keyboard. Moving a mouse on a flat surface moves the screen cursor in the same direction. When the cursor is positioned over a desired option, such as a menu choice, clicking the left hand button on the mouse indicates the user's choice to the computer.

4.22 Some packages encourage the use of a mouse by presenting menus or other options in the form of a picture or icon. The mouse can be used to move the cursor to the appropriate icon, and clicking the left hand button makes the desired selection. Newer packages also have uses for the right hand button.

BPP
PUBLISHING

5   DATA RETRIEVAL

5.1   Once data has been input to a system a user may wish to refer to the data, to **look up an item of information**. In most cases he or she will not want a printout of the data, but will simply want to check an item as quickly as possible. The most effective way of doing this is to call an item up on screen, for example, to answer queries from customers about their accounts.

5.2   The method of retrieving data for display on screen (or for printing out) varies from one application package to another. A search facility (the ability to search through files quickly and easily to find data) is provided by many commercial packages. In Sage for example, the user could check the details of a specific supplier's account by selecting:

- The Suppliers option from the main menu
- Clicking once on the supplier concerned
- Entering the details of what transactions are required, eg Date Range
- The transactions are then displayed

The procedure for checking supplier account details is covered later in this Text.

6   OUTPUT

6.1   There are three methods of output available in most computer systems.

- The screen or monitor
- Printed output (hard copy)
- Output to a computer file (to be stored on disk and/or sent via e-mail)

6.2   The VDU screen allows the user to review an individual record or a small piece of information very quickly. **Screen output** is for immediate viewing and is lost when the user moves to another 'page'.

6.3   Printed output (**hard copy**) can be reviewed and re-visited very easily, distributed to different recipients, written on by hand and filed away.

6.4   There are a number of different **types of printer**.

(a)   **Dot matrix printers** are used with continuous feed computer paper, and so are ideal for printing out long reports. The print quality is often not particularly good and the dots that form each character can be clearly seen. Dot matrix printers are used where reports are printed on *multi-part* stationery. Multi-part stationery allows **more than one copy** of a document, such as an invoice, to be **printed at the same time**.

(b)   **Bubble jet or inkjet printers** are quicker and quieter. They are not suited to printing very long reports, but produce better quality output than dot-matrix printers. They use A4 paper.

(c)   **Laser printers** are **more expensive** and offer the best quality print. They too are most commonly used with A4 paper. Laser printers are best suited to tasks which require high quality presentation, such as producing reports.

6.5   Most software packages give clear **instructions to the user about printing selected output**. Prompts on screen could ask the user:

(a)   To choose **between screen display or printout.**

14

(b) To **specify the items for printing**, or **'print range'** (for example, a range of invoice numbers for printing invoices, a range of employee reference codes for printing payslips, or a range of dates to print out the details of all transactions that occurred between the specified dates).

Print layouts

6.6 The **layout** of a printed document in an accounts system, such as list, letter or report, is **specified within the program**. A layout can be altered, and new layouts can be designed, but this will normally be the responsibility of a manager or supervisor in the accounts department.

6.7 The computer user might be required to insert details into a document before printing can take place. For example, it might be necessary to key in invoice details for an invoice production system. The screen should always provide sufficient prompts to allow the user to input the data required.

Using a printer

6.8 Before you use your printer, you should feel fairly confident that you know how to operate it. In particular, be sure that you know how to:

- Switch the printer on
- Check that the printer is *on-line* (ready to print)
- Align the paper properly in the printer
- Move continuous stationery to the top of the next page (if applicable)
- Stop the printer

We shall encourage you to make a record of this information, as far as your college system is concerned, in the next chapter.

6.9 If you use a PC at work, say, check that you know how the printer is connected to the computer. You might at some time need to check the connection, if the printer is not working, to see if a faulty connection is the cause of the fault.

6.10 Printed output should be clean, clearly printed and properly aligned. If the alignment is incorrect (for example, if a single printed page is spread across two pages of continuous stationery because the paper was incorrectly positioned in the printer at the start of printing), you should print the output again. If the print quality is poor you might need a new ink cartridge in your printer.

6.11 Computer systems have a reputation for producing large quantities of paper. To save yourself time, and your company money, you should:

(a) Take sensible precautions about **aligning paper properly** and keeping your printer properly supplied with replacement printing parts (cartridges).

(b) Only print very long reports if there are office routines and procedures that call for their production.

(c) Use **screen displays** for output instead of a printout, where a screen display is sufficient.

(d) When specifying the **'parameters'** for a report, don't make reports unnecessarily long by specifying items for inclusion in the printout that you don't really need.

BPP
PUBLISHING

Output to a disk file

6.12 The third method of output available is to **output data to a disk file**.

6.13 In Sage most reports can be output to either the screen (using the **Preview** option), to a **Printer**, or to a **File**. When requesting a report, the method of output can be selected from the options given on the right of the screen.

6.14 Choosing the **File** option would allow the report to be printed at a later date, or, more likely, would allow you to **use the data in the report file in another application**, such as a word processor or spreadsheet.

6.15 In section 9 of Chapter 2 we will cover this process in detail.

6.16 It is often too expensive for an organisation to provide one printer per terminal or keyboard. A wages department is likely to have its own printer, so that confidential output is not produced where staff can see it. Other departments may not have their own printers, however, but may be linked to a central printing facility.

6.17 Long reports such as a detailed nominal ledger printout or a printout of customer statements may be printed overnight so that the printer is not effectively taken out of action during working hours.

Output to E-mail

6.18 Sage allows you to choose to send a report using e-mail from within the program. This would be done by selecting the E-mail option on the output box. To send e-mail reports from within Line 50 the e-mail addresses you which to send to must be set up within the Report Designer, and your system must have the hardware and software required for e-mail. These are technical issues outside the syllabus of this Paper – just be aware of the availability of the e-mail option. (We look at the use of e-mail in general terms in Chapter 2.)

Printing graphs and charts

6.19 Some software packages give the user an option to produce and print graphs or charts from numerical data. This is a facility with all graphics packages (software written specifically for the production of graphs and diagrams). It is also available with some other types of software, including spreadsheet packages such as Microsoft Excel.

Example

6.20   Carter Doyle Ltd had the following sales turnover in 20X7.

Quarter	Sales
	£000
1	75
2	100
3	175
4	150
Total	500

6.21   If this data were input into a program with a graph production facility, any of the following graphs or charts could be prepared.

Pie chart: Annual sales

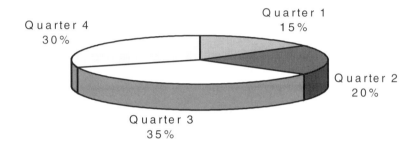

Graph: Time series

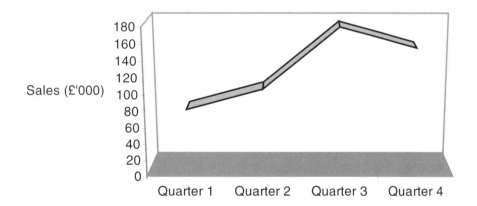

BPP
PUBLISHING

Histogram: Sales per quarter

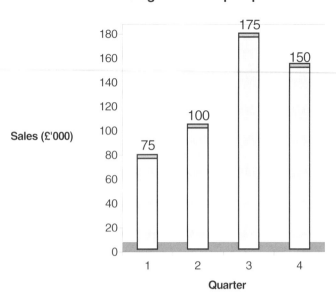

Sales (£'000)

7 **DISTRIBUTION**

7.1 Computer reports should be distributed promptly to the individuals or departments that expect to receive them.

(a) Reports should not be late - managers could be waiting for them and wanting to use them. It is usual for regular reports such as monthly reports to be printed to a specified timetable and deadline. For the reports to be up-to-date, this means having to make sure that all the relevant data has been input and processed.

(b) Reports, once printed, should be distributed promptly. When data is confidential, the reports should be sent in sealed envelopes, with the recipient's name and the words 'STRICTLY CONFIDENTIAL' clearly shown.

(c) Reports may be distributed on paper, or sent via fax or e-mail. We will look at the use of fax and e-mail in Chapter 2.

Quick quiz

1   What is computer hardware? (See paragraph 1.3)

2   What is computer software? (2.1)

3   Name a popular operating system. (2.2)

4   The data in a record is divided into separate items, called _____ ? (3.7)

5   What are the three methods of output available in most computer systems? (6.1)

2 Using PCs and Windows

This chapter contains

Learning objectives

On completion of this chapter you will:

- Understand and be able to perform some basic Windows operations
- Understand some features of word processors and spreadsheets
- Understand the features of fax and e-mail

Knowledge and understanding

1   The relationship between different software packages: accountancy packages; spreadsheets; databases; word processors.

2   The purpose and application of different software packages: accountancy packages; spreadsheets; databases; word processors.

3   Types of data held on a computer system.

4   How to save, transfer and print documents.

5   House style for the presentation of documents.

BPP
PUBLISHING

1 INTRODUCTION

1.1 The chapter aims to teach you the basics of using a PC and Microsoft Windows software.

1.2 We shall assume that you have never used a PC before and that, as far as you know, a window is something that lets in light!

1.3 For many students this won't be true. You may have been using PCs and Windows since you were at school. If so, you can skip the first few sections of this chapter. We suggest you start with sections 6 and 7, so that you understand how to load the Blitz data. Then prove your Windows competence by doing Activity 2.9 in Section 8.

Alternative methods

1.4 There are usually at least two (and often more) different ways of doing the same thing in Windows. For the most part we only describe the options that we think are the easiest for a beginner to learn. If you can find a faster way to do something, or a way that you find easier to remember, or more comfortable for whatever reason, then use it.

1.5 We are also only going to describe those features that are useful in a very general sense, or in a particular sense for the operation of the *Sage Line 50* accounting package. This chapter is not a comprehensive guide to Windows.

Activity 2.1

Find out which version of Windows you will be using on your Unit 20 course.

2 USING PCs

Turning on your computer

2.1 When you first encounter a computer system it can take some time to build up the confidence to use it without someone holding your hand. This is understandable, but remember, a computer is simply a tool that will help you perform certain tasks.

Systems at college or at work

2.2 If you are using a larger system – the one at work or college, say – make sure that your supervisor shows you precisely what buttons to push/switches to switch to get the system going and how to turn it off again when you have finished.

PCs

2.3 If your PC has separate on/off buttons for the screen and the processor, the order in which you turn them on does not really matter. If you want a rule, first turn on the hard disk drive, then the VDU screen (but there is no reason not to do it the other way round).

2.5   The *turning off* procedure needs a little care.

(a)   *Windows 95/98/Millennium Edition (ME)*

If you have Windows 95/98/ME you should close all programs and then click on the **Start** button (even though what you want to do is stop!) and choose the option **Sh̲ut Down...** .

3   WINDOWS: THE BASICS

3.1   A 'window' is a frame that appears on your computer screen. Several different frames may be visible at once, or a single window may occupy the whole screen.

3.2   In the Windows operating system the initial screen is called the **Desktop**. The next illustration shows the desktop (in the background) with a Window that has been called up using the Start button menus.

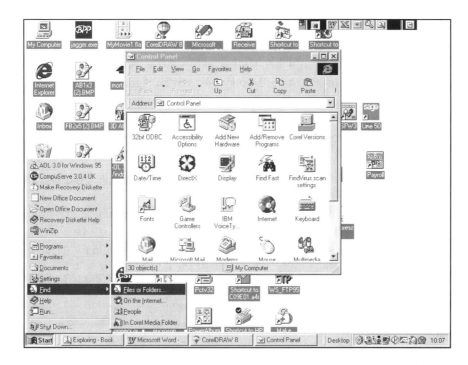

Features common to most windows

3.3   Nearly all windows have three common features

Title bar

3.4   A title, shown in a strip at the top the window. This is sometimes called the **title bar**.

Top left hand corner

3.5   Look up at the very top left-hand corner of the windows illustrated above. There is a symbol in the **top-left hand corner**. You can use this to do a variety of things, but its main use is to *close* the window. (The symbol is different depending upon which program you are using.)

Top right-hand corner

3.6   Now look up at the top **right hand** corner of a window. In Windows 95/98 you have three symbols in the top right-hand corner.

(a)   There is a line, which minimises the window, reducing it to a button on the 'task bar' at the bottom of the screen (where the Start button is).

(b)   There are two squares, one on top of the other. This makes the window a little bit smaller so you can see what else there is on your screen or look at two different windows at once. If your window is already in its 'smaller' state only one square is shown and this makes the window bigger again.

(c)   There is an **X.** This closes the window altogether.

The mouse

3.7   If you slide the mouse connected to your computer from side to side (keep it in contact with the surface you are sliding it on) you will see a white arrow (or 'pointer') moving from side to side on your screen. Here is an Activity for the complete beginner.

Activity 2.2

If you have never used a mouse before you may initially find it difficult to manoeuvre. With a little practice you will wonder why you ever had any problems.

Your first task, if you are a complete beginner, is to sit at a computer with a mouse and play with it for about five minutes.

Practice getting the arrow on screen to the place where you want it to be. Trace round the edges of the screen. Position the *head* of the arrow on top of the different shapes and symbols and words you can see on the screen. See what happens to the arrow when you lift the mouse from the surface of the mouse mat and put it down in a different place. Can you make the arrow disappear right off the edge of the screen?

Clicking and selecting

3.8   Pressing a button on a mouse is called *clicking*. Make sure that your mouse arrow is not pointing at anything other than space on the screen and then press the left button once only.

3.9   If you point the head of your mouse arrow at a particular symbol or word on the screen and click the left mouse button once, the word or the symbol's 'label' is highlighted.

3.10   This is known as **selecting**. The thing that is highlighted is 'selected', in the sense that **the next action carried out on the computer will only be done to the thing or things that are selected**. This is a general rule in any Windows program and it is an important thing to remember.

3.11   The next activity gives you some clicking practice and shows you what a menu looks like. We talked about menus in Chapter 1.

Activity 2.3

Some people find it very difficult to take a photograph without their hand shaking. Some people find clicking very difficult at first.

(a)   Being careful to click only once (otherwise you might start up a program that you don't want to start up), see if you can *select* each of symbols and words shown on your screen so that the label is highlighted.

Selecting some will result in a list of words springing out of the symbol. This is a menu. Ignore this and click with your mouse on the next symbol. The menu will disappear (or a different menu will appear: ignore this too). (Generally, to get rid of anything on the screen that you have called up and no longer want to see, press the **Esc** key on the keyboard.)

(b)   Click on the word Start and see what happens. Try clicking on things with the *right* mouse button.

Closing down the Windows operating system 95/98

3.12   You close down Windows via the **Start** button and the **Shut Down** option. When you click on this you get the following message.

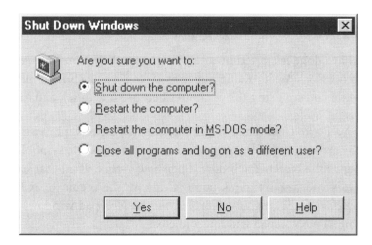

3.13   For now, however we don't want to shut down, so click on the **No** button (or **Cancel** in some versions) and the message will just disappear. Clicking on buttons to make things happen (or not happen) is something you do all the time in Windows.

4   WINDOWS: STARTING THINGS UP

4.1   We are now going to see how to start up an application in Windows. We shall also learn about two more things that you can do with a mouse.

4.2   Click on **Start,** then move your mouse pointer up the menu to **Programs,** then across to **Accessories,** then to **Notepad.** Click on this to start up Notepad.

Notepad

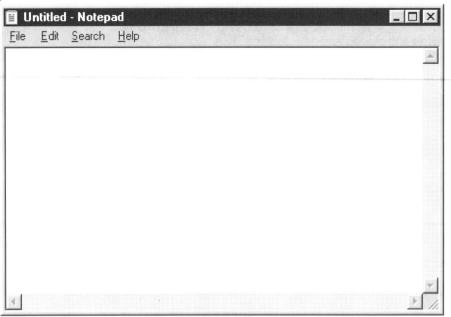

Double-clicking and making things happen

4.3 What you have done is started up an application called Notepad – a very basic sort of word processor. As its name suggests it can be useful for making notes to yourself while you are using the computer because it is quick and easy to use.

4.4 Assuming you are a complete beginner, we will briefly practise *double-clicking*. Position the arrow head of the mouse pointer over the little symbol in the top left-hand corner of the Notepad window. Then *double-click*. If all that happens is that a menu appears you weren't quick enough. Ignore the menu (or make it disappear by pressing Esc or clicking anywhere *within* the Notepad window) and try *double-clicking* again. The Notepad window will close.

5 MORE FEATURES OF WINDOWS

5.1 Start up the Notepad application. We are now going to use it to learn some more mouse skills and one or two keyboard shortcuts.

For reference, the diagram of a typical keyboard from Chapter 1 follows.

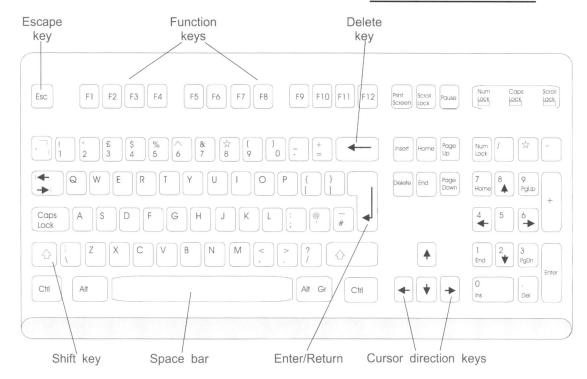

Escape key

Function keys

Delete key

Shift key   Space bar   Enter/Return   Cursor direction keys

Activity 2.4

Having started up Notepad use the keyboard to type your name, then press the Return key to take you to the next line.

Now type the numbers 1 to 10, using the number keys above the letters. Each time you type a number press either the Return key or the Enter key. (This is just to satisfy you that they do exactly the same thing.)

You should have ten lines on screen numbered 1 to 10, and a line with your name in it.

Next key in the numbers 11 to 20 on consecutive lines, but this time use the numeric keypad at the right of the keyboard. This will only work if the Num Lock light (above the keypad) is lit. If it is not, press the Num Lock key. You will find it more convenient to use the Enter key this time, since it is next to the numeric keypad.

You should now have twenty lines on screen.

Next key in the letters A to Z, on consecutive lines. Key some in as small letters (lower case) and some as capitals (upper case) using the shift key.

You should now have typed 47 lines, but you won't be able to see the first ones you typed on screen any more.

Now find *three* different ways of getting back to the line you typed (with your name in it).

Scrolling and the cursor

5.2   *Six* ways are as follows. Try them all out.

(a)   Use the direction arrow keys. Press and hold down the upward pointing arrow key to the left of the numeric keypad. The black vertical line that flashes continuously on the screen and marks your place will move slowly back up the screen until you reach the first line.

The black vertical line is called the *cursor*. Moving it in this way is called *scrolling*. You can also move it within a line by using the left and right direction arrow keys.

BPP PUBLISHING

(b) To get to the last line again press the Page Down key several times. Then to get back to the beginning press the Page Up key several times. This is a form of scrolling in larger leaps.

(c) T o get to the last line again hold down the Ctrl key and press the End key. Then to get to the *beginning* again hold down Ctrl and press Home. This takes you directly from one point to the other.

(d) Press Ctrl + End to get to the last line again. Then use the mouse. At the right hand side of the screen is a grey strip with an arrow at the top and bottom.

Position your mouse pointer at the top of this strip over the upward pointing arrow. Press down the left mouse button and hold it down. You will see a little button-like marker gradually rising up the grey strip. Your screen will scroll back to the beginning. The grey strip is called a vertical scroll bar. Note that there is a similar scroll bar (a 'horizontal' one) along the bottom edge of the screen. This is used if the line you type is too long for the width of the screen to display it all at once.

(e) Click once in the scroll bar just below the up arrow (assuming the cursor is at the last line). The little box in the scroll bar will jump about halfway up. Click in the same place again and you will be back to the beginning. This is like the Page Up/Page down option.

Note that with the scroll bar method the cursor stays where it was – only the screen display scrolls. However, if you click anywhere in one of your typed lines the cursor will instantly jump to that place.

(f) Position the arrowhead of the mouse pointer directly over the grey button in the scroll bar. Press down on the left mouse button and hold it down. Keeping the mouse button held down, move the pointer up to the top of the scroll bar (or to the bottom if you are already at the top) and release the mouse button. You will see a ghostly outline of the little grey button whizzing along in the scroll bar. It will only appear again properly when you release the mouse button. This is the mouse equivalent of the Ctrl + Home and Ctrl + End option.

This use of the mouse is called *dragging and dropping*.

5.3 You will find these scrolling techniques useful when using Sage Line 50.

Holding down the mouse button

5.4 There are two ways in which holding down the left mouse button whilst moving the mouse can be useful.

(a) For dragging and dropping, as described. This is especially handy in, for example, a more sophisticated word processing package, where you can drag and drop sentences or even paragraphs of text from one position in a document to another.

(b)   As a means of *selecting* items. For example, scroll back to first line of your Notepad screen. Notice that when the mouse pointer is in the white part of the screen it changes to an I shape. Position the pointer before (to the left of) the first character you typed (the first letter of your name) and press down the left mouse button. Keeping the button held down move the mouse downwards until you reach the last line. Then you can release it. All the characters you typed will now be highlighted.

As mentioned earlier, when something is highlighted it is *selected* as the object of the attention of all the actions that follow until it is deselected again. Press the Delete key. All your hard work will disappear! However, click on the word **Edit** at the top of the screen and then on the **Undo** option on the menu that drops down. All your hard work reappears, still highlighted!

Type the letter R. The letter R *replaces everything* that was highlighted. Undo this action in the same way as before.

Activity 2.5

How could you have 'undone' your deletion without using the mouse?

Moving and resizing windows

5.5   Position the mouse pointer arrowhead anywhere on the *title bar* of the Notepad window (the strip where it says Notepad). Hold down the left mouse button and move the mouse slightly as you do so. The edges of the window frame will go fuzzy and if you continue to move the mouse while keeping the button held down the whole window will move too. Take the Notepad window for a spin round the screen and drop it (by releasing the mouse button) in a different place to where you found it.

5.6   This may seem like a frivolous Activity, but is very useful in applications that show you a new window at the drop of a hat without the current one disappearing from the screen. You end up with lots of little windows covering up bits of each other that you want to see, so it is very useful to be able to move them around in this way. (It is a bit like shuffling pieces of paper around, a time-honoured office pastime!)

(If you accidentally click outside the Notepad window during this Activity, it will either vanish or the title bar will go dim. To re-activate Notepad, hold down the Alt key and press Tab repeatedly until you see a message saying Notepad, or the title bar goes bright again. Then release the Alt key.)

Resizing windows

5.7   It is sometimes (though not always) possible to change the shape and size of a window, too. You do this by moving your mouse pointer to one of the edges of the window. Just as it passes over the edge it changes shape and becomes a two-headed arrow, holding the frame in a vice-like grip. If you now click and hold down the left mouse button, you can pull out the side of the rectangle you are 'holding', elongating the window. Try it with the Notepad window: it is a bit tricky at first to get the point right on the edge so that it turns into a two-headed arrow, but persevere and you will get the knack.

5.8 You can resize a window in two dimensions at once if you point at one of the corners until the pointer turns into the two-headed arrow and then hold down the left button and drag.

5.9 Most people find these two features of Windows rather satisfying when they first encounter them, so don't be ashamed to play with them for a short while. As we have said, they are useful techniques.

6 FILING WITH WINDOWS

6.1 Without clearing your typing from the Notepad screen *double-click* on the symbol or on the square at the top **left-hand** corner of the window, just like you did when you were learning to double-click. Instead of the window disappearing instantly you get a message.

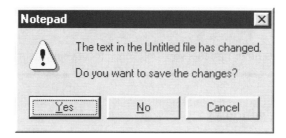

6.2 You are now going to have your first encounter with the Windows filing system.

6.3 A 'file' in a computer system is a single document (or other collection of data) of a particular *type*. A word-processed letter would be one file. A spreadsheet would be another. It is not a file in the sense of something that you put pieces of paper into. In a computer system this sort of container is called a *directory*.

6.4 If you click on **Yes** when you get the above message a new window will appear.

Save As

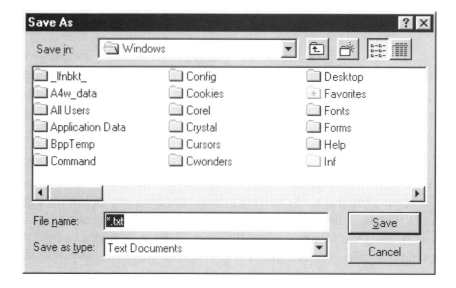

Saving files

6.5 The Save As window is common to all Windows-based applications that have a facility for storing data in a file.

6.6 When the window first appears the File Name box is highlighted. Don't type anything here yet. You can move from section to section of this window by pressing the **Tab** key. This is the key above the Caps Lock key on your keyboard. Each time you press this, a different item in the window becomes highlighted (or is surrounded by a dotted line). Try this out.

You can move back and forward between consecutive items if you wish. To move back you hold down the **shift** key – the one you would use for capital letters – and press **Tab**. Try this out too.

6.7 This use of the Tab key is an important aspect of the Sage Line 50 accounting package, so get some practice in now.

6.8 We shall now conduct you on a guided tour of the Save As window. We do so in the order in which you should make decisions or check things, not in the order of Tabbing.

Activity 2.6

Read the relevant paragraphs below and find out what part of the Save As window actually specifies where a file will be saved.

Save in

6.9 You must first decide where you want to save your file. This is like deciding what *filing cabinet* you are going to keep a paper file in. Computers store data in different 'drives'. There is a hard drive, where the data is written onto a disk which is part of the computer equipment itself, a 'floppy drive' where floppy disks can be used and sometimes a CD Read/Write drive allowing data to be he data is written onto a CD. The hard drive is usually called drive C, floppy drive A and the CD-ROM is often D.

6.10 Click on the arrow at the right of the **Save in** box. A list of the drives available will appear and you can select the appropriate drive by clicking on its name.

6.11 Select the C drive. The result will be something like this.

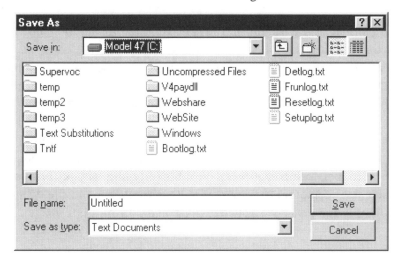

6.12 If you were going to save your file you would search for an appropriate directory and sub-directory by *double-clicking* in this way until you found one. You might have a directory on your floppy disk in the A drive called 'Notes', say. To save the file there, you would need to *double-click* in the Save in and directories boxes until the Save in box said 'Notes'.

Save as Type

6.13 As a rule you won't need to do anything with this box. It specifies the format in which the file will be saved, and it will always suggest the usual format for documents created in the application you are using. For the Notepad application the usual format is as a Text (.TXT) file. For a letter created in, say Microsoft Word, it is as a Word Document (.DOC) file. For a spreadsheet created in Microsoft Excel it is as an Excel (.XLS) file, and so on.

6.14 If you did want to change the format that Windows suggests here, you would click on the down arrow to see if data created by this application can be saved in another format. In the case of Notepad there are no real alternatives, but there *are* other possibilities in, for example, the Sage accounting package.

6.15 The file type shown in the File Type box also determines what files are listed in the box above it. In our example, there are no TXT files in the windows sub-directory, so there is nothing listed in this box.

File Name

6.16 When the window first appears this box is highlighted. It shows an asterisk, a full stop and three letters. In place of the asterisk you must choose a name for your file. You are not actually going to save it on this occasion (unless you want to), but you should know the basic rules for file names.

(a) The name should be something sensible that will help to identify the file if you want to find it again at a later date. Although Windows 95/98 allows long file names, it is often more efficient to use shorter names.

(b) If you want to create a series of files of the same type and on similar subjects, it is helpful to number them sequentially. If you are sure there are going to be fewer than ten such files you can use 1, 2, 3, etc, but it is usually better to be safe and use 01, 02, 03, because the Windows filing system sorts numbers in order of the first digit. If you numbered some files 1, 2, 3, etc up to 10 they would be sorted in the order 1, 10, 2, 3, etc.

(c) The format of the file must always be reflected in the file name by the three characters after the full stop. This is known as the file *extension*. There is no need for you to type an extension yourself. You can just type something like **NOTES01** in the file name box and Windows will automatically give the extension specified in the File Type box, in this case **.TXT**.

6.17 If there were existing files listed in the box below the File Name box you would be able to just click on one of them and it would appear in the box above where you could edit it. This can sometimes save a bit of typing. If you try to save one file with the name of another, however, it will overwrite the old file. Windows warns you about this and gives you a chance to change your mind.

Activity 2.7

You are going to save ten files. Devise a file name for each file incorporating part of your name (or your initials, or something that identifies you) and consecutive numbers.

Switching between applications

6.18   Before you close Notepad it is worth learning a very useful keyboard trick. Without closing Notepad, click on the Start button, go to Accessories and start up the Calculator.

Alt + Tab

6.19   Now press and hold down the Alt key, then press the Tab key once, but do not let go of the Alt key. A grey box will appear in the centre of the screen showing all open applications.. Now let go of the Alt key. You will instantly transfer to the application named in the grey box. Do this again, but this time before letting go of the Alt key press Tab several times. Each time you do so the name in the grey box changes, and if you release the Alt key you are taken to the application named in the box. Use this trick to find your way back to Notepad.

Closing down

6.20   This concludes our guided tour of the Save As window. You can just click on the **Cancel** button, then close File, Exit and answer No when asked if you wish to save your changes.

Windows Explorer

6.21   One of the most important applications in Windows 95/98 is **Windows Explorer**. Amongst other things, this allows you to see what directories and files are on a disk, make copies of files and disks, move files around from one directory to another, look at the files in a directory in date order, or name order, or file type order, and to search for files.

6.22   It is quite possible, however, that your college system prevents you from using Explorer. This will be to stop people accessing files and directories that do not belong to them.

6.23   However, your tutor will probably be willing to give you a demonstration. They work in much the same way as the Drive and Directory and File list boxes that we have just been looking at.

7   LOADING THE BLITZ DATA

7.1   In this section we explain how to use the Sage data contained on the CD that accompanies this Text. You **do not need to load the data while reading this section**. The instructions provided later in this book, at the start of each assignment, tell you when to load the data.

7.2   Blitz is the name of the fictional company on which the case study in the remainder of this book is based. The CD contains data files to be used with either

Sage Line 50 or Sage Instant. To use this data **you need to have access to Sage Line 50 or Sage Instant - the CD does not contain Sage software** (BPP is not entitled to give away Sage software!).

7.3　The data is held on the CD in standard **Line 50** and **Instant back-up files**. Each back-up file has been named to make it clear which assignment it relates to. You load the data that represents the starting point for each Assignment by starting Line 50 or Instant and then restoring the relevant back-up.

Loading the Sage data

7.4　The latest version of Sage **Line 50** (at the time of publication) is version 7. As many users are still using Line 50 version 6, we have provided a set of data in **version 6** format and a set in **version 7** format.

7.5　The latest version of Sage **Instant** (at the time of publication) is version 6. The Sage Instant data is provided in **version 6** format.

7.6　When working through the remainder of this book you will come across instructions such as 'load the data for Assignment 1'. You should then...

Step 1　Ensure the **CD is in your CD-ROM drive** (you will not see anything happen after inserting the CD – it is not designed to auto-run).

Step 2　**Start Sage Line 50 or Sage Instant.** If you do not know whether you have Line 50 version 6 or Line 50 version 7 read the box that pops up immediately after you start Line 50.

Step 3　From the Sage main menu select **File, Restore.** You will see a box similar to that shown below. Click on the down arrow next to the Drives box, then select the letter of your CD-ROM drive.

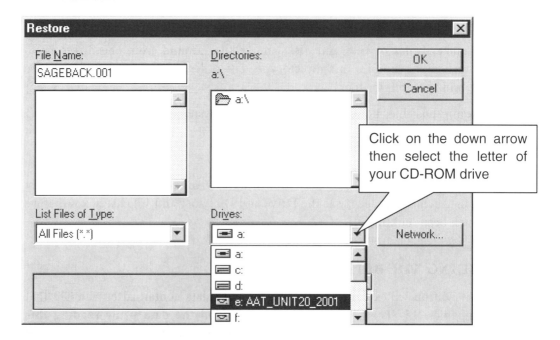

Step 4   You should now be able to see the contents of the CD in the directories window – as shown below. (In the diagram below the CD-ROM drive is drive E – your drive may use a different letter.)

Double-click the folder that relates to the Sage software you are using;

If you are using Instant double click **instantdata_ver6**

If you are using Line50 version 6 double click **line50data_ver6**

If you are using Line50 version 7 double click **line50data_ver7**

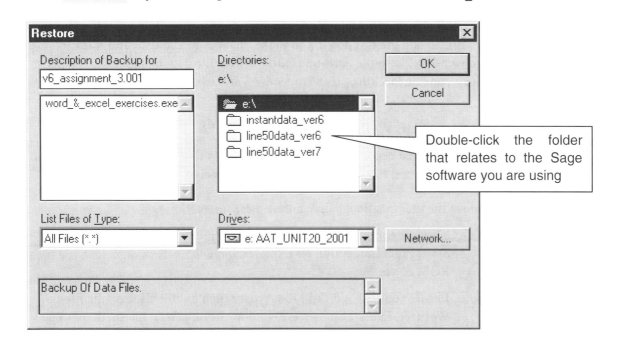

Step 5   We now need to choose the Assignment to restore from the large white box below the File Name box. The **Assignment number is the number before the dot**. For example, if we are using Line 50 version 6 and we wish to load Assignment 3 we would click once on v6_assignment_**3**.001 to highlight it, and then click on **OK**.

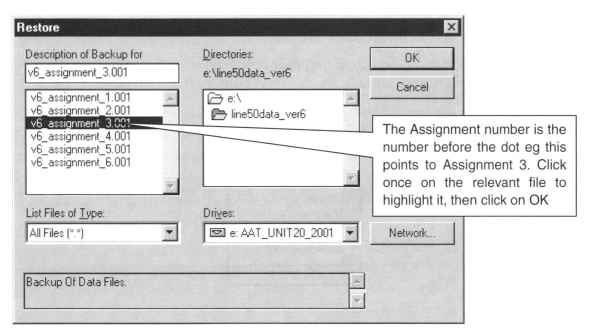

BPP PUBLISHING

Step 6   You should now see a box telling you the **Restore has been successful**. Click on OK. The assignment is now loaded.

(As a check, if you click on Customers you should see a list of Blitz's customers.)

Overwriting Blitz data

7.7   Whenever you load up an Assignment (by restoring the relevant file) Sage **overwrites** any existing data. You cannot prevent it from doing this because that is what it is designed to do! If you make changes to the data and want to save them you should use the back-up facility to save the data to a floppy disk. (Refer to the section on 'backing up' in Appendix 3 at the back of this book.)

8   LOADING THE WORD AND EXCEL FILES

8.1   The CD-ROM that accompanies this book includes five Microsoft Word files and four Microsoft Excel files. The files are used in exercises throughout the book.

8.2   To unload the files to a floppy disk follow these instructions.

Step 1   View the contents of the CD-ROM in Windows Explorer. (eg Click on Start, Programs, Windows Explorer and double-click onto your CD-ROM drive.)

Step 2   Ensure you have a disk in the A drive then double click on the file Word_&_Excel_exercises.exe. Follow the on-screen instructions. (You will need to click OK, Unzip then OK – in that order.)

Step 3   You should see the following.

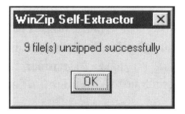

Click OK, then click on Close.

8.3   If you view the contents of the floppy disk in Windows Explorer you will see the files available for use in Word (the .doc files) or Excel (the .xls files).

9   USING A WORD PROCESSOR

9.1   We could devote a whole book to the many facilities offered by a modern word processing package. All we are going to do here is give you a brief overview and then set you an Activity.

Word processing

9.2   We are going to tell you a bit about Microsoft Word, one of the most commonly used word processors. There is little difference between the main competitors these days: manufacturers are quick to copy each others' good features, and it is in their interests that users find it easy to transfer from another system to the one that they make.

9.3   If you start up Word you will be presented with a window something like (but not exactly like) the following.

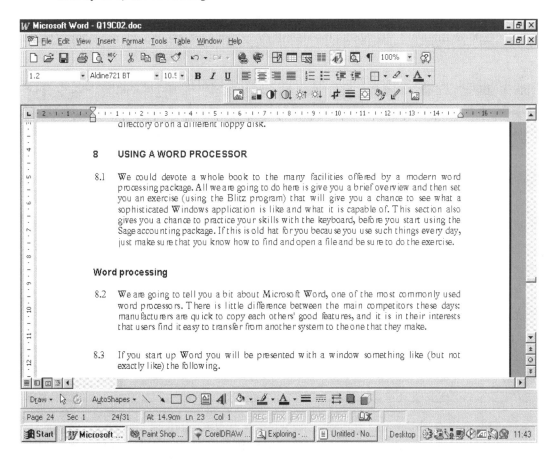

9.4   The main part of the screen is the area where you type, of course. At the top of the screen there is a bank of buttons and arrows that do useful things like **embolden** or *italicise* a word or words that you have selected, change the font style or ₛᵢzₑ of selected text, or place text in the centre of the page, or set it to one side of the page. A host of other things can be done and you can create your own customised buttons to do them if you like.

In recent versions of Word, if you let the mouse pointer linger over a particular button (without clicking on it) a little label soon pops up telling you what it does. This is more fun than reading a book about it so we won't describe the buttons further.

BPP
PUBLISHING

Activity 2.8

Open your word processor, type in something (copy a paragraph of this book if you like) and then *select* a portion of text (see below if you can't remember how) and try clicking on different buttons.

9.5 The ruler below the buttons is used to set the left and right margins of the page and to indent paragraphs. You do this by dragging and dropping the triangular markers that you can see at either end of the ruler. The paragraphs on this page that you are reading now, for example, are indented by moving the lower of the two left-hand triangles in to the 1 mark.

9.6 The menu choices just below the title bar of the screen offer a huge range of further options. We are going to look at several of the most commonly used.

File: Open

9.7 Click on the word **File** and a menu will drop down which includes the item **Open**. If you click on this, a window like the following will appear.

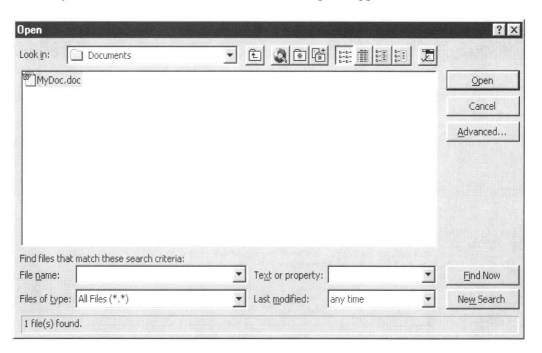

9.8 This is very much like the Save As window that we looked at earlier. To open a particular file you would click on the **Look in** box arrow to specify the drive (if it is not the one shown already) then *double-click* in the directories box to pick the directory. A list of all the Word type files in the chosen directory will appear. Click on the file name that you want and that name will appear in the File Name box. Then you click on OK to open the file.

Double-clicking on a file name has the effect of both selecting it and clicking on OK to open it.

File: Save As

9.9 This is menu option is the same as the one we looked at when we were experimenting with Notepad.

9.10 The important point to add here is that you can open a file that has one name, make some changes to it, and then save it with another name. The effect is that the file you originally opened remains in its original form, but the file with the new name retains all of your changes. Thus you could open a file containing a letter to Mrs Smith called Smith.Doc, change the name and address details, and save it as Jones.Doc. You would end up with *two* files – one called Smith.Doc and the other called Jones.Doc.

File: Close

9.11 Once you have finished with your file you must close it. Click on **File** and then on **Close** in the drop down menu. If you haven't already done so you will be asked if you want to save any changes you made.

File: Print

9.12 If you have a document open and you wish to print it, click on the **Print** option in the **File** menu. The following box will appear.

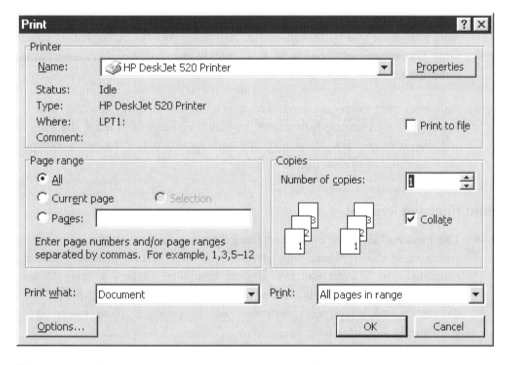

9.13 There are options to print more than one copy of the same document, to print only the page that your cursor was on when you clicked on the Print option or to print specific pages of your document. Just click in the relevant white spaces or on the arrows to make changes to any of the settings that come up when the window is first displayed.

9.14 An important point to check before you click on OK is the first line, which tells you which printer the document will be printed on.

Edit: Cut, Copy and Paste

9.15 The cut, copy and paste facilities are so useful that there are probably toolbar buttons for them as well as menu items. They are used as follows.

(a) Select some text. Do this by positioning the mouse pointer at the beginning of the first word, holding down the left mouse button and, keeping the button held down, moving the mouse to the end of the last word (not forgetting any punctuation marks) and then releasing the button. This portion of text will now be highlighted.

(b) Click on **Edit** at the top of the screen. A menu drops down.

(i) To retain the highlighted text in its current place and also to make a copy of it which is retained temporarily in the computer's memory, click on **Copy.**

(ii) To remove the highlighted text from its current place, but also keep it temporarily in the computer's memory, click on **Cut.** The highlighted text will disappear.

(c) Move the cursor to the point in your document where you want to move the highlighted text or place a copy of it. Do this using the direction arrow keys or by pointing and clicking with the mouse.

(d) Click on Edit again and choose **Paste.** The text you highlighted will reappear in this new place.

9.16 Note that what you paste will be the last thing you cut or copied. If you cut out some text meaning to put it in later, but before you get there you cut or copy something else, the first thing you cut will be lost.

9.17 Note also that there are keyboard shortcuts for cutting, copying and pasting. These are listed on the **Edit** menu. In Word you can even *drag* the selected text and *drop* it in the new place. Try this with a sentence of the text you typed in at the beginning of this section.

Edit: Find and Replace

9.18 The **Find** and **Replace** options on the **Edit** menu are very useful. Suppose you had a document that included lots of references to a certain product made by your company: the 'Widget 98', say. If your company releases a new 'Widget 2000' version of the product, it will be a slow process to scroll through the entire document and retype every instance of the product name when you see it. Fortunately you don't have to.

(a) Click on **Edit** and then on **Replace.**

(b) A window appears that allows you to type in one box 'Widget 98' and in another 'Widget 2000'.

(c) You then have a choice of buttons to click.

(i) The **Find next** button will take you directly to each successive instance of 'Widget 98' in the document.

(ii) The **Replace** button will replace a particular instance of 'Widget 98' with 'Widget 2000'.

(iii) The **Replace All** button will automatically replace *every* instance of 'Widget 98' with 'Widget 2000'. This sounds better than option (ii), but there may be cases where you only want *some* of the examples of 'Widget 98' replaced.

You might think that it would be simpler still to find '98' and Replace All with '2000', but give this some thought: there may be other instances of the number 98 in the document, such as 'This is the new improved version of the well-loved Widget 98'.

Format: Paragraph

9.19   This item on the **Format** menu offers you (amongst other things) a better way of spacing out paragraphs than pressing return several times to leave blank lines.

9.20   Clicking on the **Paragraph** option in the **Format** menu brings up a window with a Spacing section which allows you to specify the number of 'points' (small units of vertical space) before paragraphs and after them. For example there are '18 pts' between this paragraph and the previous one.

Tools: Spelling

9.21   Finally we come to what is the best feature of word processors for bad spellers and clumsy typists. Click on **Tools** and then on **Spelling** in the drip down menu. Word will work right through your document seeing if the spelling matches the spelling of words in the computer's dictionary. If not it suggests alternatives from which you choose the correct one. For example, if you type 'drp', the choices you are offered include 'drip', 'drop', 'dry' and 'dip'. Do you think this paragraph has been spell-checked?

9.22   People sometimes forget that computer spell-checkers only recognise mistakes if they don't match a word in the computer's dictionary. For example, if you type 'form' instead of 'from' the computer will not realise you have made a mistake. It is also easy to make mistakes with a spell-checker if you are too eager to accept its first suggestion. The previous paragraph has a deliberate example.

Activity 2.9

Unload the Word and Excel activities onto a blank floppy disk in the way described earlier in this chapter.

(a)   Open the file 0Ex01. If you are using a word processor other than Microsoft Word you may have to follow simple instructions on the screen for converting the document into another format. Accept all the default options offered: in other words just say yes to everything your computer suggests.

(b)   Look through the document quickly and then *save* it with an appropriate new file name (but not with the name of any other file already on the disk).

(c)   Embolden the subject heading 'New solutions from Good Solutions'.

(d)   Type the following new paragraph at the beginning of the letter:

Widget users will be pleased to hear of the release of *Widget 2000*. This is the new improved version of the well-loved Widget 98.

(e)   Move the three lines 'The Widget 2000 is based ... rest follow' to the end of the *current* first paragraph of the letter.

(f)   Rearrange the features listed so that 'Same day delivery ...' comes first, and 'No leakage' comes before 'Stackable for easy storage'.

(g)   Alter the font of the letterhead and make it stand out in some way. Reposition the letterhead as you think appropriate.

(h)   Alter any other aspect of the layout of the letter that you think could be improved.

BPP PUBLISHING

(i)   Correct any mistakes that you can find.

(j)   Make sure that the letter all fits onto one page.

(k)   Run a final spell check when you are satisfied that the letter is otherwise perfect.

(l)   Save the letter and produce another copy to be sent to Ms Ann Richard, Spokes & Co Ltd, 99 Denton Drive, Mulcaster, Yorkshire, MS3 9RG. Save this second copy with a different filename.

(m) If you have access to a printer, print out a copy of both letters.

Finally close any open files and exit from your word processor.

House style

9.23   Some organisations use the same font and formatting options for all documents. This ensures consistency and presents a professional image. If your organisation has a house-style ensure you know how to apply it to your documents.

10   USING SPREADSHEETS

10.1   Spreadsheets are covered in greater depth at AAT Intermediate level. However, there are several activities involving simple spreadsheet tasks in the Blitz case study.

10.2   A spreadsheet is essentially an **electronic piece of paper** divided into **rows and columns** with a built in pencil, eraser and calculator. It provides an easy way of performing numerical calculations.

10.3   The main examples of spreadsheet packages are Lotus 1-2-3 and Microsoft Excel. We will be referring to Microsoft Excel, as this is the most widely-used spreadsheet.

10.4   When a 'blank' spreadsheet is loaded into a computer, the VDU monitor will show lines of empty rows and columns. **Rows** are always **horizontal** and **columns vertical**. The **rows** are **numbered** 1, 2, 3 . . . etc and the **columns lettered** A, B C . . . etc.

10.5   Each square is called a '**cell**'. A cell is identified by its reference according to the row or column it is in, as shown below.

	A	B	C	D	E	F	G	H
1	A1	B1	C1	D1	E1	F1	G1	H1
2	A2	B2						
3	A3		C3					
4	A4			D4				
5	A5				E5			
6	A6					F6		
7	A7						G7	
8	A8							H8

10.6   The screen **cursor** will highlight any particular cell - in the example above, it is placed over cell C6.

10.7   The contents of any cell can be one of the following.

(a) Text. A cell so designated contains words or numerical data (eg a date) that will not be used in computations. On newer versions of all popular spreadsheets, text can be formatted in a similar way to what is possible using a WP package. Different fonts can be selected, text can be emboldened or italicised, and the point size of the lettering can be changed.

(b) Values. A value is a number that can be used in a calculation.

(c) Formulae. A formula refers to other cells in the spreadsheet, and performs some sort of computation with them. For example, if cell C1 contains the formula =A1-B1 this means that the contents of cell B1 should be subtracted from the contents of cell A1 and the result displayed in cell C1. Note that a formula starts with a specific command or choice or symbols in most packages to distinguish it from text.

   (i) In Excel, a formula always begins with an equals sign: =

   (ii) Where a long row or column of cells (referred to as a range) is to be added together, a '**sum**' **function** can be used. In Excel this would be entered as =SUM(B7:B18)

Some hands-on skills

10.8 The instructions here refer to **Excel 97**. Later versions of Excel also work in the way described here, although they contain extra features.

10.9 Load up your spreadsheet by finding and double-clicking on the Excel **icon** or button (it will look like an X), or by choosing Excel from somewhere in the **Start** menus (maybe from within the **Microsoft Office** option).

Moving about (F5)

10.10 Press the function key labelled **F5** at the top of the keyboard. A **Go To** dialogue box will appear with the 'cursor' (a flashing line or lit up section) in a box. Delete anything that is in the box with the Delete key and then type C5 (or c5 – case does not matter) and press Enter. The 'cursor' will now be over cell C5. This is the **active cell** and it will have a thick black line all round it.

10.11 Press **Ctrl** + ↑ and then **Ctrl** + ←. (This means that you hold down one of the keys marked Ctrl and, keeping it held down, press the other key.)

10.12 The cursor will move back to cell A1. Try holding down Ctrl and pressing each of the direction arrow keys in turn to see where you end up. Try using the **Page Up** and **Page Down** keys and also try **Home** and **End** and Ctrl + these keys. Try **Tab** and **Shift + Tab**, too. These are all useful shortcuts for moving quickly from one place to another in a large spreadsheet.

Entering data and the active cell

10.13 Get your cursor back to cell A1. Then type in 123. Then press the ↓ key. Note that the cell below (A2) now becomes the **active cell**.

10.14 Type 456 in cell A2 and then press the → key. The cell to the left (B2) is now the active cell.

10.15 Get back to cell A1. Above cell A1 you should be able to see a rectangle at the top left *telling* you that you are in cell A1 and, to the right of this a line containing the numbers 123. In other words this line at the top of the screen shows you the **cell reference** and the **contents** of the currently **active cell**.

Editing data (F2)

10.16 Assuming you have now made cell A1 the active cell, type 45. Note what happens both in the cell and in the line above. The previous entry (123) is replaced by the number 45. Press ↓. The active cell is now A2 (check in the line at the top of the screen).

10.17 Suppose you wanted to **change the entry** in cell A2 from 456 to 123456. You have four options. Option (d) is the best.

(a) **Type** 123456 and press **Enter**.

To undo this and try the next option press **Ctrl + Z**: this will always undo what you have just done.

(b) **Double-click** in cell A2. The cell will keep its thick outline but you will now be able to see a vertical line flashing in the cell. You can move this line by using the direction arrow keys or the Home and the End keys. Move it to before the 4 and type 123. Then press Enter.

When you have tried this press Ctrl + Z to undo it.

(c) Click once on the number 456 in the line that shows the active cell reference and cell contents at the top of the screen. Again you will get the vertical line and you can type in 123 before the 4. Then press Enter, then Ctrl + Z.

(d) Press the **function key F2**. The vertical line cursor will be flashing in cell A2 at the *end* of the figures entered there (after the 6). Press Home to get to a position before the 4 and then type in 123 and press Enter, as before.

10.18 Now make cell A3 the active cell. Type **1 2** (a 1, a space, and then a 2) in this cell and press Enter. Note that because the software finds a space it thinks you want **text** in this cell. It **aligns it to the left**, not the right. If you ever need to enter a number to be treated as text, you should enter an **apostrophe** before it. eg '1.

Deleting

10.19 Get to cell A3 if you have not already done so and press **Delete**. The contents of this cell will disappear.

10.20 Move the cursor up to cell A2. Now hold down the **Shift** key (the one above the Ctrl key) and keeping it held down press the ↑ arrow. Cell A2 will stay white but cell A1 will go black. What you have done here is **selected** the range A1 and A2. **Anything you do next will be done to both cells A1 and A2.**

10.21 Press Delete. The contents of cells A1 and A2 will disappear.

10.22 EXERCISE: USING EXCEL AND WORD

Mr Tim Nicholas would like a memo giving details of total gross pay, total National Insurance, and total overall payroll cost for the month, and any differences from the previous months totals. A similar memo was prepared last month and saved in the file **StaffCostsMem.doc**.

On October 2 2000, Mr Nicholas handed you the following information and asked you to prepare the memo.

Month 2

	Total Gross	Employers Nat. Ins.
1 T. NICHOLAS	3,000.00	300.00
2 S. LYNCH	2,125.00	212.50
3 A. PATEL	1,650.00	165.20
4 J. ESCOTT	1,500.00	150.00
5 A. CROPPER	850.00	59.64
6 A. VAUGHAN	875.00	61.32
7 K. KNIGHT	900.00	63.00
8 L. LEROY	1,083.33	108.40
9 L. BROWN	1,100.00	110.00
10 M. KORETZ	1,083.33	108.40
11 N. PARKER	1,083.33	108.40
12 G. TURNER	0.00	0.00
13 M. KOTHARI	1,067.00	106.90
14 N. FAROUK	968.00	97.00
15 L. FARROW	927.00	86.73
16 E. PARKINSON	182.00	0.00
17 N. HAZELWOOD	1,350.00	135.20
18 C. STANLEY	1069.00	107.10
19 S. BABCOCK	983.33	63.28
20 D. COOMBES	1,150.00	60.48

Unload the Windows exercises onto a blank floppy disk if you have not already done so.

Open the file **StaffCostsMem.doc** with your word processor and **StaffCosts.xls** with your spreadsheet package. Save each file with a different name (eg StaffcostsSep00....).

(a) Using **StaffCosts.xls,** enter this month's figures and details in the appropriate columns. The totals will be calculated automatically.

(b) Copy the spreadsheet into the memo and make any other changes that you think are appropriate.

Hint: Highlight the relevant cells in the spreadsheet and click on **Edit, Copy**. Then switch to the memo in Word, place the cursor where you would like the figures to appear and click **Edit, Paste**.

(c) If possible, print out a copy of the memo.

10.23 SOLUTION: USING EXCEL AND WORD

This sort of task is very common day to day work for an accountant in a modern office. A suggested solution can be found in the file **StaffCostsAns.doc**.

11   FAX AND E-MAIL

Fax

11.1   Fax (or facsimile transmission) involves the transmission by data link of exact duplicate copies of documents. The original is fed into the fax machine, which 'reads' it and converts it into electronic form so it can be transmitted over the telephone. It is printed by the recipient's fax machine. Fax has largely replaced older systems such as telex.

11.2   The latest fax machines can also be used as **scanners** to scan data into a PC, as **printers** for PC output and as **photocopiers**.

11.3   Alternatively a PC can be fitted with a **fax modem**, allowing data to be transmitted directly from the PC without going through a separate fax machine.

11.4   However, users of PCs fitted with fax modems may easily forget that when they switch off their machine at the end of the day it will **not be able to receive fax messages**, unlike a stand-alone fax machine, which tends to be left on-line 24 hours.

Activity 2.10

Ensure you can send documents using the fax machine at your work, or, if applicable, at college. Find out if the machine has a memory facility that stores documents for sending later.

Electronic mail (E-mail)

11.5   The term 'electronic mail', or **e-mail**, is used to describe various systems of sending data or messages electronically via a telephone or data network and a central computer.

11.6   E-mail has the following **advantages**.

(a)   **Speed** (transmission, being electronic, is almost instantaneous). E-mail is far faster than post. It is a particular time-saver when communicating with people overseas.

(b)   **Economy** (no need for stamps etc). E-mail is reckoned to be 20 times cheaper than fax.

(c)   **Efficiency** (a message is prepared once but can be sent to thousands of employees at the touch of a button).

(d)   **Security** (access can be restricted by the use of passwords).

(e)   Documents can be retrieved from **word-processing** and graphics packages.

(f)   Electronic **delivery and read receipts** can be requested.

(g)   E-mail can be used to send **documents and reports** as well as short memos, for instance by **attaching** a file.

11.7 Typically information is 'posted' by the sender to a central computer which allocates disk storage as a **mailbox** for each user. The information is subsequently collected by the receiver from the mailbox.

(a) Senders of information thus have **documentary evidence** that they have given a piece of information to the recipient and that the recipient has picked up the message.

(b) Receivers are **not disturbed** by the information when it is sent (as they would be by face-to-face meetings or phone calls), but collect it later at their convenience.

11.8 Each user will typically have **password protected access** to his own inbox, outbox and filing system. He can prepare and edit text and other documents using a **word processing** function, and send mail using **standard headers and identifiers** to an individual or a group of people on a prepared **distribution list**.

11.9 E-mail systems may serve one department or the whole organisation. It is also possible to connect an e-mail system to outside organisations.

11.10 E-mail use is now widespread both **within organisations** and **between** them – via the Internet.

Activity 2.11

There are many types of e-mail system. Perhaps the most common is Microsoft Outlook. Ensure you can send a message using the e-mail system at your work or college. Find out how to attach a file (such as a spreadsheet) to your message.

12   GLOSSARY OF COMMON TERMS

12.1 You have now completed Part A of this Text. Before you move on to Part B make sure that you know what each of the terms listed on the next page means, or what each item does. Write in the answer yourself. There are some spare boxes for your own use.

BPP
PUBLISHING

Part A: Data processing

Application	
Button	
Click	
Cursor	
Directory	
Double-click	
Drag and drop	
Drive	
Enter or Return	
File	
Icon	
Menu	
Scroll	
Select	
Shift	
Tab key	
Window	

Quick quiz

1 List three different ways you can scroll on a computer screen. (See paragraph 5.2)

2 What type of file is a .doc file? What type of file is an .xls file? (6.13)

3 For what purpose would you press the Alt and Tab keys at the same time? (6.19)

4 In Microsoft Word, under what menu option is the Find and Replace function? (9.18)

5 List five advantages of e-mail over paper based mail. (11.6)

Answers to activities

Answer 2.5

You could have held down the Ctrl key and pressed Z. This is known as a keyboard shortcut. Most menus in Windows programs tell you what the keyboard shortcuts are: click on Edit again to bring up the menu and you will see Ctrl + Z alongside the Undo option.

Answer 2.7

Here are some suggestions for people named Steve Morris, John Smith and Jamie Lee Curtis.

SteveM01	SmithJ01	JLC_001
SteveM02	SmithJ02	JLC_002
SteveM03 etc	SmithJ03 etc	JLC_003 etc

Answer 2.9

The letter is shown in our answer on the next page.

Good Solutions Limited

58 Alfriston Road
London
NW4 6SG

Mr P Wyzovski
Mulchester House
West Frintleigh
Devon
WF4 7QD

Date: As postmark

Dear Mr Wyzovski

New solutions from Good Solutions

Widget users will be pleased to hear of the release of *Widget 2000*. This is the new improved version of the well-loved Widget 98.

Good Solutions has long been recognised as the premier supplier of widgets to meet every need of discerning manufacturers. The Widget 2000 is based on industry-standard specifications and is used by many leading companies, such as ICI, GEC, Bosch, Ford Motors, and London Electricity. *Good Solution's* Widgets are still the only widgets that are compatible with hydraulic splinter technology. We lead, the rest follow.

The Widget 2000 is a multi-purpose widget. Features include:

- Same day delivery in many areas
- Choice of finishes
- Light and transportable
- No leakage
- Stackable for easy storage
- Guaranteed for 12 months

Good Solutions won the Queen's Award for Industry in 1999.

If you would like a sample Widget 2000 and further information, call Tim Davis on 020-8269 8246 or fill in the prepaid postcard enclosed.

Yours sincerely

Tim Davis
Marketing Director

Part B
Using accounting software

3 Introducing the case study

This chapter contains

1   Using Sage Line 50 or Sage Instant Accounting

2   The case study

3   Loading the data for assignments

4   Account reference codes

5   The nominal ledger

6   Conclusion

Learning objectives

On completion of this chapter you will:

- Understand the basic keys and other tools used to enter data into Sage

- Be able to load the data for the Assignments in this book

- Be aware of the nominal ledger codes we will be using

Knowledge and understanding

1   The relationship between different software packages.

2   The purpose and application of different software packages.

3   Types of data held on a computer system.

4   Location of information sources.

BPP PUBLISHING

1 USING SAGE

1.1 Sage is a 'user-friendly' software package and is designed to help you as much as possible. This first section describes some important features that you will use all the time.

Getting access to Sage

1.2 Check with your tutor or supervisor about how to gain access to the software package. The procedure is likely to be as simple as that described below for a stand-alone PC, but it may be different if your college has a larger system.

1.3 Click on the Start button and search through the menus until you find Sage. Alternatively there may be an **icon** on the 'desktop'. If so, just **double-click** on it.

Activity 3.1

Make sure that you can easily locate the Sage Line 50 or Instant icon (or Start option) on your system (on whichever computers you are likely to use, if there is a choice of more than one).

You may wish to make notes of how to find Sage, in which case write them neatly in the space below so you always have this information with you when you are using this book.

....

....

....

....

....

....

....

Password

1.4 The software *may* have been set up by your college so that you have to enter a password before you can get into the package. **BPP do not recommend this for the purposes of the Blitz case study**.

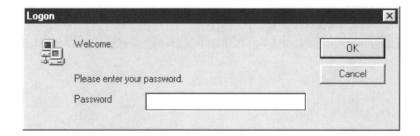

1.5 If asked for a password, you will have to ask your tutor what the password is and **learn it**. As you type the password you will see a series of tiny *'s appear in the box rather than the actual letters you type – there would be little point in having a password if the computer gave away what you were typing!

1.6 Once you have typed in the password correctly you can either click on the OK button or press Enter. The first screen will disappear and you can start your Sage session.

1.7 If, when you are at the password stage, you decide not to proceed, click on Cancel or press Esc. This will return you to the opening Windows screen.

1.8 If you get the password wrong the computer will just beep at you or display a message telling you the password is invalid if you try to click on OK or press Enter. If you know you have made a mistake when typing the password use the Delete key to cross out the row of *'s and start again.

1.9 Once you have gained access to the package the Sage screen will look something like this. Notice the menu bar (File, Edit, View etc) and the row of icons or buttons beneath (Customers, Suppliers, Nominal, etc).

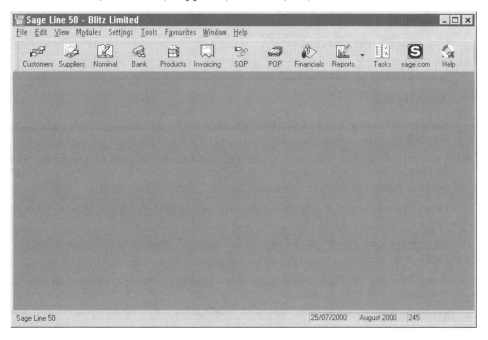

Activity 3.2

Don't be afraid to play with the Sage package. Use the CD-ROM to load up any Assignment you like (see Chapter 2 Section 7 for detailed instructions) and then click on any of the buttons and menu options you fancy and look at what appears on screen. Each time you can press the **Esc** key to clear away what appeared and return to the main screen.

Buttons or icons

1.10 When you use Sage, the first task is to click on a button and choose the appropriate part of the program for the work you will be doing. When you click on a button a further window will then appear, specifying more detailed areas of work within your initial selection. Again you click on a button within this new window to select an option. The selection process goes on until you have reached the program or 'routine' that you wish to use.

1.11 When you have reached the program or routine you want to use, there will be a screen display and it should be fairly clear, from instructions on the screen or from the position of the cursor, what you are expected to do next. You might, for example, enter transaction details into the computer, or give instructions for extracting information from the files. You will be helped throughout by 'prompts' from on-screen messages and instructions. The cursor will show you at any time the position you have reached on the screen with entering data or instructions.

Using the keyboard and the mouse

1.12 The package can be used with a keyboard alone, but generally it is best to use a **mixture** of keyboard and mouse to enter transaction details and to give instructions to the computer.

1.13 When you are using a keyboard, you must be familiar in particular with the **Tab** key. The **Esc** (or Escape) key is also useful.

(a) The **Tab** key is used to move on to the next item on screen. Using the **Shift** key and the **Tab** key together moves you back to the previous item on screen.

(b) The Escape key (**Esc**) can be used to close the current window and move back to the previous window.

Activity 3.3

Click on the button labelled **Customers** and then on the new button that appears labelled **Record**.

Find the cursor: it should be in a box labelled A/C. Press **Tab** several times (slowly) and watch the cursor move from one box to the next. At some times it will highlight a button such as Save instead of appearing in a box.

Now experiment with the Shift + Tab combination and watch the cursor move in reverse order.

What happens if you place your mouse pointer in a particular white space on the screen and click?

Press **Esc** when you are happy that you understand the tools you have available for moving the cursor around the screen.

Correcting errors

1.14 It is easy to make errors when data is input.

(a) If an error is spotted immediately, you will usually be able to wipe out the incorrect data using the **delete** key.

(b) If an error occurs whilst you are entering a transaction record, and you spot the mistake before the transaction is saved or posted, you can alter the details or cancel the transaction entirely and start again, using the **Discard** option.

(c) If errors are spotted much later, you will need to make an appropriate input to correct the error. Correcting errors by this means is described in a later chapter.

Activity 3.4

Click on **Customers.** If there are any customers listed note down the A/C code (eg ADAMSE) of the first one. Now click on **Record**, and type 000000 (six noughts) in the A/C box and press **Tab**. Now click on **Discard**. What happens? Then clock on Close.

Exiting from Sage

1.15 When you have finished working on Sage, you should exit from the system properly, to avoid the risk of corrupting data in the system. To exit Sage, you click on the word **File** in the top left-hand corner of the screen. The last option on the menu that drops down when you do this is **Exit**. Click on this word.

Do you wish to Backup your Data?

1.16 A message will then appear on the screen asking you whether you wish to back up your data. In a 'live' system, you would back data up at regular intervals - probably daily. In a training system, your course supervisor might instruct you to select No. If you choose No (by clicking on the No button or pressing N) you will exit from Sage, and you will be returned to the Windows desktop screen.

1.17 When you start doing the assignments in this book you may well want to make a copy of your work on a floppy disk. Procedures for **backing up** and restoring data are described at the end of this book in Appendix 3.

2 THE CASE STUDY

2.1 The assignments in Part D of this workbook are based on a case study of a fictional North London company, Blitz Limited. The case study is set in late 2000 and early 2001.

2.2 Blitz Limited was established in August 2000 by two friends, Maria Green and Tim Nicholas. Each has put £20,000 into the company, and they are worker-directors.

2.3 The company provides cleaning services. Much of its business comes from office cleaning and other contract cleaning services (such as factory cleaning). However, the company also provides window cleaning services for businesses and domestic cleaning services for private individuals.

When does the case study begin?

2.4 The case study begins in October 2000, just over one month after the company has started operations. It has had a fairly busy September, receiving 27 invoices from various suppliers and has issued 35 invoices to customers. Apart from payments of wages and salaries, there were no cash transactions in September, and all invoices are as yet unpaid.

2.5 At the beginning of October 2000, Blitz Limited has 27 supplier accounts on its purchase ledger and 35 customer accounts on its sales ledger.

3 LOADING THE DATA FOR ASSIGNMENTS

3.1 The data for the assignments in this workbook has been arranged so that you can load the starting data for any assignment at any time and in any order.

3.2 To refresh your memory, go back to Chapter 2 and:

- Read section 7
- Do Activity 2.9 in section 9

Overwriting Blitz data

3.3 Every time you restore an Assignment a fresh copy of the data is loaded. The program overwrites any data that was there previously, so you can, for example:

(a) Load Assignment 1 and make any entries you like, even if they are complete nonsense, and then load assignment 1 again to get a fresh clean version. In other words you can *experiment with the data* as much as you like.

(b) Load Assignment 1, then load Assignment 2. Restoring Assignment 2 will overwrite the data for Assignment 1 and replace it with the data for Assignment 2.

Activity 3.5

(a) Load the data for assignment 1. Click on Suppliers. What is the code of the first supplier listed?

(b) Load the data for assignment 2. Click on Suppliers. What is the code of the first supplier listed?

(c) Click on New and use the Supplier Record Wizard to create a new supplier record with the name and *Refn* 111111. (Leave all other details blank by clicking Next each time, then Finish.) What is the code of the first account listed now?

(d) Re-load the data for assignment 2. Click on Suppliers. What is the code of the first supplier listed now?

Looking at the opening data

Suppliers ledger data

3.4 Firstly, re-load Assignment 1. Then look at the opening data in the suppliers ledger accounts, click on the **Suppliers** button in the main window (second from the left). The following window will appear.

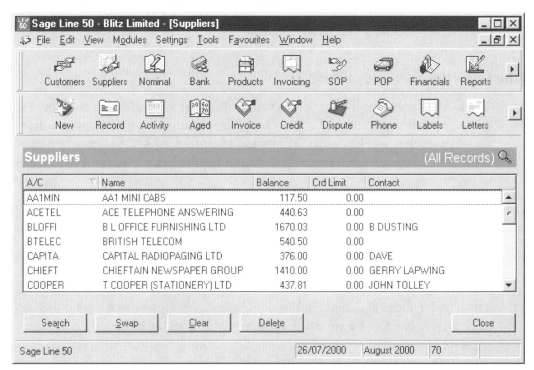

3.5 In the Suppliers window you should then click on the **Aged** button (second row of icons, fourth from left). Enter 30/09/2000 in the Report date and Payments Up To boxes, and click OK.

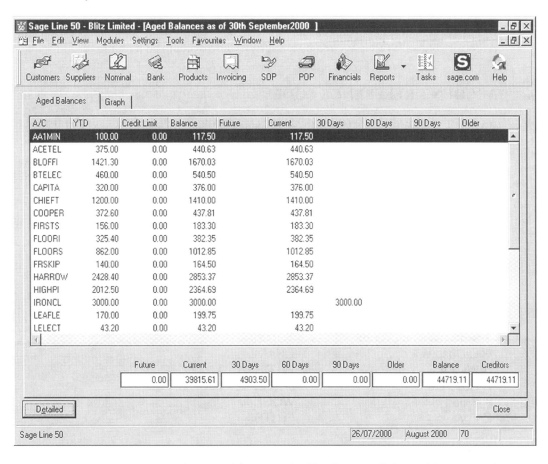

3.6 When you have had a look at this press the Esc key or click on **Close** to make this window disappear. Now click on the **Activity** button (next to the **Aged** button) and accept the date range you are offered by clicking on **OK** or pressing Enter.

3.7 You may receive a warning stating 'Terms have not been agreed on this Account'. If you don't receive the warning go to paragraph 3.8. If you do receive the warning just click OK - Blitz is a new company and has not yet finalised terms with suppliers.

3.8 The next screen you see shows you details of how the balance on an account is made up. To see details for another account click on the *button* at the right of the box labelled A/C. A list of all the supplier accounts will drop down. Just scroll around and *double-click* on any account name to see the activity for that account.

3.9 Alternatively, if you prefer not to use the mouse, press the function key F4. This will bring down the menu of accounts. You can use the up and down cursor keys to scroll from one account to another and press the **Enter** key when the account you want is highlighted.

Customers ledger data

3.10 To look at data in the customers ledger, you follow the same procedure. It is usually good practice to close any windows that you are not using. Do this by pressing the Escape key until you get back to the main window. When you get there, click on the **Customers** button.

3.11 From the Customers window, you should then select the **Aged** button or **Activity** button and follow the same procedures as above for the Suppliers ledger. The first customer account on the file for Assignment 1, for example, is for E T ADAMS.

3.12 Alternatively, in either the Suppliers or Customers windows you can click on the Account you wish to view, then click Activity and accept the date range.

4 ACCOUNT REFERENCE CODES

4.1 As you may already have realised, in our case study, Blitz Limited uses the first six significant letters (or numbers) in the supplier's or customer's name to create their code. For initials and surname, the first six significant letters are taken from the surname. If there are less than six characters in the name (and initials), the code is made up to 6 digits with Xs.

Examples

Name	Account reference code
Matthias Scaffolding	MATTHI
Ace Telephone Answering	ACETEL
B L Office Supplies	BLOFFI
The Tomkinson Group	TOMKIN
R C Chadwick	CHADWI
A Wyche	WYCHEA
A Rose Ltd	ROSEAL
P Wood	WOODPX
C Fry	FRYCXX

4.2 If you select Customer or Supplier, then highlight an account and click on the Activity button you can view past transactions on an account – this is useful if a customer or supplier has an account query. Try the following Activity.

Activity 3.6

Load the data for Assignment 1, then start up Sage. A customer, Mr E A Newall, has telephoned Blitz to say he has not received an invoice for some domestic cleaning work. He would like to know how much the cost will be. Can you answer his query?

5 THE NOMINAL LEDGER

5.1 If you have not already done so, load the opening data for Assignment 1 now - following the instructions given in section 7 of Chapter 2.

5.2 Blitz Limited is using the 'default' nominal ledger account codes provided in the Sage software. The sales account codes 4000, 4001, 4002 and 4100 have been renamed. A list of the codes is given in Appendix 1 to this book.

5.3 To ensure your system is operating using the date that the case study is set in, we will change the system date. Close all Sage windows except the main window, then select **Settings, Change Program Date** from the pull-down menu. Insert the date 30/09/2000 and click OK.

Looking at the opening data

5.4   To view the current Nominal ledger balances on screen you simply click on the **Nominal Ledger** button.

5.5   If you want a 'hard copy' trial balance report close the Nominal window and click on the **Financials** button and then on the **Trial** (Balance) button. Choose the Period September 2000 and choose whether you want to print the report or preview it on screen. Then click on **OK**. (Ensure you have changed the Program Date as explained in paragraph 5.3 before running the report.)

5.6   The trial balance to the end of September follows.

Blitz Limited
25 Apple Road
London
N12 3PP

Nominal Ledger Trial Balance

Acct	Name	Debit	Credit
0020	PLANT AND MACHINERY	5734.50	
0030	OFFICE EQUIPMENT	1620.00	
0040	FURNITURE AND FIXTURES	1421.30	
0050	MOTOR VEHICLES	16220.80	
1100	DEBTORS CONTROL ACCOUNT	22620.43	
1200	BANK CURRENT ACCOUNT	33946.07	
2100	CREDITORS CONTROL ACCOUNT		44719.11
2200	Sales Tax Control		3369.03
2202	Purchase Tax Control	6022.38	
2210	P.A.Y.E.		1370.00
3000	ORDINARY SHARES		40000.00
4000	SALES - CONTRACT CLEANING		16597.40
4001	SALES - WINDOW CLEANING		1970.40
4002	SALES - DOMESTIC SERVICES		683.60
5000	MATERIALS PURCHASES	3703.83	
6201	ADVERTISING	2200.00	
6203	P.R. (LIT. & BROCHURES)	170.00	
7001	DIRECTORS SALARIES	1707.03	
7003	STAFF SALARIES	475.75	
7004	WAGES – REGULAR	4941.15	
7005	WAGES – CASUAL	480.00	
7100	RENT	3000.00	
7103	GENERAL RATES	1240.00	
7200	ELECTRICITY	43.20	
7400	TRAVELLING	100.00	
7500	PRINTING	500.00	
7501	POSTAGE AND CARRIAGE	89.50	
7502	TELEPHONE	1155.00	
7504	OFFICE STATIONERY	372.60	
7700	EQUIPMENT HIRE	296.00	
8202	CLOTHING COSTS	650.00	
		108709.54	108709.54

Activity 3.7

Your supervisor has asked you for details of cash received into the bank account and paid from the bank account since the company was established. With assignment 1 loaded, can you provide this information using the Activity facility? The nominal ledger code for the bank account is 1200.

6   CONCLUSION

6.1   You should now be able to do the following.

(a)   Use the BPP CD-ROM to load data for the Assignments.

(b)   Refer to individual accounts in the Suppliers ledger, Customers ledger or Nominal ledger in order to answer queries about transactions in the account.

(c)   Produce a Trial Balance.

(d)   Key in data at lightning speed! (*If you require practice using the keyboard try the exercises contained in the Excel file* **DataEntryTests.xls** – *this will be on the floppy disc you used when studying Chapter 2 section 8.*)

Activity 3.8

If you have been reading through this Chapter while not sitting at a suitably equipped computer, make a note to do all of the activities **hands-on** as soon as you get the opportunity.

Quick quiz

1   How do you exit from Sage? (See paragraph 1.15)

2   What does the F4 key do within Sage? (3.9)

3   What method does Blitz Limited use to devise customer and supplier account codes? (4.1)

4   What range of accounts make up the Sales accounts in the Blitz nominal ledger? (5.1)

5   How do you print a trial balance from Sage? (5.7)

Answers to activities

Answer 3.4

The 000000 should disappear.

Answer 3.5

(a)   AA1MIN

(b)   3DTECH

(c)   111111

(d)   3DTECH. You have a fresh copy of the assignment 2 data, free of any entries you made yourself.

This Activity is to encourage you to experiment with any entries you like, safe in the knowledge that you cannot damage the Blitz data.

Answer 3.6

The query is from a credit customer, so you begin by clicking on the Customers button. To find Mr Newall's account use the down arrow in the scroll bar to the right of the list of accounts. When you see NEWALL, click on that name to highlight it, then click on the Activity button. Accept the Defaults suggested by clicking on OK. The next screen will show you the current balance on Mr Newall's account.

The display on screen should show you that there is only one invoice outstanding, an amount for domestic cleaning invoiced on 22/09/2000 for £77.55.

Answer 3.7

The supervisor's request is for the Transactions on the Bank Current account, nominal ledger code 1200. Select the Nominal button, scroll down to account 1200, highlight it, click on the Activity button. Accept the Defaults. You should see, on screen, the following information.

1200 Bank Current Account

No.	Tp	Date	Ref	Details	Amount	Debit	Credit
1	BR	19/08/2000		M Green - shares	20000.00	20000.00	
2	BR	19/08/2000		T Nicholas - shares	20000.00	20000.00	
8	JC	16/09/2000	xxxxx	Wages and salaries	6053.93		6053.93
						40000.00	6053.93
						33946.07	

The Tp column shows the type of transaction. BR is a bank receipt. JC is a journal entry (credit entry). The three figures at the foot of the display show total debits and credits and the balance.

4 Supplier invoices and credit notes

This chapter contains

1   The Suppliers window

2   New suppliers

3   Supplier details

4   Entering details of invoices received

5   Entering details of credit notes received

6   Reports

7   Conclusion

Learning objectives

On completion of this chapter you will be able to:

- Set up accounts in the purchase ledger for new suppliers

- Record invoices received from suppliers

- Record credit notes received from suppliers

- Post entries (for invoices or credit notes received) to the purchase ledger and the nominal ledger

- Produce a listing of entries for invoices received and credit notes received

Knowledge and understanding

1   The relationship between different software packages.

2   The purpose and application of different software packages.

3   Types of data held on a computer system.

4   Location of information sources.

BPP
PUBLISHING

1 THE SUPPLIERS WINDOW

1.1 The Suppliers window, which is shown below, is displayed on screen when you click on the **Suppliers** button in the main window.

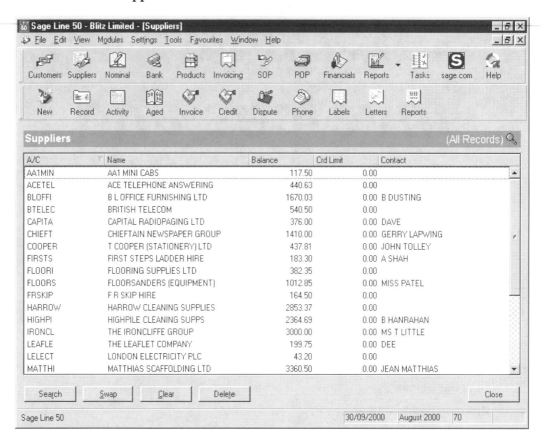

2 NEW SUPPLIERS

2.1 When an invoice is received from a new supplier, an account for the supplier must be set up. There are three ways of entering new supplier accounts.

(a) Using the Supplier **Record** button.

(b) Using the **Invoices** button.

(c) Using the **New** button from within Suppliers to access the Supplier Record Wizard.

2.2 The **Record** button method is described here. Experiment with the other two methods yourself.

3 SUPPLIER DETAILS

3.1 To set up an account for a new supplier click on Supplies. Then, ensure no existing supplier is highlighted and click on the **Record** button.

3.2 This option allows you to insert details of a new supplier (that is, create a new supplier account) or to amend details of an existing account, for example to change the supplier's address or telephone number.

3.3   Existing supplier accounts can also be deleted from the ledger in certain
       circumstances. When you click on the **Record** button, the following display will
       appear on screen.

       Note that different aspects of supplier details are depicted as index cards (Details,
       Defaults, Graphs etc). You click on the index tab to get the section you want.

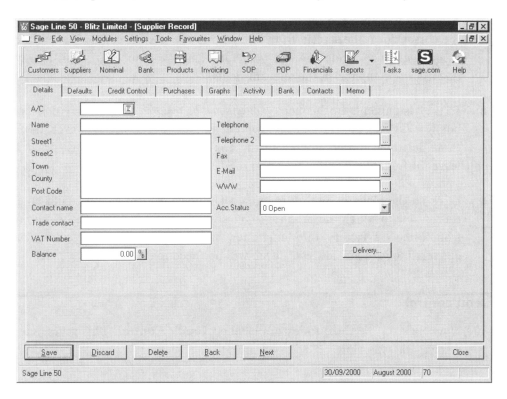

Details

3.4   The cursor starts at the **A/C box**. The supplier's reference code should be entered
       here. The maximum length for the code is eight digits. The coding system used by
       Blitz Limited uses six characters.

3.5   When you enter a code for a new supplier and press **Tab**, the words **New Account**
       will appear in the grey area next to the **A/C box**.

3.6   The cursor will have moved down to the next line, and you can insert the
       supplier's name. Press **Tab** to move from the name line to the address section.
       Press the **Shift** key plus **Tab** to move *up* to the previous line. If you want to leave a
       line blank just press **Tab** again to move on to the next line.

       Here is a typical set of entries that you might make.

Name	Lexington Supplies
Street 1	Billington House
Street 2	25-29 Dorchester Avenue
Town	London
County	
Postcode	W12 5TL

BPP PUBLISHING

Activity 4.1

Load up Assignment 6 and using the A/C code LEXING enter all of these details as a new supplier account and save your entries. Between which two codes does the new account appear?

3.7 After you have entered the supplier's name and address, use the **Tab** key to move the cursor down the screen, from one item to the next. A contact name (in case of account queries), trade contact, telephone and fax numbers, e-mail and website details can be entered in the relevant fields.

3.8 In the assignments in this book *you will not be required* to enter any details in the box for **Vat Reg No** (it is not relevant at Foundation level). However, in practice these details would be entered in the box if required. You can just press **Tab** to leave the field blank and move on to the next field.

3.9 Click on the Delivery button to enter a **Delivery Address**. You would enter here the address to which the supplier in question normally delivers the goods you buy from him – a factory in Manchester, say. Blitz Limited has all its supplies delivered to its main address, so you will not need to enter anything here.

Credit control

3.10 Now click on the third index tab labelled **Credit Control**. This gives you a new screen – shown below.

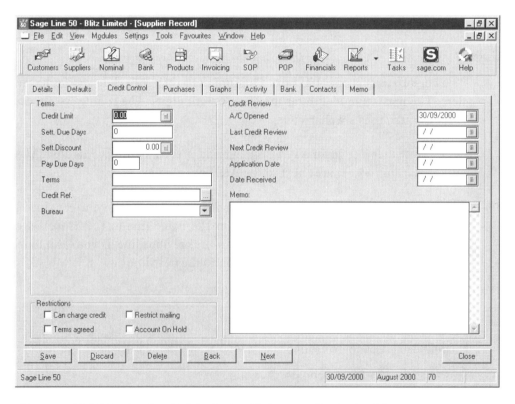

3.11 You would fill in the **Credit Limit** line if the supplier had told you that they were unwilling to allow your account balance to exceed a certain value before you paid them some money.

3.12 The **Sett Due Days** and **Sett Discount** lines go together. A supplier might offer you a 10% discount if you pay an invoice within, say, 7 days. In this case you would enter the number 7 in the **Sett Due Days** box and 10.00 in the **Sett Discount** box.

3.13 The entry in the **Pay Due Days** box is the number of *days* that you have to pay an invoice: typically a supplier might expect payment within 30 days. The **Terms** box is for a narrative description: 'Payment on delivery', or whatever is appropriate. When Terms have been agreed with a supplier the **small Terms agreed** box should be 'ticked'.

3.14 You need not be concerned with the **Credit Ref** and **Bureau** boxes. If you are interested, use the Sage on-line help facility to find out their purpose.

Defaults

3.15 The Defaults index tab allows you to specify certain details about how a transaction with the supplier will normally be posted. For example if one of your suppliers were Yorkshire Electricity you would probably be reasonably sure that all transactions on this account should be posted to the Electricity expense account in the nominal ledger.

If you make an entry in the **Def N/C** box when you first set up the Yorkshire Electricity account, then when you next have an invoice from Yorkshire Electricity the program will automatically suggest to you that it should be posted to the 'default' nominal account you specified when the account was set up. (You can, however, choose a different nominal code at the time when you are posting the transaction.)

3.16 Sage has a box for **Disc%**. This is for discounts other than settlement discounts. It is not used in the Blitz case study.

3.17 The **Def Tax Code** box will offer you a pull down list of possible VAT codes that apply to this supplier. In the assignments in the Blitz case study the default code is **T1 – 17.5%,** which is the standard rate of VAT at the time of preparation of this book.

3.18 Below the **Def Tax Code** box is a box labelled **Currency**. The default in the case study is '**1 Pound Sterling**'. If you click on this box and its downward pointing arrow you will be offered a number of other options such as French Francs or German Marks. The Blitz case study only uses UK currency, so you can just accept the default for this box.

3.19 In the assignments in this book *you will not be required* to enter any details in the boxes for **Analysis.** These are useful for management accounting purposes, but not part of the standards of competence at AAT Foundation level. In each case press **Tab** to leave the field blank and move on to the next field.

3.20 The other index tabs are not used in the assignments in this book, but you might find it interesting to have a look at them and see what happens when you click on various buttons. Don't be afraid of experimenting: you can always get a fresh copy of the data using the CD-ROM.

Checking and saving your work

3.21 When you have entered all the details that need to be entered you should *check* what you have on screen against the document you are working from (against the details given in this book in the case of the assignments).

(a) If you have made just one or two errors just press **Tab** until the entry is highlighted and type in the correct entry. If just one character is wrong it is quicker to click on the entry, and move the cursor using the cursor keys until it is in the appropriate place, delete the wrong character and insert the correct one.

(b) If you have made a complete hash of the entries it may be better to start all over again and be more careful next time. In this case click on the button labelled **Discard.** The screen will be cleared and you can start again.

(c) If you are happy that all your entries are correct click on **Save**. The new supplier will be added to the Suppliers ledger.

(d) If you click on Save and only then realise you have made a mistake in posting the details you can call up the details you posted again by selecting the supplier code from the main Suppliers window, click on **Record** and edit out your mistakes. Alternatively you can call up the account and click on **Delete** to remove it entirely. However you can only delete a supplier in this way if no transactions have yet been posted to that account.

Activity 4.2

(a) What is the post-code for account AA1MIN?
(b) What is the contact name for account TROJAN?
(c) What is the full account name and telephone number of the account COOPER?

Activity 4.3

Set up a supplier account for the following supplier in the same way as details have been entered for existing Blitz supplier accounts. Refer to the paragraphs above if you don't know whether you need to put an entry in a particular box or how to make the entry.

Lineker Leisurewear Limited
Bernard House
647 Spenser Street,
Birmingham, BH1 2OD
Contact: Frederic Ferinella
Phone: 0161 123 6543
Credit limit: £1,500

---

4 ENTERING DETAILS OF INVOICES RECEIVED

4.1 When invoices are received from suppliers, the details of each invoice must be entered in the Suppliers Ledger, in the appropriate supplier's account.

The Invoices option

4.2 To enter supplier invoice details, you should click on the **Invoice** button in the **Suppliers** window. The following window will be displayed.

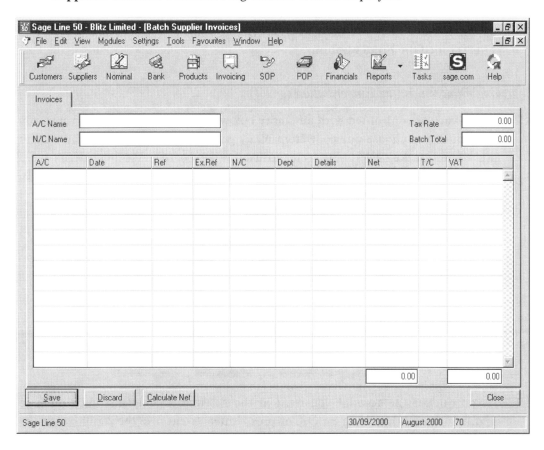

4.3 Suppose your company receives an invoice from a firm of public relations and marketing consultants as follows:

Invoice details	£	Nominal ledger item
Sales promotion expenses	2,000	Sales promotions
Advertising costs	1,500	Advertising
Public relations	600	PR
	4,100	

This invoice needs to be split into its three elements, £2,000 to charge to sales promotion expenses (nominal ledger account code 6200), £1,500 to advertising costs (N/C code 6201) and £600 to PR (N/C code 6203). You would enter three separate lines in the Supplier Invoices window.

4.4 You can enter as many lines as are necessary on each invoice. You can invoice *several different suppliers* on the same screen.

4.5 You can scroll back up and edit transactions if you realise you have made a mistake before you **Save** the invoice. If you want to delete an entire line, tab to it or click in it anywhere and then press function key F8. Other function keys are useful too. See Appendix 2 at the end of this book for a list.

4.6 Once you have finished entering the details of an invoice you click on **Save** and the screen is cleared ready for the next supplier's invoice.

A/C

4.7 Initially the cursor will be in the box labelled **A/C.** If you know the *code* for the supplier you can just type it in and press Tab. If you know some of the details for the supplier but you can't quite remember the code, Sage offers you a handy tool for finding out what you need to enter. At the right of the A/C box is a button. This is called the **Finder** button.

Searching for accounts: the Finder button (or F4)

4.8 When you are confronted with an empty box with the Finder button because you are required to choose one code from many possibilities. Click on the button (or press **function key F4** if you prefer to use the keyboard). Another alternative if you know, say, that the code begins with G, is to type G and then press Enter. In each case you will be presented with a selection window.

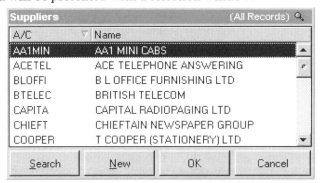

4.9 If you can see the account you want in the list immediately just click on it to highlight it and then click on OK or press Enter. If not, use the scroll bar or the cursor keys to scroll up or down until you see the name you want, then click on it and click OK.

Activity 4.4

Click the relevant buttons until you reach the Supplier Invoices window and then press F4. What appears in the A/C *Name* box at the *top* of the window when you select the account code BLOFFI and click on OK or press Enter? What if you type in the code MUSWEL?

Searching for accounts: the Search button

4.10 The **Search** button at the foot of the Finder window offers you a means of searching for accounts that fulfil certain conditions. Let's say, for the sake of argument, that you are in charge of the purchase ledger for accounts of suppliers who come from Watford. Click on the Search button and you will see the following screen.

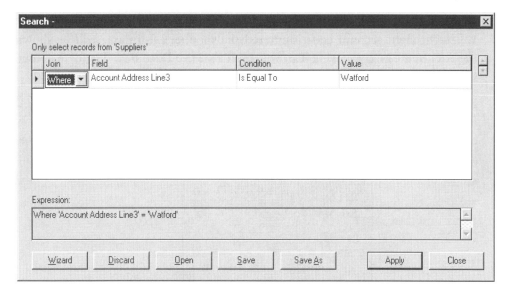

4.11 Click the down arrow to the right of the Join heading and select **Where**. Tab to the white square below the heading Field. From the drop down menu select **Account Address Line 3**. Tab through the condition field, ensuring it is set to 'Is Equal To'. In the Value field type *Watford*. Click on **Apply**, then click on **Close**. You will be returned to a window which shows only the names of those suppliers whose records indicate that they are located in Watford. If you are trying this out using Blitz data there will be now be only three account names: BLOFFI, FLOORS and UNIFOR.

4.12 You can search on more than one criteria. For example, from within the Suppliers finder window click on **Search** again, the criteria entered previously will show. Press **Tab** four times and you will be on a new line. Using the drop down menus under each heading select **And** (hit Tab), **Balance** (Tab), **Is Greater Than** (Tab), and type in 1000.00. Click **Apply** and **Close**. The suppliers in Watford with balances over £1,000.00 will be displayed.

4.13 Wherever you see the **Search** button within Sage the same principles for searching and selecting records apply.

4.14 When you close the Suppliers Record window you will notice that the 'filter' you designed still applies. Therefore, only those records that meet the criteria appear in the Suppliers window. To view all records click on the magnifying glass button. (2 Records found)🔍

4.15 There are symbols that may help you with searches. For example, if you wish to find all accounts with a post code that begins with W a search on W in the postcode line would not find any records. You can, however, search using W* - the asterisk is a 'wildcard', standing for **any other character** or characters. Try it.

4.16 The magnifying glass symbol in the suppliers window (pictured in paragraph 4.14) has the effect of switching between all suppliers record and just those records that meet the Search Criteria. Try the button out.

Activity 4.5

Try out the techniques described in paragraphs 4.11 to 4.16 for yourself.

BPP
PUBLISHING

Date

4.17 When the right account code is entered the supplier's full name will be shown in the A/C Name box. Pressing Tab will highlight the **Date** box. The date you enter should be the date *on the supplier's invoice*.

> Sage has a delightful feature for entering dates. When the cursor enters the date field another Finder button appears. If you click on this or press F4 a little calendar appears and you just have to *double-click* on the date you want. Use the arrows at the top to scroll through the months and years if necessary.

> The calendar is fun, but it is probably quicker to type in the date using the numeric keypad. This is a matter of personal preference.

Ref

4.18 Press Tab again and you are taken to a box headed **Ref**. You can leave this blank but it is best to use it for the supplier's invoice number for reference purposes. There is also an extra reference box **Ex Ref** for an additional reference if required.

Entering the invoice details

4.19 Pressing Tab once more takes you to the parts of the invoicing screen that do what you would think of as the double entry in a manual system. The entries you make are as follows.

(a) The nominal ledger code (**N/C**). This is the account in the nominal ledger to which the purchase or expense relates. You can use the search facilities described above to find the nominal code you want.

> A good shortcut here, if you have an approximate idea of the nominal account code, is to type in the approximate number and then press Enter, or function key F4, or click on the Finder button. This brings up the Nominal Accounts list starting from the number you typed. So, for example, if you know an invoice is an overhead and that overhead account codes are in the range 7000 to 7999 you can type in 7 and press F4.

(b) The **Dept** box can be used to analyse the information further. This is not used in the Blitz case study, so just press Tab again.

(c) In the **Details box** you type details of the goods or service supplied. Try typing a long sentence and see how the text scrolls across as you reach the end of the box.

(d) In the **Net** box key in the amount of the invoice item *excluding value added tax* (the net amount). Just key in figures, with a decimal point between the pounds and the pence. Don't try to key in a £ sign. You don't need to key in zeros for pence at the end of a round figure amount.

- Keying 123 gives you 123.00
- Keying 123.4 gives you 123.40
- Keying 1230 gives you 1230.00

(e) The code for the VAT rate (**T/c**) will automatically show T1, though you can alter this if necessary. The VAT codes used in the Blitz case study are:

T0   Zero-rated items (VAT = 0%)
T1   Standard-rated items (VAT currently = 17.5%)
T9   Transactions to which VAT does not apply

You will be told what code to use at AAT Foundation level.

(f) The **Tax** is calculated automatically from the net amount of the invoice already entered and the VAT tax code.

The Calculate Net button

4.20 If you prefer, instead of entering the net amount of the invoice in the **Net** box, you can enter the total amount, *including VAT. Before* pressing Tab, click on the **Calculate Net** button or press function key F9. The program will now deduct VAT *at the standard rate* from the invoice amount you have keyed in, and display the VAT automatically in the **Tax** column.

4.21 When the VAT has been calculated and you have entered all the invoice details, press Tab again, and the cursor will move down to the next line of the screen. Details of another invoice item can then be entered on this line.

4.22 Note that running totals of your entries are shown at the foot of the Net column and the VAT column. You can compare the totals with the total shown on the invoice once you have posted all the items. If the totals are not the same there is a mistake somewhere. If it is your mistake you can scroll back up or tab to the error and correct it.

4.23 Remember that a whole line can be deleted by clicking on it or tabbing to it and pressing function key F8. Only use the **Discard** button if you wish to scrap *all* the details you have just entered on the screen.

Activity 4.6

Load **Assignment 6** and enter the following invoice details, following the instructions given in paragraphs 4.17 to 4.23. You should not end up with any question marks, but use the features of the Sage package to calculate the correct figures for you.

A/C	Date	Refn	N/C	Details	Net	T/C	VAT
NEWLIT	01/10/2000	SW369	5000	Materials	100.00	T1	??.??
IRONCL	04/10/2000	214876	7701	Repairs	???.??	T1	??.??

The gross amount of the second invoice is £240.

Required

Find out the total amount of VAT for the two transactions, and what the N/C codes 5000 and 7701 stand for.

Save the details, once you have checked the answer.

Posting the invoice details

4.24 When you have entered details for all the items on the invoice(s) you are processing and you are satisfied that they are correct, click on the **Save** button. **Saving the transaction posts the invoice**.

4.25 When you post the details of an invoice, the **program**:

(a) Updates the individual account of the supplier in the Suppliers Ledger;

(b) Updates the appropriate accounts in the Nominal Ledger. The accounts that are updated are the Creditors Control Account, the VAT Control account and the various purchases, expense or fixed asset accounts to which the invoices relate (as specified in the transaction details by your choice of N/C codes). The double entry posting to the nominal ledger will be:

Debit   Nominal Ledger Account selected
Debit   Purchase Tax Control, code 2202
Credit   Creditors Control Account, code 2100

Note that in Sage there are two VAT control accounts, one for VAT on purchases (debits), the other for VAT on sales (credits).

Activity 4.7

When you have done Activity 4.6 find out the debit or credit balances on the Nominal Ledger accounts 2100, 2202, 5000 and 7701 and the Suppliers ledger accounts NEWLIT and IRONCL and make a note of them.

Now reload a fresh copy of Assignment 6. How do the balances on the accounts differ? Explain each of the differences.

5 ENTERING DETAILS OF CREDIT NOTES RECEIVED

5.1 When a credit note is received from a supplier, the supplier is acknowledging that, for one reason or another, he has charged too much. Credit notes can be issued when goods are returned to the supplier as faulty or unwanted, or when there is a dispute about an invoice and the supplier agrees to reduce the bill.

5.2 Details of credit notes received from suppliers must be entered in the Suppliers Ledger, in the account of the appropriate supplier. The procedures are very similar to those for entering details of purchase invoices.

(a) Click on the **Credit** button in the Suppliers window.

(b) The screen will display a new window just like the Supplier Invoice window, except that the details of the credit note appear in red as you enter them.

5.3 The procedure is the same as that already described for entering details of purchase invoices. You must make sure, however, that:

(a) The nominal ledger code you select (N/C) is the same as the code that was chosen for the original purchase invoice details.

(b) The VAT code (T/C) is also the same as for the original purchase invoice.

5.4 Some other points should also be noted.

(a) Enter the **Date** on the credit note, not 'today's date'.

(b) The **Ref** item is for the credit note number, which you can copy from the credit note itself.

(c) The **Details** item can be used for recording brief details of the reason for receiving the credit note.

5.5 After you have entered the details of your credit note(s) click on **Save** as before. When you Save a credit note, the program:

(a) Updates the account(s) of the individual supplier(s) in the purchase ledger.

(b) Updates the Creditors Control Account and the other relevant accounts in the nominal ledger.

Activity 4.8

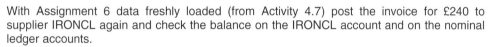

With Assignment 6 data freshly loaded (from Activity 4.7) post the invoice for £240 to supplier IRONCL again and check the balance on the IRONCL account and on the nominal ledger accounts.

Then post a credit note for the same amount to the IRONCL account and check that the balances have reverted to their previous level.

---

6 REPORTS

6.1 When you have entered a day's batch of invoices you can print a list of the details, with totals. These listings are sometimes called 'Day Books'. In Sage, logically enough, they have names like 'Supplier Invoices' report, 'Supplier Credits' report and so on.

6.2 To produce a Supplier Invoices report or a Supplier Credits report, click on the Reports button in the Suppliers window. A new window will appear as shown over the page.

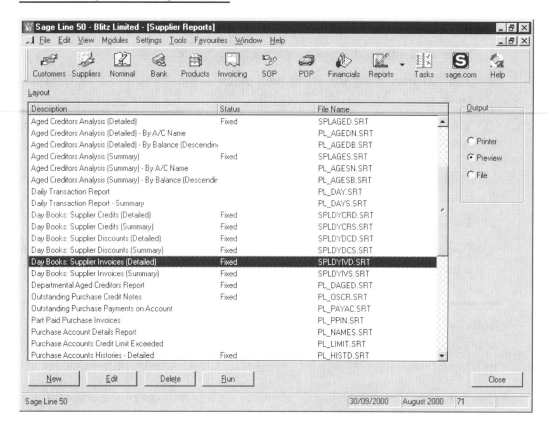

Output

6.3 Begin by choosing how you want your report to be output. There are three alternatives, from which you choose *one* by clicking in the white circle next to the appropriate label in the Output section of the screen. A black bullet will appear in the circle when you do this.

(a) *Printer.* This sends your report straight to a printer to be printed out. The usual Windows Print window will appear, allowing you to choose what part of the document you want printed, what printer you want to send it to and so on. Printing things using Windows applications is explained in Chapter 2.

(b) *Preview.* This option brings up a screen display of the information that you can edit to some extent for printing purposes. For example you might want to change the font style or the width of the margins.

(c) *File.* This option allows you to save a copy of the report on disk. The usual Windows **Save As** window will appear and you will have to choose a name for report and specify the directory in which you want it to be saved. Again, see Chapter 2 if you have forgotten how to use the Save As window.

Report type

6.4 The main box on the screen contains a list of all the different types of report that the package is set up to produce. All you have to do is click on the type of report you want or scroll down to it, using the cursor keys ↓ or ↑ until it is highlighted. Pick Day Books: Supplier Invoices (Detailed), if you are trying this out on screen as you read.

You now click on **Run.**

Criteria

6.5 You must now choose what transactions you want to appear in your listing. There are five main criteria for doing this.

(a) By specifying a supplier range (the accounts you wish to be included).

(b) By specifying a date range (the date or dates of the transactions you wish to list).

(c) By specifying a transaction range (the range of transaction numbers for which you require a listing).

(d) By specifying a department range.

(e) By specifying a nominal account range.

Supplier range

6.6 Accept the defaults (by 'Tabbing' through) if you want transactions with all suppliers to be included in the report. However, you may want a report of transactions with suppliers in a certain range eg A – D. If, for example, you had a query from a specific supplier about invoices sent to you in the last month you would specify the appropriate date range, leave the transaction range as it is (ranging from the first to the most recent transaction) and then enter the supplier code in *both* boxes in the **Supplier** section. Note that you can click on the Finder button (or press F4 when the cursor is in the appropriate box) if you are not sure of the account code.

Specifying a date range

6.7 Press Tab if necessary until the first box in the date section is highlighted. As a default this may show the date 01/01/1980, but it is unlikely that you will want to accept this. The second box may show a date like 31/12/2019. Again it is unlikely that you will want to accept this.

6.8 Instead you should key in the earliest date for transactions you wish to list and then the latest date. Key in each date using *two digits* for the day of the month, two digits for the month of the year and two digits for the year (there is no need to type slashes or the full four digit year, the program will insert these automatically).

Examples	*Enter*
6th April 2000	060400
15th May 2000	150500
2nd November 2000	021100

6.9 Suppose today is 5 October and you have just entered invoices received from suppliers with various dates from 30 September to 2 October. In the first Date Range box enter 30092000 then press Tab. In the second box type 02102000. You can use the calendar button if you prefer.

6.10 You are now ready to produce your report. Just Click on **OK** and wait for the report to be output in the way you specified earlier.

Specifying a transaction range

6.11 Choosing the date range for a listing of purchase invoices or supplier credit notes can be a problem because the invoices or credit notes will have different dates. When an invoice has a date that is now several weeks old, it could be very difficult to be sure of including it in a report by specifying the date range, without listing other invoices you have already processed in the past.

6.12 You can specify the invoices (or credit notes) you wish to list by specifying their transaction numbers. These are unique numbers, automatically allocated to each entry into the system by the program. To specify a transaction range, you should remember to *take a note* of the first transaction number for the invoices and the credit notes when you start to process them. The second box in the Transaction section shows the total number of transactions entered so far on the system (purchase ledger, sales ledger and nominal ledger). Your next transaction will be the next number in the sequence. For example, if the box shows that 70 transactions have been processed (number of entries = 70) your next entry will be transaction 71.

You can find the last transaction number by clicking on **Financials** in the main window and jumping to the end of the list that appears.

6.13 The Transaction boxes on screen will display a transaction range from 1 to 9999999 (or to the most recent transaction number). You should alter the range, to specify the transactions you wish to list.

6.14 Don't worry about mixing purchase invoices and credit note transaction numbers. The report will contain only one type of transaction or the other (ie invoices only or credit notes only), depending on the type of report you have selected.

6.15 You are now ready to produce a report of transaction within the range specified. Just Click on **OK** and wait for the report to be output in the way you specified earlier.

Nominal account range

6.16 The procedure is the same if you wanted to know about all transactions posted, say, to nominal account codes 7000 to 7999, or code 1200 to 1200 (ie account 1200 only).

6.17 Again when you have specified the range you want you are ready to produce your report as before.

Activity 4.9

Load a fresh copy of Assignment 6 data. Run the report Day Books: Supplier Invoices (Detailed). Make sure that the data range covers the period from 1 August 2000 to 30 September 2000.

What are the totals shown and what is the number of the last transaction listed.

6.18 If you use the Preview option for Output, Sage will open a Report or 'File View' window for the report. You can switch between the report and the program itself by clicking on the word **Window** at the top of the screen and then clicking on whichever window you want.

Closing a Report or File View window

6.19 Buttons at the bottom of the screen give you a variety of options for moving about in the report, viewing it in different ways, saving it, printing it, or just closing the report window.

7 CONCLUSION

Experiment ...

7.1 This is an important chapter because it introduces many of the widely used features of the Sage package. Spend some time going over what you have read, ideally while sitting at a computer. Try calling up windows and making entries in the way we describe. You won't break the software by experimenting with its features and you can always call up a 'clean' copy of Blitz case study data.

... and try an Assignment!

7.2 If you think you can follow the instructions in this chapter, **you should now be able to attempt Assignment 1** at the end of this Interactive Text. If you haven't yet attempted the **Activities** in this and the previous chapter, you should do these first.

Quick quiz

1   List three possible methods of setting up a new supplier account. (See paragraph 2.1)

2   What is the purpose of the Defaults tab in the Supplier Record? (3.16 - 3.20)

3   What is the Search button within the Finder window used for? (4.10)

4   Why are credit notes issued? (5.1)

5   What three alternatives exist for outputting a report from Sage? (6.3)

Answers to activities _____

Answer 4.1

It should appear between LERWIC and MATTHI.

Answer 4.2 _____

(a)   N14 6TS

(b)   Candy Spicer

(c)   T Cooper (Stationery) Ltd, 01582 405592

Answer 4.3 _____

Check the details you have entered on screen very carefully to make sure that all the spelling and numbers are exactly as you see them here. Have you got the right combination of letters and numbers in the post-code, for instance?

Answer 4.4

You should get BL OFFICE FURNISHING LTD and MUSWELL HILL COUNCIL.

Answer 4.5

(a) This is a hands on activity.

(b) FLOORI, HARDIN and LERWIC. This will only work if you follow the instructions given above and avoid the pitfalls.

Answer 4.6

You should get the answers £53.24, Materials Purchases and Office Machine Maintenance.

(Incidentally, unless we tell you otherwise, it does not normally matter whether you save information entered for activities or close without saving.)

Answer 4.7

These are the results you should get.

Account	With new transactions Dr	With new transactions Cr	Fresh Assignment 6 data Dr	Fresh Assignment 6 data Cr	Difference Dr	Difference Cr
2100		8034.78		7677.28		357.50
2202	7030.74		6977.50		53.24	
5000	6336.89		6236.89		100.00	
7701	204.26				204.26	
IRONCL		240.00		0.00		240.00
NEWLIT		789.63		672.13		117.50

The differences are entirely due to the transactions you posted in Activity 4.7. You should trace through each figure until you are happy about this, using your knowledge of double entry from Units 1 and 2. Ideally, write out all the T-accounts.

This Activity is to reassure you that Sage follows the same principles of double entry as a manual system and to highlight how much easier it is to use a computerised package.

Answer 4.9

The last transaction listed should be number 194. You should get the following totals.

Net	Tax	Gross
54,742.89	8,119.29	62,862.18

5 Customer invoices and credit notes

This chapter contains

1 The Customers window

2 New customers

3 Producing invoices

4 Invoicing for services provided

5 Invoicing for the sale of goods

6 Producing credit notes

7 Printing invoices and credit notes

8 Updating the ledgers

9 Updating the ledgers without producing invoices

10 Reports

11 Customer queries

12 Conclusion

Learning objectives

On completion of this chapter you will be able to:

- Set up accounts in the customers ledger

- Produce invoices and credit notes

- Post details of customer invoices and credit notes in the customers ledger and the Nominal ledger

- Extract information from the sales ledger

Knowledge and understanding

1   The relationship between different software packages.

2   The purpose and application of different software packages.

3   Types of data held on a computer system.

4   Location of information sources.

1   THE CUSTOMERS WINDOW

1.1   We will now look at another of the buttons from the **main** window. The **Customer** button in the main window brings up a Customers window which is very similar to the Suppliers window which we explored in the previous chapter.

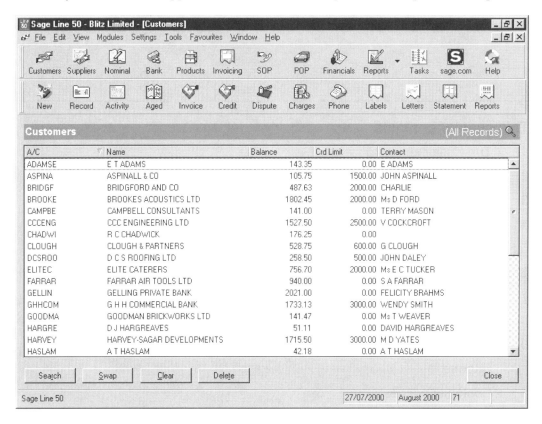

2   NEW CUSTOMERS

2.1   When an invoice has to be produced for sending to a new customer (ie a customer who has not been invoiced before by your company), an account for the customer must be set up in the customers ledger. There are four ways of entering new customer accounts in the ledger:

(a)   Using the **Record** button in the Customers window.

(b)   Using the **Invoices** button in the Customers window.

(c)   Using one of the buttons in the **Invoicing** window.

(d)   Using the **New** button from within Customers to access the Customer Record Wizard.

2.2   The **Record** button option and the Wizard option are similar to the options for entering details of new supplier accounts in the purchase ledger described in the previous chapter.

2.3   The option to set up new customer accounts from the **Invoices** button in the *Customers* window also works in a similar way to the method described in the context of the *Suppliers* window in Chapter 4.

2.4   Note that the **Invoices** option from within the Suppliers window would only be used if the actual invoices were not going to be printed from Sage. In the Blitz case study we will be producing Invoices and Credit Notes using Sage, therefore we will be using the **Invoicing** option from the **main** window.

Activity 5.1

If you have forgotten what a 'record' looks like, or what details are needed, load up any Assignment you like, click on **Customers** then on **Record** and select any account to remind yourself.

Credit limits

2.5   For the purpose of the case study and Assignment 2 you will be required to enter an amount for the maximum credit that will be allowed to the customer (ie the maximum value of goods or services that will be supplied on credit at any time). This amount should be entered as the 'Credit Limit' in the appropriate box.

2.6   How you enter new customer accounts from within the **Invoicing** window is described later in this chapter.

3   PRODUCING INVOICES

3.1   If you select the **Invoicing** button from the **main** window the following box will appear.

BPP
PUBLISHING

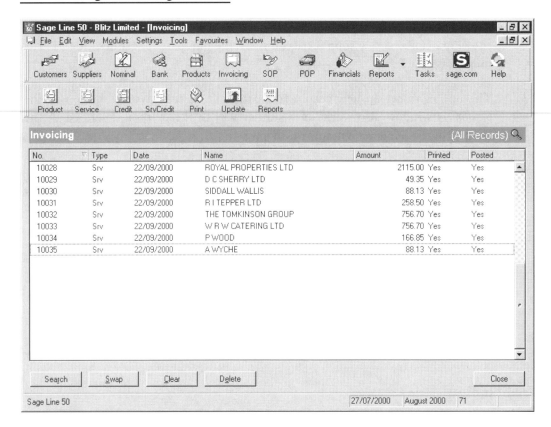

3.2 The **Product** button and the **Service** button in the Invoicing window can be used to:

   (a) Set up accounts for a new customer in the customers ledger.
   (b) Record details of invoices for sending to customers.
   (c) Print the invoices.

3.3 As you process invoices the blank space in this window will gradually be filled up with key details of each invoice, providing a handy numerical index of all invoices in the system. The **Swap** and **Clear** buttons affect which items are selected (highlighted) in the main part of the screen. Test these functions for yourself. The **Search** button will be explained later in this chapter.

Invoicing for goods or services?

3.4 Invoices to customers can be for goods supplied on credit or services supplied on credit. Blitz Limited in the case study is essentially a service company, but does sell some cleaning materials on credit to customers.

3.5 The following options are available in the Invoicing window.

	Pop-up Label	*Use*
(a)	Product	To invoice for the sale of goods or a product
(b)	Service	To invoice for the supply of services
(c)	Credit	To produce a credit note for goods
(d)	Service Credit	To produce a credit note for services
(d)	Print	To print invoices or credit notes
(e)	Update	To post invoices and credit notes to the ledgers
(f)	Reports	To produce lists of invoices in various stages of production

Invoice and credit note numbering

3.6 Invoices should be numbered sequentially. The program therefore allocates a number to each invoice automatically as you work, by adding 1 to the number of the previous invoice.

The Sage windows for Invoicing

3.7 Invoices (and credit notes) are built up in sections, and the appropriate details must be entered in each section.

    (a) There is a main input window, which is used to enter the customer's account reference code (and, for new customers, other details such as name and address).

    (b) Windows can be called up:

        (i) For entering line-by-line details for the invoice, such as the details of the goods or services provided and the price.

        (ii) To specify the *nominal code* to which the transaction should be posted.

    (c) An Order Details screen can be displayed, for entering certain order details, such as specifying the delivery address, if this differs from the invoice address.

    (d) A Footer Details window can be displayed, for entering details to appear in the bottom part of the invoice, such as the price for carriage outwards (ie delivery cost), if any, and discounts. This needn't be used if there are no such details to add.

Activity 5.2

Familiarise yourself with the above by clicking on **Invoicing** in the main window and seeing what happens when you click on the various buttons and options available. Press **Esc** to get back to the initial Invoicing screen whenever you like.

---

4 INVOICING FOR SERVICES PROVIDED

4.1 Invoices for services can be produced using the **Service** button in the Invoicing window. When you click on this button, the window shown below will appear.

4.2 This window is used to enter the details for one invoice. Each invoice is for the sale of one or more services or items. There is a separate line for the details of each item, in the main (central) part of the screen.

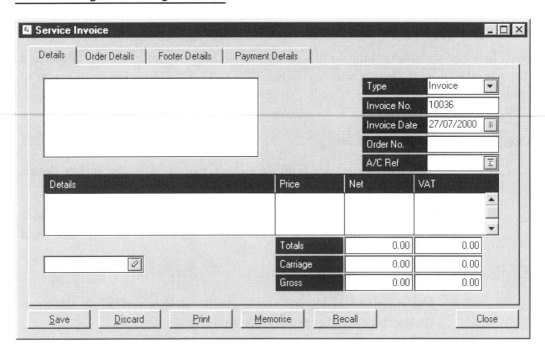

The customer account

4.3 The cursor begins in the **A/C Ref** box where you enter the customer's account reference. You can type in the code directly if you know it, or just type *part* of the code if you can make a good guess at it. If you type in your guess at the code and press Tab, a list of Customer Accounts will appear with the nearest code to the one you guessed at highlighted. If this is correct, click on OK or press Enter to accept the code. If not you will have to scroll up or down the list in the usual way to find the customer you want.

4.4 If you have no idea of the code, this first box has the Finder button it to help you find it. Click on this button or press function key F4 to display the list of Customer Accounts. Scroll down the list using the cursor keys or the scroll bar until you find the one you want then click on OK or press Enter. The customer code will appear in the A/C Ref box and the full name and address will appear in the box in the top left hand corner.

4.5 If the invoice is to be sent to a new customer, bring up the Finder list and click on the **New** button at the bottom of the Finder window. A screen will appear that is just like the one you met in the previous chapter for entering new Supplier records. Enter all the details for the new account and click on **Save**. You will then be returned to the customer accounts list and the account that you have just set up will be highlighted. Press Enter or click on OK to accept this.

4.6   Once you are satisfied that you have the correct customer account code in the A/C Ref box press Tab. This will take you to the **Details** section of the screen, but before we proceed there are a couple of things to check.

Invoice number

4.7   The invoice number is already shown on the screen. This is automatically entered as the next number in sequence after the previous invoice produced by the system.

4.8   It should usually be unnecessary to alter this number. However, the number can be altered if required simply by typing in a new number. (Use Shift and Tab to 'go backwards' to the Invoice No.)

Invoice Date

4.9   The screen will display today's date (ie the date in the computer system). To accept this date, press Tab. Another invoice date can be entered, if required. As the Assignments in this book are set back in the Year 2000, you will need to enter an appropriate date for every invoice. (Note: If you are going to enter many invoices with the same date, use the **Change Program Date** function under the **Settings** menu option from the main menu.)

Activity 5.3

Load up the data for **Assignment 1** and then enter these details in a service invoice, following the instructions above.

A/C Ref: WRWCAT
Invoice number: 20000
Date: 25 November 2000
Details: Contract cleaning
Amount: £100.00 plus VAT

What is the name and address details of the customer concerned?

The Details box

4.10   Having entered the date, press Tab until you get to the main part of the screen. In the details box enter a description of the service that has been delivered. In the Blitz case study this will be something like 'Window Cleaning' or 'Domestic Services'.

4.11   Before tabbing on from the Details box to the Price box you *must* do one of two things (the choice is yours).

       (a)   Press function key F3.

       (b)   Click on the little button with a pencil symbol that you can see *below* the Details box next to the box that says 'Item 1 of 0'.

       A third option is to Tab on to the Price box and then *double-click* in the Details line you have just entered. We do *not* recommend this because it is then too easy to forget about filling in all necessary details.

4.12   Whichever you do, the following window will appear.

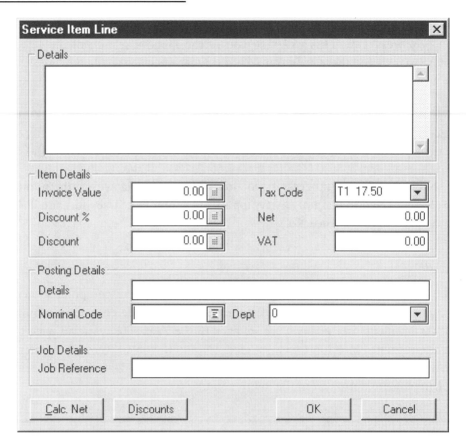

4.13   This window shows the text you entered in the details box in the main Service Invoice window. This is how the text will appear on the invoice and you can edit it or add to it if you like.

4.14   As mentioned above, this is the chance to change the Tax code if you need to do so. The VAT will be recalculated if you Tab down to the Tax Code box and specify a different code to the standard T1 (click on the arrow beside the Tax code box for other options). You won't normally need to do this.

4.15   You can also enter the Invoice Value and any *additional* Discount details (*not* settlement discount, which is handled elsewhere). If you click on the buttons beside these boxes (or press F4) a little drop-down calculator appears.

<-	C	Ce	/
7	8	9	×
4	5	6	-
1	2	3	+
0		.	=

This can be operated either with the mouse, or better, by using the *numeric keypad* on the keyboard. It is useful if, say, you are preparing an invoice for 7 items at £9.36 each and you don't trust yourself to do the maths in your head (!).

4.16   In fact you can bring up a calculator window at *any* time, just by pressing F2. To enter the result of a calculation into a field in a Sage screen you can press Ctrl + C, to copy the value from the calculator, then click on the field in question and press Ctrl + V.

Nominal code

4.17   This box is where you specify the nominal code for the invoice.

4.18   Each item on the invoice can have a different nominal ledger code if appropriate (in other words different items on the same invoice can be given different nominal ledger sales account codes). For each item (each line of Details you enter in the main Service invoice window) the code for the appropriate nominal ledger sales account should be entered using the Service Item Line screen.

4.19   In the Blitz Limited case study, the nominal ledger codes that are used are:

Code	Nominal ledger account
4000	Sales - Contract Cleaning
4001	Sales - Window Cleaning
4002	Sales - Domestic Services
4100	Sales - Materials

4.20   Rather than memorising these accounts, an easy approach is to key in the number 4 alone and then press Tab (or use function key F4). This brings up the list of Nominal Accounts with number 4000 highlighted. If Contract Cleaning is not the account you want then just scroll to find Window Cleaning or whatever. Once the nominal account you want is highlighted press Enter or click on OK and this account number will be entered in the right box.

4.21   There is also the option of specifying a Department for management accounting analysis purposes. This facility is not used in the Blitz case study so once you have entered the nominal code you can just press Enter or click on OK to be returned to the main Service invoice window.

Price and VAT

4.22   Press Tab once you have entered the details for an item and its nominal code and you will be taken to the **Price** box. Enter the amount of the invoice *excluding VAT* and press Tab again. The Net and VAT amounts will be calculated automatically. By default VAT will be 17.5% of the Net Amount you entered. (If you need to change this you can return to the Service Item Line window and do so.)

4.23   You are now taken to the next line of Details and you can follow the same procedure to enter a second invoice item and a third, and so on.

Activity 5.4

Load up the data for **Assignment 6**. Prepare the following service invoices (you have to find out the Nominal code yourself). Click on **Save** when you have entered the details for each invoice.

No.	Date	A/C	Details	N/C	Price
10053	25/11/2000	ADAMSE	Window cleaning	?	£100
10054	25/11/2000	GARDEN	Contract cleaning	?	£100

When you have finished press **Esc** (or click on **Close**) to return to the initial Invoicing screen. Scroll down to the bottom and make a note of the amount of each of the invoices you entered.

Explain the results.

PUBLISHING

Order Details

4.24 Occasionally, you might want to include extra details about the order on the invoice, for example:

(a) To specify a delivery address when this differs from the invoice address.

(b) To specify payment terms (eg 'PAYMENT REQUIRED WITHIN 30 DAYS OF INVOICE DATE').

4.25 To add these details, you should click on the **Order Details** index tab. A new window will appear on screen, and you should use this to specify the details you wish to add or alter. Press Tab to move from one field (item) to the next, or when you do not wish to input any details for the field.

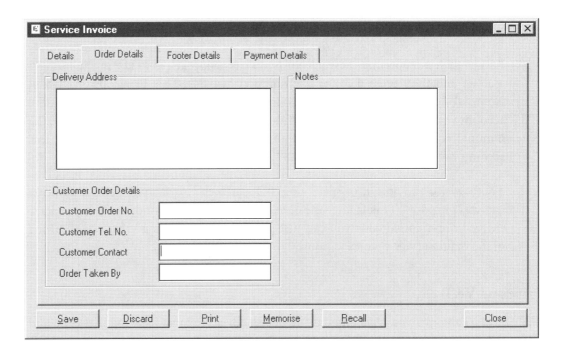

Customer Order No.

4.26 This box can be used to enter any customer reference for the order, such as the order number used by the customer when placing the order.

Customer Tel. No./Contact

4.27 The customer's telephone number and contact name will be displayed automatically.

Delivery Address

4.28 The delivery name and address can be entered here, when this is different from the name and address on the invoice (and in the records in the customer's account in the customers ledger).

Notes

4.29 Notes can be added, to appear on the invoice. These can be used, if required, to bring special information to the customer's attention; for example '5% DISCOUNT FOR SETTLEMENT WITHIN 7 DAYS OF INVOICE DATE'.

4.30   When you have inserted the special order details you require click on the next index tab at the top of the window.

Footer Details

4.31   If you wish, you can also add details to the bottom of the invoice for:

(a)   Charging for the delivery of goods (Carriage).

(b)   Providing details of any discounts offered to the customer for early payment (Settlement Terms).

(c)   Giving every item on the invoice the same tax code, nominal ledger code or department code (Global).

Of these, only (a) is described in this chapter.

4.32   If you wish to add footer details to an invoice, click on the **Footer Details** index tab. A new window will appear, as shown below.

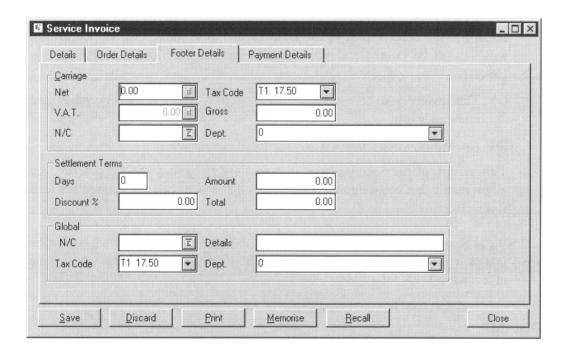

Carriage

4.33   The amount of charges for carriage outwards can be entered in the Net box at the top of the window. The charge for carriage, *excluding VAT*, should be keyed in.

Tax code (T/c)

4.34   Unless told otherwise use the same tax code for VAT as for the main invoice. It should usually be T1, meaning that VAT is chargeable at the standard rate of 17.5%.

Nominal code

4.35   Enter the nominal ledger code for the Carriage Outwards account in the nominal ledger. In the Blitz Limited system, this code is 4905. Otherwise you may need to click on the Finder button beside this box to find the right code.

Activity 5.5

Load up the data for Assignment 6. Enter the following details, referring back to the previous paragraphs for instructions if necessary.

No.	Date	A/C	Details	N/C	Price
10055	31/12/2000	OWENLO	Sundry	4101	£100

Delivery address: 14 Woodgate Street, Barnet, N16 3BB
Order no.: 14879
Telephone number: 020-7734 2843
Customer contact: Jennifer
Carriage: £5
Settlement discount: 5% if settled within 30 days

What is the total amount of the invoice as shown on screen? Did any discrepancies arise as you were doing this activity, and if so what should you do about them?

Saving the invoice details

4.36 When you have entered all the details of the invoice (which might or might not include footer details) click on the **Save** button. This adds the main details of the invoice to the index shown in the main Invoicing window. The Service Invoice window will be cleared and you can start entering details for a new invoice. However:

(a) The invoice you have saved is *not yet posted* to the customers ledger and nominal ledger.

(b) An invoice is not printed.

This feature of the Sage package very sensibly recognises that in practice you might realise that you want to change the details to be posted and printed at a later stage.

4.37 We shall see how to *print and post* invoices *later in this chapter*. It is important *not* be in a rush to post things to the ledgers. You have *saved* all your hard work, so none of it is wasted.

Discard

4.38 As an alternative to Saving the details you have entered, the **Discard** button allows you to cancel all the details of the invoice you have just entered. It is sometimes easier and safer to start again than trying to edit a hopelessly wrong set of entries.

Editing saved entries

4.39 You can change any of the entries you have made so far, so long as you haven't posted them (updated the ledgers). Click on the relevant invoice (which you will now see listed in the main Invoicing window) and then click on the **Service** button again. Alternatively, just double-click the invoice you wish to edit.

Activity 5.6

(a)   Load Assignment 6 and find out the balance on the Customer account WOODPX.

(b)   Enter the following service invoice details (accept the invoice number offered by Sage and find out the nominal code for yourself). Then click on **Close** and respond **Yes** to the question 'do you want to save changes?'

Date	A/C	Details	Price
31/12/2000	WOODPX	Domestic services	£600

(c)   Find out the balance on the customer account WOODPX.

5   INVOICING FOR THE SALE OF GOODS

5.1   To produce an invoice for the sale of products, you can use the **Product** button in the Invoicing window. When you click on this button, the screen will display windows similar to those that appear when you select the **Service** invoice option.

In the Blitz case study all invoices and credit notes are processed as Service Invoices or Service Credits. The reason for this is that, as a cleaning company, Blitz is essentially a service provider.

The few sales of materials Blitz does make are processed on 'Service' invoices for simplicity and consistency. For example, a customer can then be invoiced for cleaning services and purchases of cleaning materials on the same invoice.

However, it is perfectly acceptable to invoice these sales using the Product invoicing option. The important thing, from an accounting point of view, is to ensure sales of products are **posted to the correct nominal account** - in Blitz's case account 4100 - Sales Materials.

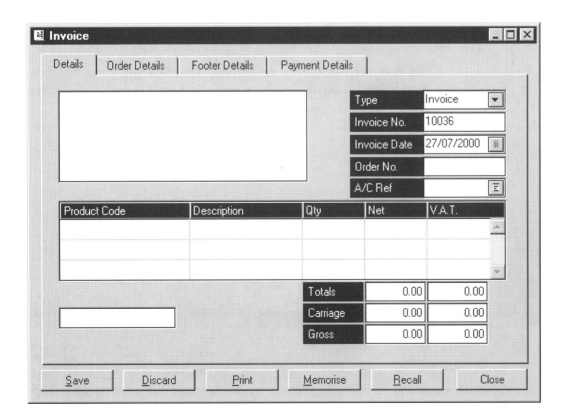

5.2   This operates just like the Service window with the following exceptions.

Product code

5.3 Once you have entered the A/C Ref and pressed Tab you will be taken to the **Product Code** box in the central part of the window. On each line of the screen, you can enter details of sales for a product. One line of details should be entered for each item sold.

5.4 Enter the code for the product. If you don't know what the code is you can use the Finder button beside the Product Code heading or press function key F4 when the cursor is flashing in the Stock Code column. A window will appear with a list of stock items and their codes. There is also the facility to set up a new stock item if you wish. This is much like setting up a new customer or supplier account. When the stock item you want is highlighted, press Enter or click on the OK button and this code will be shown in the Product Code field in the main screen, together with its description.

5.5 A company might not use product codes in its Sage system, perhaps because, like Blitz Ltd in the case study, selling materials is just a sideline, or because stock is set up on a different system. There may also be times when an item sold is 'non-standard' and does not have a stock code because it is not usually carried in stock. In this case you can make one of three entries in the Product Code field.

M This simply allows you to type a message in the Description box. You might want to type something like *'Thank you for ordering the following items'* before listing out the items ordered with their prices.

S1 This code is used for a non-stock item to which VAT applies.

S2 This code is used for a non-stock item to which VAT does not apply.

5.6 You will only use the **S1** code in the Blitz case study. Type in S1 and press Tab. A window headed Product Item Line will appear. This is shown below.

5.7 If you think this is rather like the screen that appears when you press F3 when you are preparing a Service invoice, you are right. In fact this window will also appear if you *double-click* in the relevant line.

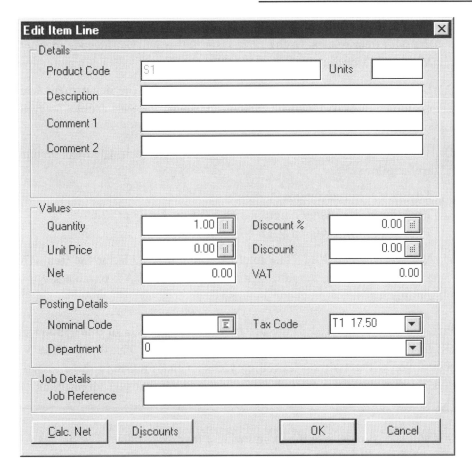

5.8   The entries to make are as follows.

(a)   *Description.* One line's worth of description can be entered. You can follow this with two lines of *Comments* which might describe the item further, or make it clear that it is a non-stock item, or explain how the item is packaged ('box of 12'), or whatever else you like.

(b)   Once you have entered your description and comments, Tab down to the *Quantity* box and key in the number of items you are selling. Note that if the item is sold and priced in, say, boxes of twelve you should key in the number of *boxes*, not the number of individual items.

(c)   Pressing Tab takes you to the *Unit Price*. This is the price of one unit of sale (eg a box), not of an individual item.

Suppose for example an item's price is £2 per can and cans are sold in boxes of 12. If you were selling somebody 36 cans you could enter this in two ways.

	Method 1		*Method 2*
Quantity	36	Quantity	3
Unit Price	2	Unit Price	24

Method 2 is generally preferable. To make things crystal clear on the invoice you might include the words 'box of 12 cans' in your description or comments

(d)   *Discount %.* This is zero, unless the customer is entitled to a trade discount on the net price; for example, a discount for bulk purchasing. You can simply Tab on to the next item when there is no trade discount. If you do offer a discount of, say, 2%, key in 2.

(e) *Nominal Code*. This is the nominal ledger code for the sales account to which the sales item relates. In the Blitz system, this will be the code for the Sales – Materials account, which is code 4100.

(f) *Department*. This can be used to enter a code for the department which has made the sale. In the Blitz system, department codes are *not used*, and you should leave this item blank simply by pressing Tab.

(g) The same *Tax Codes* apply as described previously. In the Blitz system, these are as follows.

   T0   for zero-rated items
   T1   for standard-rated items (with VAT currently at 17.5%)
   T9   for items to which VAT does not apply

(h) *Net, Discount and VAT*. The total net amount payable for the item (Quantity × Unit Price), the amount of discount and the VAT payable are displayed automatically.

5.9   Once you have completed all the details you want to enter in this window click on OK. If you have forgotten to specify the Quantity, the Tax Code or the Nominal account you will get a message telling you so. Click on OK in the message box or press Enter to clear the message, type in the entry that you forgot, then click on OK.

5.10 This will take you back to the main Product invoice window. The details you have just specified will now be shown in the relevant boxes. The cursor will be flashing in the Description box and you add whatever details you like. Once you have done this and you are satisfied that the figures are correct (change them if not), press Tab until you reach the next line of the invoice.

5.11 The main invoice screen also gives you options for Order Details and Footer Details. These features were described in the previous section of this chapter.

5.12 When the invoice is complete and correct Save it by clicking on the **Save** button and the screen will be cleared ready for the next invoice. If you have entered details of all the invoices you have to process click on Close or press Esc to get back to the main Invoicing window.

Activity 5.7

On 21 October 2000 a customer R I Tepper Ltd purchased 4 cases of Gleamo. One case contains 12 tins and costs £10.68.

Re-load Assignment 6 and enter this transaction as a **Product** invoice number 10065, following the instructions given in the preceding paragraphs (use Product Code 51).

What is the total amount of the invoice? Which nominal code should be used?

6   PRODUCING CREDIT NOTES

6.1   The Invoicing window also offers you Credit Note options. Processing credit notes is similar to processing invoices.

6.2 Click on the **Credit** button or **SrvCredit** button in the Invoicing window and a new window will appear that looks and works exactly like the windows just described.

6.3 To prepare a credit note for *goods* sold, proceed as described in the previous section of this chapter.

6.4 To produce a credit note for *services*, use the Service Credit (**SrvCredit**) button, which is just like preparing a Service invoice.

7 PRINTING INVOICES AND CREDIT NOTES

7.1 To print invoices and credit notes you have two main options.

(a) At any time during the preparation of an invoice you can print out a hard copy to see what it looks like on paper. If you don't like what you see and *you have not yet updated the ledgers* (ie posted the invoice) you can make permanent changes to it. If you do like what you see, you can then Save the invoice and go on to the next one.

To print out a copy of the invoice while you are preparing it click on the **Print** button at the bottom of the Product invoice window or the Service invoice window. Further windows will appear as explained below.

(b) You Save each invoice or credit note before leaving the input screen. A list of invoices and credit notes will be shown in the main Invoicing window and from this you can select invoices to print.

The Print button (on the main Invoicing screen)

7.2 If you are going to use the **Print** button you must first select which invoices you want to print out. One way of doing this is simply to highlight the invoice(s) concerned in the index list in the main Invoicing window by clicking on them. This is the easiest option if you only want to print one or two invoices.

7.3 If you want to highlight *all* the invoices in an index list quickly, first use the **Clear** button at the bottom of the main invoicing window (this takes away any odd highlighting there might be) and then click on the **Swap** button (this will now highlight *all* the invoices). Every time the **Swap** button is clicked it changes highlighted invoices into unhighlighted invoices and vice versa.

The Search button

7.4 You may want only to print or look at some invoices and credit notes rather than all of them. To cope with this problem you can use the **Search** button at the bottom of the main invoicing screen. Click on this and the following window will appear.

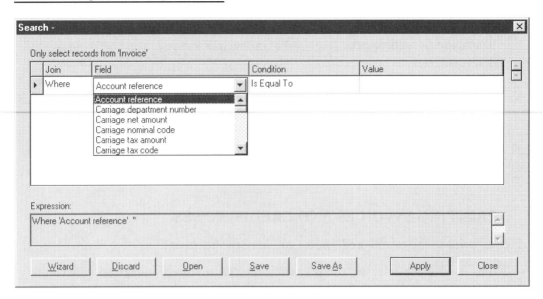

7.5 The search button appears in many places throughout Sage and always works in the same way. Re-read paragraphs 4.10 – 4.15 of Chapter 4 now, then attempt Activity 5.8.

Activity 5.8

Load Assignment 5 and click on the Invoicing button. Use the Search button to produce the following lists in the Invoicing window.

(a) A list of Service invoices with an Invoice Total greater than £1,500.00, with an invoice number less than 10040.

(b) A list of invoices or credit notes that have not been posted.

(c) A list devised by you using the wildcard symbol (*).

(d) A full list of all invoices and credit notes on the system.

Printing

7.6 After clicking the Print button in the main Invoicing window, another window will appear, like the following.

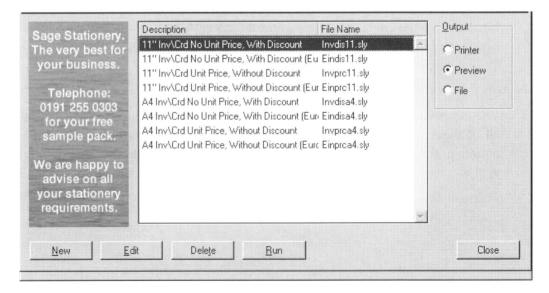

7.7 You are given the options of sending the invoice(s) straight to the Printer, seeing a Preview on screen or creating a File copy of the invoice. (The file option has nothing to do with posting the invoice to the ledgers: it is a file copy of the invoice document.)

7.8 You get a list of possible layouts for your invoice in the Description box. We suggest you use the layout INVDIS.

You have two of each of these – one set for 11" paper and one set for A4 paper. Ask your tutor which your printer uses.

Alternatively your tutor might tell you to use a special layout designed by your college to suit its type of printers.

7.9 On the next page is an example of how an invoice might appear on headed paper using the format INVDIS.

7.10 When you have selected your layout, click in the **Preview** circle and then click on **Run**. A screen display of your invoice will shortly appear. Click on **Zoom** and then Page Width to get a decent view of your invoice. If you are happy with what you see click on **Print.**

Managing the printer

7.11 When you click on the **Run** button the usual Windows Print window will appear. This gives you various options (number of copies, print quality and so on) partly depending on the type of printer(s) you have available. Look back at the section in Chapter 2 on printing if you are not sure what to do here.

Extra copies

7.12 Once you have printed an invoice or credit note a Yes will appear in the Print column in the main Invoicing window. This is a useful check if you are not sure whether or not an invoice has been printed, but *you can still print out a duplicate copy* of the invoice if you want to. An invoice might get lost in the post or damaged before it is sent, for example. To print another copy just select the invoice in the main Invoicing window, click on the **Print Invoices** button and proceed as usual.

Activity 5.9

Load Assignment 6 and print out your own copy of the invoice shown on the following page.

---

8 UPDATING THE LEDGERS

8.1 When you click on the **Save** button after processing an invoice or credit note, the details are *not* posted to the customers ledger or nominal ledger.

BPP
PUBLISHING

Invoice	Page 1

BLITZ LTD

25 APPLE ROAD

LONDON

N12 3PP

<table>
<tr><td>
D J HARGREAVES
6 COLLEGE PARK
LONDON
NW10 5CD
</td></tr>
</table>

Invoice No.	10042
Invoice/Tax Date	08/10/2000
Cust. Order No.	
Account No.	HARGRE

Quantity Details	Disc%	Disc Amount	Net Amount	VAT Amount
Domestic services	0.00	0.00	43.50	7.61

Total Net Amount	43.50
Total VAT Amount	7.61
Carriage	0.00
Invoice Total	51.11

8.2 To post the details to the ledgers, you must click on the **Update** button in the Invoicing window. Just like printing, you can post many invoices (or credit notes) all at the same time, or you can select individual ones for posting. The following window will appear.

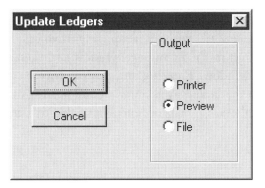

8.3 This procedure will generate a report telling you what has been posted. Decide whether you want a printed report or just a screen display or preview, or if you want a file copy of the report. Then click on OK or press Enter.

8.4 The Update Ledgers report is a list of the invoices or credit notes you have just posted to the ledger, showing details of each item posted. The listing shows:

- Invoice number or credit note number
- Invoice date
- Customer's account code
- Transaction number given to the entry by the accounts
- Product code, if any
- Nominal ledger code for each transaction
- Department code (if any) for the transaction
- Description of the goods or services sold (and quantity)
- Net amount of the invoice (or credit note)
- Tax code for the VAT
- Amount of the VAT
- Total of each invoice and a grand total for all invoices posted

---

Activity 5.10

Re-load up Assignment 5 and confirm the balances on the following accounts.

GOODMA	0.00
HASLAM	0.00
Sales – Window cleaning (4001)	2,634.40

Now enter the following details exactly as instructed and **Save** each invoice.

Invoice.	Date	A/C	Details	Nominal code	Amount (net)
10053	25/10/2000	GOODMA	Window cleaning	4001	£100.00
10054	25/10/2000	HASLAM	Window cleaning	4001	£100.00

(a) What is the balance on the three accounts now?

(b) In the Invoicing window click on **Clear** at the bottom of the screen and then on the option **Update Ledgers**. Say **Yes** to the message that appears and choose whether you want a print-out or just a screen preview.

What is the balance on the three accounts now?

---

9 UPDATING THE LEDGERS WITHOUT PRODUCING INVOICES

9.1 In some companies, invoices could be produced manually or by means of a different system. When this situation occurs, the accounting system is used to post invoice and credit note details to the customers ledger and nominal ledger, but not to produce invoices.

9.2 To update the ledgers without producing invoices, you should click on the **Customers** button in the main Sage window and then on the **Invoices** button in the Customers window. Entering and posting invoice and credit note details can then be done in the same way as entering and posting details of invoices and credit notes from suppliers. These procedures have already been described in Chapter 4.

10 REPORTS

10.1 When you have entered a batch of invoices or credit notes (or several batches of invoices or credit notes) you can print a list of the details, with totals. This is often called a day book listing. In Sage the relevant *Day Books* reports are called *Customer Invoices* and *Customer Credits*. These can be generated by clicking on the **Reports** button in the *Customers* window, then selecting the report required eg Day Books: Customer Invoices (Detailed).

10.2 The procedure is exactly the same as the one described for producing Suppliers listings in the previous chapter. You can choose between detailed and summary reports, and specify a particular Date Range, Transaction Range, Customer Account Range or Nominal Account Range, just as before.

11 CUSTOMER QUERIES

11.1 Customers often telephone the accounts department of a company with queries about invoices or credit notes. These queries can often be answered by looking up the invoice details on the system. Typical queries could be:

(a) I haven't received the credit note you promised. Have you sent it yet?

(b) I haven't had an invoice from you yet. Can you tell me how much will it be?

(c) I haven't received your invoice yet. It might be lost in the post. Can you send me a duplicate copy?

Invoice or credit note details

11.2 You can look up the details of an invoice or credit note, to find out:

(a) Whether it is on the system.
(b) Whether the invoice or credit note has been printed (and presumably sent).

You can also obtain details of the invoice or credit note. To look up these details, you can use **Invoicing** button to display a complete list of all invoices then use the **Search** button to specify the customer's account code as your condition (for example you would set your criterion as, say, Where Account Reference Is Equal to ADAMSE. You can narrow the field further by specifying additional criteria, such as a date range.

Example

11.3 You receive a telephone enquiry from David Hargreaves, asking about an invoice that had been expected but not yet received. You might know the customer's account reference number already. In the case study of Blitz Limited, the customer's code would start with the first letters of the surname. There are two ways of finding the details you want.

(a) Call up the Invoicing window, set your Search criteria as Account Reference Is Equal to HAR★ and click on **Apply** and then on **Close**. All accounts with codes beginning with the letters HAR will be shown. Highlight the account and click on the **Service** button. You will probably get a warning telling you that the invoice has been posted and that amendments will not be saved. You only want to *look* at the details, so just click on OK and the invoice window that you used to prepare the invoice will be displayed once more.

(b) Alternatively click on the **Customers** button in the main Sage window. This too has a **Search** button and you might find it quicker to use this than to scroll right through the list. Once you find the account code for D Hargreaves click on it to highlight it, click on **Activity** and on **OK**. You will see on screen details of the account. However this will not tell you whether the invoice has been printed yet. Take a note of the number and use the Invoicing window to find this information.

Duplicate invoices

11.4 We saw how to print extra copies of invoices in section 7 of this chapter.

12 CONCLUSION

12.1 If you can follow the instructions in this chapter, you should be ready to attempt **Assignment 2**.

Quick quiz

1 List four methods for setting up a new customer account. (See paragraph 2.1)

2 Are you able to change the default invoice number allocated by Sage if required? (4.8)

3 List the four nominal ledger codes Blitz Limited uses for sales revenue. (4.20)

4 How do you post invoicing accounting entries to the nominal ledger? (8.2)

5 How would you print a Sales Ledger day book listing? (10.1)

Answers to activities _____

Answer 5.3

The screen should show the full details in the white box at the top left.

    W R W CATERING LTD
    11 STATION PARADE
    BARNET
    HERTS
    BT5 2KC

Answer 5.4

You should have got an amount of £117.50 for ADAMSE (N/C 4001) and of £116.63 for GARDEN (N/C 4000). Although the net amount of both invoices is £100, GARDEN's record is set up to receive settlement discount of 5% and so the Sage package automatically charges VAT on the discounted amount (£100 – 5% = £95).

£95 × 17.5% = £16.63

Very well done if you were able to explain the results without looking at this solution. You can check the records of ADAMSE and GARDEN to confirm that one is set up to receive settlement discount and the other is not.

Answer 5.5

You should have got the amount £122.51. First, set up the customer's record to receive 5% settlement discount. Delivery address, order number, telephone number and contact name should be entered on the Order Details tab, but not before you have checked why the phone number shown above is different to the one contained in the customer record (020 7734 2043). The number may have changed, or it may have been entered into the system incorrectly, or it may just be an additional number. Likewise you should check whether the customer's record should be permanently amended to show the contact name Jennifer.

The other details are entered on the Footer details tab.

Answer 5.6

The initial balance should be £0.00. The balance should still be £0.00 at the end of the activity, because you have not posted the invoice.

Answer 5.7

You should get the answer £50.20. The nominal code is 4100.

Answer 5.8

(a) Only eight invoices should appear.
(b) No invoices should appear.
(c) Did you get the result you expected and wanted?
(d) Credit notes 1 to 4 and invoices 10001 to 10052 should all appear.

Answer 5.10

(a) It is the same as when you started because you have not posted anything yet.

(b) GOODMA now has a balance of £117.50. HASLAM has a balance of £117.50. The Sales – Window Cleaning account has increased by £200 to £2,834.40.

6 Payments to suppliers

This chapter contains

1 Source documents for recording payments

2 Locating invoices for payment. Aged analysis

3 Posting payments

4 Discounts

5 Credit notes

6 Payments on account

7 'One-off' payments: cheque requisitions

8 Producing cheques

9 Reports

10 Queries about payments

11 Conclusion

Learning objectives

On completion of this chapter you will be able to:

- Identify the source documents you will need to process a payment to a supplier

- Identify invoices in the Suppliers ledger that are due for payment

- Post payments to the appropriate Suppliers ledger and Nominal ledger accounts

- Record and post payments

- Produce reports and remittance advices

- Deal with queries from suppliers

Knowledge and understanding

1 The relationship between different software packages.

2 The purpose and application of different software packages.

3 Types of data held on a computer system.

4 Location of information sources.

1 SOURCE DOCUMENTS FOR RECORDING PAYMENTS

1.1 Cheques for payments may be produced manually or printed from within Sage. Regardless of which method is used, the signing the cheques need to know that payment has been authorised. Therefore, they need to see the source documents which may include:

(a) The *invoice* or *invoices* for payment, and possibly a statement from the supplier listing all invoices still outstanding and unpaid;

(b) Any *credit note* or *credit notes* from the supplier; and

(c) Possibly *goods received note*, to confirm receipt of the goods that are being paid for.

1.2 The invoice must be signed or initialled by an *authorised* person, giving authority for the invoice to be paid. This signature could be written on the invoice itself, and dated. If any invoice has not been properly authorised, it should be referred to your supervisor.

1.3 A payment could be made for which there is an authorised *cheque requisition* form, instead of an invoice from a regular supplier with an account in the Suppliers Ledger. The procedures for recording such transactions in the accounts are different, and are explained later.

2 LOCATING INVOICES FOR PAYMENT – AGED ANALYSIS

2.1 If your supervisor tells you, say, to pay all invoices that have been outstanding for over one month, your first task would be to find the relevant source documents.

(a) If your department keeps unpaid invoices in date order in a separate file, this is usually a simple manual task. You can take the invoices for payment out of the file.

(b) Alternatively, you can identify which suppliers to pay by checking the records in the Suppliers Ledger. The most efficient way of doing this is to use an Aged Analysis.

2.2 An aged analysis is a listing of all accounts or selected accounts with the invoices analysed according to how long they have been outstanding.

2.3 Click on **Suppliers** and then on **Aged.** You will get the following dialogue box.

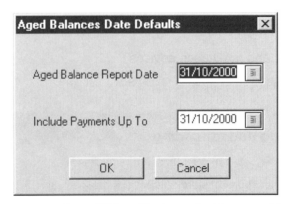

(a) *Aged Balances Report Date*. This will show the Program Date which will be today's date unless you have changed it (under Settings, Change Program Date).

You should enter the date you want to use to calculate the aged balances: the program will count back 30 days, 60 days, 90 days and so on from this date and analyse the balances accordingly. In the example above you would enter 31102000 and you would get balances that were 30, 60, 90 etc days old as at 31/10/2000.

(b) *Include Payments Up To.* You might have paid lots of invoices in early November but this might not be relevant to your report on the state of affairs at the end of October. You might only wish to include payments made up to 31/10/2000 (or another date): if so specify this here.

2.4 Click on **OK** and the following report will appear – the figures shown below were obtained using Assignment 1 data.

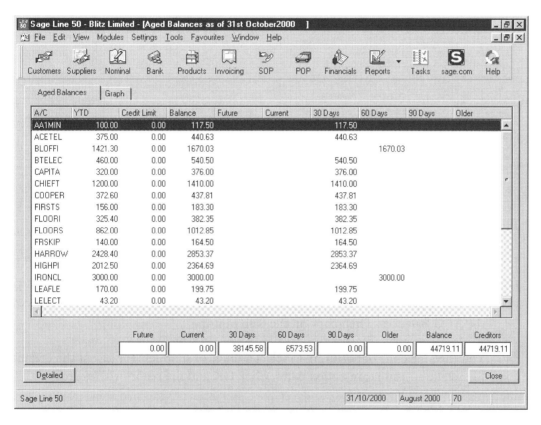

2.5 You can see at a glance how long each amount making up the current balance on each account has been outstanding.

Future

2.6 Sage is not clairvoyant, but if you are using dates for your reports that are prior to the real date it will know what transactions have been posted between your report date and the real date. Therefore an Aged Balances report will show you the total of such transactions in a **Future** column. For example, if you received and posted £5,000 of new invoices on 1 November, but ran a report on that day for 31 October the report would show an amount of £5,000 in the Future column.

Print-outs

2.7 It may well have occurred to you that it would be handy to have a *print-out* of this information. If you scroll through the list you may also feel that accounts with nil balances may as well be excluded. Such a report can be obtained by using the

107

PUBLISHING

Reports button in the Suppliers window. Get back to this by closing the Aged analysis window: just press Esc or click on Close.

2.8 Now click on the **Report** button. A Supplier Reports window appears, as follows.

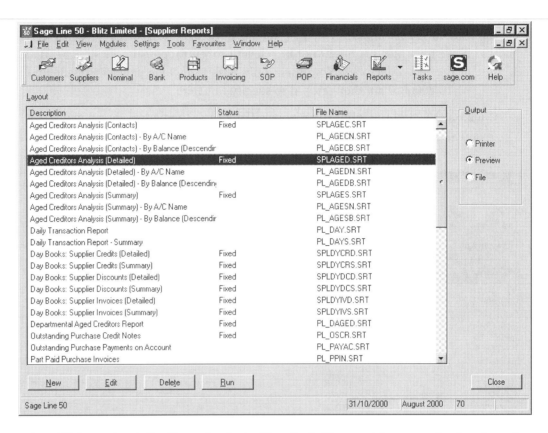

2.9 Click on Aged Creditors Analysis (Detailed) if you wish to see the invoices that make up the balance, or Aged Creditors Analysis (Summary) if you just wish to see the Aged Balances. Then click on the **Run** button.

2.10 You then have the opportunity to select a range of suppliers (or accept the defaults to include all), and transaction dates. Click OK and the report will be produced.

Activity 6.1

The Search button was explained in the previous chapter in relation to customers, but can also be used in the Suppliers Window. To practice using the Search button, load up the data for Assignment 2 and try getting listings of Suppliers' accounts according to a variety of criteria: all those with codes in the alphabetical range P to S, say, or all those with a balance over or under a certain amount, all those that do not have an address in London, or anything else you think of.

3 POSTING PAYMENTS

3.1 When payments are processed to suppliers accounts entries are made to:

- The suppliers' individual accounts in the Suppliers Ledger
- The creditors control account in the Nominal Ledger (debit)
- The bank account in the Nominal Ledger (credit)

3.2   To post a payment, you should have the following data:

(a)   The nominal ledger code for the bank account. In the Blitz case study, this is code 1200.

(b)   The supplier's account reference code.

(c)   The date of the payment.

(d)   If possible, the cheque number.

(e)   Usually, the cheque amount.

3.3   If you want to check the previous transaction details on a supplier's account before recording the payment, you can use the **Activity** button.

Allocation of payments to invoices

3.4   Normally, a payment is made to pay off one or more outstanding invoices. Instead of just recording a payment in the supplier's account, the payment should be allocated to the invoice or invoices to which it relates.

How to post payments

3.5   If you Click on the **Bank** button in the main Sage window a bank accounts window will appear with a number of buttons and a list of all the company's bank accounts. Highlight the Account the payments will be made from - in this case the Bank Current Account.

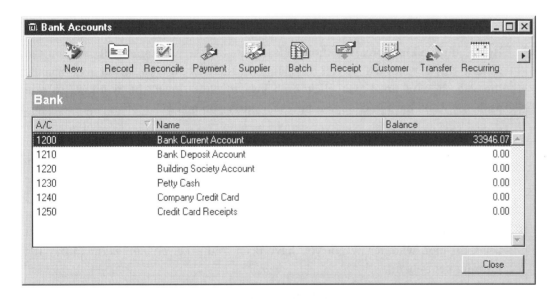

3.6   Click on the **Supplier** button and you will get a new window the top of which looks very much like a cheque book and the lower half of which tells you about outstanding invoices on a supplier's account.

BPP
PUBLISHING

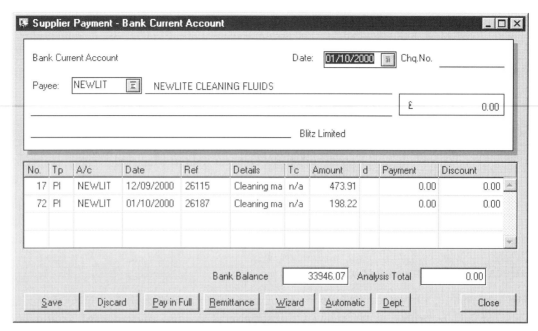

Most of the headings are self-explanatory. As you will see, the **Tp** column in the lower half of the screen identifies the type of transaction as a purchase invoice (PI), a purchase credit note (PC), or a purchase payment on account (PA).

3.7   When you first see this screen all the details will be blank and the cursor will be flashing in the **Payee** box. Here you type the supplier's code number (use the Finder button if you don't know the precise code). Press Tab. The supplier's full name will appear alongside the Payee box and the details of any outstanding invoices will appear in the lower half of the screen. The illustration above shows you what this will look like.

3.8   By default the **Date** box will show today's date (or the program date), but you can change this if you wish. If you do change it, the new date you enter will become the default date until you click on Close to shut down the window, so you probably won't have to change it for every entry you make.

3.9   When the date is the one you want, press Tab again and in the **Chq No.** box enter the number of the cheque you are posting. You will have to do this for *every* payment. Do not neglect to enter the cheque number: it will then show up in the records and it is a very useful reference.

3.10   Press Tab again and you are taken into a box with a pound sign. What you do next depends upon whether or not you have been told precisely *how much* to pay the supplier beforehand.

(a)   If you know that the cheque you are entering is to be for, say, £500, *type in* 500 and press Tab.

(b)   If you have been told to pay certain invoices, type nothing: just press Tab.

3.11   Look at the illustration above showing details for Newlite Cleaning Fluids. Two outstanding invoices are shown, one for £473.91 and the other for £198.22, a total of £672.18. The information and instructions you might have could be as follows.

(a)   A cheque for £473.91 is to be sent to Newlite Cleaning Fluids. **OR**

(b)   Any invoices received from Newlite Cleaning Fluids in September 2000 should be paid. **OR**

(c) The balance on the Newlite Cleaning Fluids account should be paid in full.

Predetermined cheque amount

3.12 If you have been told the amount of the cheque, type it into the box with the pound sign. Press Tab and two things will happen.

(a) Very satisfyingly, the amount that you typed in figures (eg '473.91') will appear in words ('Four hundred seventy-three Pounds and 91p'), just like on a real cheque.

(b) You will be taken to the first **Payment** box in the lower half of the screen. The amount shown (highlighted) in this box will at this point be 0.00. Look also at the Analysis Total box at the bottom of the window, which also shows 0.00 at this point.

3.13 Now click on the **Pay in Full** button at the bottom of the screen. The amount in the first Payment box (next to the invoice Amount box) will change to £473.91. The amount in the Analysis Total box will also change to £473.91. This, of course, is the total amount of the cheque you are paying.

3.14 The cursor, meanwhile will have moved down a line to the next Payment box and 0.00 will be highlighted. If you click on the Pay in Full button nothing will happen. Click on the Pay in Full button as much as you like but this will not change. This is because there is no difference between the amount in the £ sign box (the amount of the cheque) and the amount in the Analysis Total box: all the money available has already been allocated.

Remittance advices

3.15 If you want to print out an advice to send to the supplier indicating the invoices that are being paid you *must* do this now, before Saving the invoice. This is explained in more detail below.

Posting payments

3.16 You can now click on the **Save** button. The payment is then posted and the screen is cleared for the next payment. Payments will only be posted if the amount in the analysis total box equals the amount of the cheque.

Activity 6.2

(a) Load the data for Assignment 3. Change the program date to 31/10/2000 (from the main menu choose Settings, Change program Date). What is the balance on the Supplier account NEWLIT and the Bank account (1200)?

(b) Enter the details for a cheque to NEWLIT for £473.91 dated 10 October 2000, cheque number 010203. Print out a remittance advice, then save your entry.

(c) What is the balance on the account NEWLIT and the bank account now?

Paying specific invoices

3.17 Our second scenario suggested that you had been told to pay invoices with a September 2000 date only. If you look back to the Newlite illustration you will see that the only invoice that fits into this category is the one for £473.91. You proceed as follows.

(a) When you reach the box with the pound sign, just press Tab, leaving the box blank.

(b) The cursor will move to the September 2000 invoice's Payment box with an amount 0.00 highlighted.

(c) Click on the Pay in Full button. The amount in the first Payment box will change to £473.91, and so will the amount in the box with the pound sign showing the amount that the cheque will be for, and the amount in the Analysis Total box.

(d) The cursor will move to the next Payment box, beside the outstanding invoice amount of £198.22.

(e) You *do not* want to pay this second invoice because it is not a September 2000 invoice. Therefore (unless you first want to print a remittance advice note) just click on the **Save** button. The payment is posted and the screen will clear for the next entry.

Activity 6.3

Load Assignment 3 again. Change the program date to 31/10/2000. Following the above, pay any invoices received from Newlite Cleaning Supplies in September 2000. Cheque number is 010203. Also pay any received from British Telecom in September 2000. Cheque number is 010204.

Paying off the balance

3.18 The final scenario suggested that you were told to pay off the balance on the account. The procedure is exactly the same as the procedure for paying specific invoices, except that instead of Saving at step (e) you click on Pay in Full. You continue to do this for each invoice listed until all the invoice Amount boxes on screen have an equivalent amount in the Payment box. The cheque amount and the amount in the Analysis Total box will increase by the amount of each invoice that you Pay in Full. When all the invoices shown are paid, print a remittance advice if you want to and then click on the **Save** button.

3.19 To finish processing payments click on the **Close** button or press Esc.

Part payments

3.20 If you had been instructed, say, to pay Newlite Cleaning Fluids an amount of only £150 (perhaps because of some dispute with the supplier) this would not cover either of the two invoices that are outstanding. In this case you make a part payment. The procedure is exactly as for any other predetermined cheque amount. Enter the amount of the cheque in the pound sign box then press Tab until you reach the Payment box of the invoice you want to part pay. Type £150 in the Payment box. When you save the payment the outstanding amount will be reduced by £150.

3.21 If you want to pay the whole of some invoices but only a part of others. Tab through the box with the pound sign, leaving it blank. When you are in the

Payment box for an invoice you want to pay in full, click on the Pay in Full button. When you are in the Payment box of an invoice you want to *part* pay, *type in* the amount you want to part pay yourself and press Tab. The amount of the total cheque, and in the Analysis Total box, will increase accordingly every time you do this.

Activity 6.4

Load Assignment 3 again. Change the program date to 31/10/2000.

Pay off the balance on the Newlite Cleaning Fluids account. Cheque number is 914785.

Pay Prairie Couriers Ltd £50.

What is the balance on these two accounts, now?

3.22 A remittance advice can be sent with a payment to a supplier, indicating the invoices that are being paid, together with discounts taken and credit notes being used. It is, quite simply, a statement to show what the payment is for.

3.23 To produce and print a remittance advice, once you have entered (but *not saved*) the details of a payment click on the **Remittance** button. The following window appears.

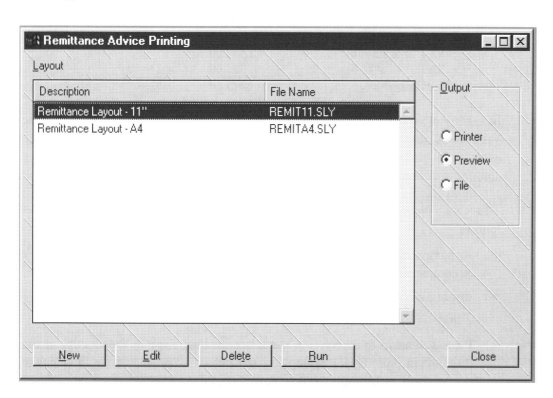

3.24 You must pick one of the default layouts, REMIT11 or REMITA4, depending on your printer's paper size, or use another one (perhaps one set up by your college). Choose what sort of Output you want – printed, preview or file – and then click on Run.

Activity 6.5

Load Assignment 3. Change the program date to 31/10/2000.

Pay Newlite Cleaning Fluids £198.22. Cheque number is 246264.

Print a remittance advice.

4 DISCOUNTS

4.1 As mentioned in Chapter 4, some suppliers offer a discount for early payment of an invoice. For example, payment terms of '30 days net, 3% discount 7 days' means that the invoice should be paid in full within 30 days, but a discount of 3% is available if payment is made within 7 days of the invoice date.

4.2 When such a discount (a 'settlement discount') is taken, you will need to calculate the amount of the discount. VAT rules stipulate that VAT should be charged on the discounted *net* amount (whether or not the discount is taken). Check that you can do the calculation accurately. For example, suppose that a supplier offers a 3% settlement discount for the following invoice.

	Taking the discount £	Not taking the discount £
Net amount	1,600.00	1,600.00
Discount (3%)	(48.00)	
VAT-able amount	1,552.00	
VAT at 17.5%	271.60	271.60
Total payable	1,823.60	1,871.60

4.3 In other words, if you pay up within 7 days you can save your company £48. The VAT authorities are also happy, because your supplier's accounts show a VAT *output* (sales) tax amount of £271.60 and yours show a VAT *input* (purchases) tax amount of £271.60, whether you take the discount or not.

4.4 To record a payment when a settlement discount is being taken the procedure is as follows.

(a) As before, click on **Bank** in the main window and then **Supplier** in the Bank Accounts window. Enter the supplier code, date and cheque number.

(b) When you get to the box with the pound sign in it leave it blank by pressing Tab to take you on the Payment box. Make no entry here.

(c) Press Tab again to take you to the Discount box. Type in the amount of the discount in pounds (for example type in 48.00). You may have to calculate this yourself, or it might be shown on the invoice already.

(d) Press Tab. The amount in the Payment box will automatically be calculated as the amount of the invoice minus the discount. The cursor will move to the next payment line.

(e) **Save** the payment as usual.

Activity 6.6

Load Assignment 3. Change the program date to 31/10/2000.

Pay off the full balance on the account SAMURA, taking a discount of 5% on the total amount owing. The cheque number is 222354

How much do you actually pay? What is the VAT element?

5 CREDIT NOTES

5.1 When a credit note has been posted to a supplier's account, this can be offset against an invoice that is being paid. For example, if a supplier has submitted an invoice for £100 and there is a credit note for £25, only £75 has to be paid to settle the account. Credit notes that have been posted to suppliers' accounts will appear with invoices in the list on the cheque screen.

5.2 To use a credit note, enter the details on the cheque in the usual way, leaving the cheque amount box with the pound sign blank by Tabbing through it. Press tab until you reach the *credit note's* Payment box. Click on the **Pay in Full** button. You will see the amount in the Payment box change to the amount of the credit note – in the example given it would be £25. However, look at the *Analysis Total* box. This will have changed to a *negative* amount equal to the amount of the credit note (–25, in the example). The amount in the cheque amount box will be 0.00 at this point.

5.3 Now Tab up or down to the Payment box of the invoice you want to pay. Click on **Pay in Full**. The amount in the invoice's Payment box will now be equal to the amount of the invoice (£100, say), but the Analysis Total box and the cheque amount box will show the amount of the invoice less the amount of the credit note: £75 in our example.

5.4 If the amount of the credit note is greater than the amount of any outstanding invoice, proceed as follows. Without entering a cheque amount, Tab down to the Payment boxes of the invoices in question and click on Pay in Full. Then Tab to the Payment box of the credit note and *type in* the amount shown in the Analysis Total box. Press Tab.

5.5 The cheque amount will then be nil – in other words no cheque needs to be sent. This will be relatively rare, but if it happens Tab back up to the cheque number box and clear any number you typed there by pressing Delete. When you click on **Save** this has the effect of clearing off the invoices that have been offset against the credit note, and reducing the amount of credit outstanding.

Activity 6.7

Load up Assignment 3. Change the program date to 31/10/2000 if necessary.

Pay Trojan Secretarial Services £141. Cheque number is 147853.

6   PAYMENTS ON ACCOUNT

6.1   Occasionally, a payment might be made to a supplier 'on account', before an invoice is received. When this happens, the amount shown in the cheque amount box will still be greater than the amount shown in the Analysis Total box, even after you have paid any invoices you want to pay in full.

6.2   To make a payment on account, enter the supplier, date and cheque number details and then *type into* the pound sign box the total amount you want to pay.

6.3   When the total cheque amount is entered Tab down to the Payment box and click on **Pay in Full** for each invoice in the normal way. When you have finished, assuming that you do not want to generate a remittance advice (see below), click on **Save**. A message like the one shown below will appear. Click on Yes (or key in Y or press Enter) to accept this.

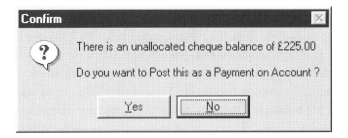

6.4   If you do want to send a remittance advice you must do this *before* you click on Save. Use the **Remittance** button in the way already described.

Offsetting payments on account against invoices

6.5   Later, when invoices have been received, the payment on account should be offset against them. This is done in the same way as using a credit note. Without entering a cheque amount, Tab down to the Payment boxes of the invoices in question and click on Pay in Full. Then Tab to the payment on account item, and *type in* the *smaller* of:

- The total of the payment on account.
- The amount now shown in the Analysis Total box.

6.6   If the payment on account is not large enough to cover the newly-received invoices there will now be an amount shown on the cheque to make up the difference.

If the amount of the payment on account still exceeds the amount of any invoices received the cheque amount will be nil – in other words no cheque will be sent. Again, this will be relatively rare, but if it happens Tab back up to the cheque number box and clear it by pressing Delete. If you click on **Save** this has the effect of clearing off the invoices that have been offset against the payment on account, and reducing the amount of the outstanding payment on account.

Activity 6.8

Load up Assignment 6. Change the program date to 31/10/2000.

Pay the Leaflet Company £500 (cheque number 278400), part of which is a payment on account. Note down how much.

Post an invoice for leaflets dated 5 November 2000 (number WE4582) received from The Leaflet Company for £700 (gross). The Nominal account is the Printing account.

Change the program date to 15/11/2000 and clear the balance on this supplier's account (cheque number 278487).

Required

(a)   How much was the payment on account?
(b)   What is the amount of the cheque needed to clear the balance?

7   'ONE-OFF' PAYMENTS

7.1   Payments are sometimes made against a cheque requisition, not an invoice.

(a)   If an invoice will be received in due course, the payment can be entered as a payment on account, as described above.

(b)   If there will not be an invoice, *there should be no entry for the transaction in the suppliers ledger*, because the suppliers ledger is for credit transactions only.

7.2   A cheque payment for a bank transaction that will not be processed through the suppliers ledger should be recorded directly to the nominal ledger accounts. The payment should be processed as follows.

(a)   Click on the **Bank** button in the main window.

(b)   If different bank accounts are used for nominal ledger payments and Supplier payments, make sure the correct one is highlighted. (Only one account is used in the Blitz case study.)

(c)   Click on the **Payment** button in the Bank Accounts window.

7.3   The following screen will appear.

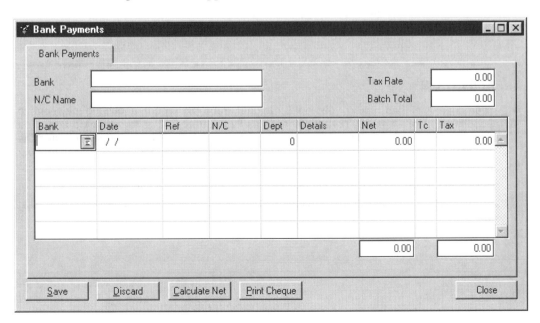

BPP PUBLISHING

7.4   The cursor begins in the Bank column with the usual finder button. This is because many businesses make non-suppliers ledger payments from a separate bank account to the main one for purchases, although this does not apply in the case of Blitz, where you would simply choose A/C 1200 as usual.

7.5   Enter the **Date** in the usual way. The **Ref** should be the cheque number.

7.6   Press Tab again to take you to the **N/C** box. Here you enter the nominal ledger account code for the account to which the payment refers. For example, a cheque payment for the hire of a motor car should be given the nominal account code 7401 in the Sage system. This is the account code for Car Hire expenses. As usual, a list of codes can be displayed on screen by clicking on the Finder button or pressing the F4 function key.

7.7   In the Blitz case study you can Tab straight through the **Dept** box, but you should type in an appropriate brief description of what the payment is for in **Details**.

7.8   In the **Net** box you have two options.

        (a) Enter the *net amount of the payment (excluding VAT)* and press Tab. The cursor will move to the **T/c** (Tax code) box. The default code T1 for standard rate VAT will already be shown and the **Tax** box will already show VAT calculated at this rate. You can, however alter the tax code (usually to T0 for zero rated items). If you do this and press Tab the VAT will automatically be recalculated at the appropriate rate.

        (b) Alternatively you can enter the *total payment inclusive of VAT* in the **Net** box. Before pressing Tab click on the **Calc Net** button at the foot of the window. This will automatically calculate VAT at the standard rate and divide the total amount that you entered into net and VAT amounts. The tax code T1 will be shown in the **T/c** box. You can change this to another rate (in which case the figures will be recalculated) if necessary.

7.9   When you click on **Save** the transactions will be automatically posted to the appropriate nominal ledger accounts:

Credit: Bank Account (probably code 1200)
Debit: Nominal ledger account specified in the N/C field for the transaction.

Activity 6.9

Your supervisor has asked you, on 5 October 2000, to record a cheque payment to Goodtime Ltd for £1,410.00 (£1,200.00 net plus £210.00 for VAT at the standard rate.) The cheque is for UK Entertainment (nominal ledger code 7403). There is no invoice, and the request for payment has been submitted on a cheque requisition form. The cheque number is 345432.

Record this transaction. (It does not matter which Assignment you have loaded.)

8   PRODUCING CHEQUES

8.1   To print cheques using Sage follow the following instructions.

Step 1   The date of your printed cheques are retrieved from the computer system date. To create post-dated cheques, change your computer's system date.

Step 2   From the main Sage toolbar, choose the Bank option.

Step 3   *From the Bank Accounts window, select the account that you want to make the payments from - 1200.*

Step 4   Click on the Cheques button. The Print Cheques window appears listing all remittances for all purchase invoices), purchase credit notes and purchase payments on account that have not been printed before and have blank references. Remittances for bank payments that selected to print the cheque during processing are also shown.

Step 5   To restrict the transactions that appear to a certain date range, select the Date Range checkbox and enter the range you require.

Step 6   If you want to include cheques that have already been printed, select the Show Printed Items checkbox. If you have already printed a cheque it appears in a different colour in the Print Cheques window and a 'Y' appears in the Prn column.

Step 7   The starting cheque number is automatically entered for you. You can change this number if required.

Step 8   Select the transactions you want to print cheques for.

Step 9   Print the cheques you have selected by clicking on the Print button. If you have not selected any transactions cheques will be printed for all listed transactions.

Step 10   Select the layout you require and click Run. The cheques are printed and you are asked to confirm that they have all printed correctly. If your cheques have printed correctly, each cheque is given a reference number.

9   REPORTS

9.1   To see on screen a list of all the *transactions* on the bank account, click on **Nominal,** highlight account number 1200 and click on **Activity,** and then on OK.

To get an equivalent print-out, click on **Nominal** as before, click on **Reports,** and choose Nominal Activity from the options you are offered. You will need to specify the relevant date range and account range (1200 to 1200).

9.2   To get reports on *payments* click on **Bank** in the main window, ensure the account you want is highlighted (A/c 1200 in the Blitz case study), and then click on **Reports**. The following window will appear.

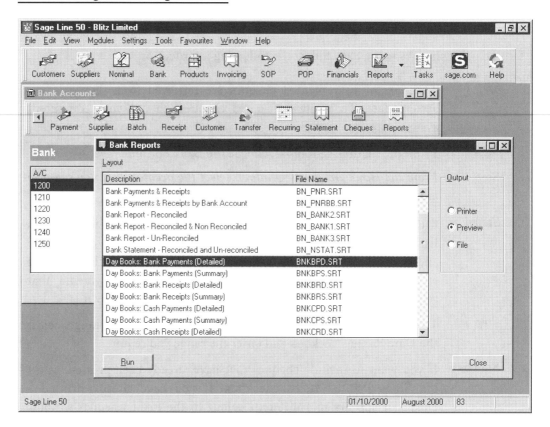

9.3　In the context of this chapter you would probably want Day Books: Bank Payments (Detailed). Highlight this, click on **Run** and (if necessary) specify the range(s) you want your report to cover.

10　QUERIES ABOUT PAYMENTS TO SUPPLIERS

10.1　You might be asked to deal with a query from a supplier who wants to know when you are going to pay an outstanding invoice.

10.2　Simply highlight the account in the main supplier window and click on Activity. this should show you how much is owed to the supplier, and for how long the payment has been outstanding or when invoices were paid.

11　CONCLUSION

11.1　If you think you can follow the instructions in this chapter, you should now be ready to attempt Assignment 3.

11.2　If you haven't yet done the exercises in this chapter, you can do so before you start the Assignment.

Quick quiz

1　List three possible source documents that may be required to be viewed before payment is made to a supplier. (See paragraph 1.1)

2　What is an Aged Analysis report? (2.2)

3　What accounting entries are posted when payments are posted to supplier accounts? (3.1)

4　What is the nominal ledger code for the bank account in the Blitz case study? (3.2)

5　What is a remittance advice? (3.22)

6: Payments to suppliers

Answers to activities

Answer 6.2

(a)   The initial balances should be:

NEWLIT: £672.13
Bank   £33,946.07

(b)   You cannot print out a remittance advice after you have saved a bank transaction.

(c)   The balances should now be:

NEWLIT: £198.22
Bank   £33,472.16

Answer 6.4

The balances should be nil and £55.16.

Answer 6.6

The cheque is for £3,044.75. The discount has to be allocated between three separate items: £82.50 + £56.25 + £21.50 = £160.25. You should have used the (F4) calculator button.

There is no VAT on insurance. You could check this by finding the transaction numbers (Suppliers … Activity), which are numbers 76, 77 and 78 and then looking up these numbers by clicking on Financials.

Well done if you got this activity right.

Answer 6.7

You should take advantage of the credit note.

Answer 6.8

(a)   £300.25
(b)   £399.75

7 Receipts from customers

This chapter contains

1 Receipts of invoice payments

2 Credit notes and customer receipts

3 Discounts

4 Returned cheques

5 Refunding paid invoices

6 Writing off small amounts

7 Account balances

8 Payments with order (bank receipts)

9 Reports

10 Conclusion

Learning objectives

On completion of this chapter you will be able to:

- Record the receipt of payments from credit customers

- Deal with bounced cheques and refunds

- Record the receipt of payments from credit customers

- Extract information regarding payments and customer accounts

Knowledge and understanding

1 The relationship between different software packages.

2 The purpose and application of different software packages.

3 Types of data held on a computer system.

4 Location of information sources.

BPP PUBLISHING

1   RECEIPTS OF INVOICE PAYMENTS

1.1   When customers make payments for invoices, the receipt should be recorded in the Customers ledger. The information you will need to post a receipt is as follows.

(a)   The nominal ledger code of the bank account into which the payment will be made. In the Blitz case study, this code is 1200.

(b)   The name of the customer and the customer's account reference code.

(c)   The date of the receipt.

(d)   The customer's cheque number (although this is not essential).

(e)   The cheque amount.

(f)   The amount of early settlement discount taken, if any.

1.2   You will also usually be given information about which invoice (or invoices) is being paid. The customer will possibly give the invoice reference number, or send a remittance advice note with the payment. The customer should also identify any credit notes that are being used.

1.3   Click on the **Bank** button in the main Sage window. As you learned in the previous chapter this gives a list of all the company's bank accounts. If there is more than one, highlight the one to which customer receipts are posted (probably account 1200, as in the Blitz case study) and then click on the **Customer** button. The following window will appear.

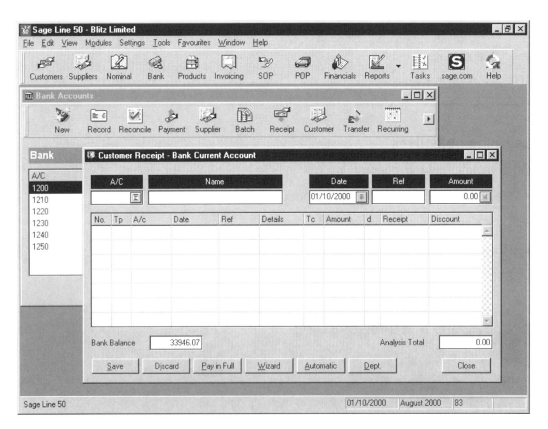

1.4   The cursor will be positioned at the box for A/C at the top left-hand side of the window. Here you enter the customer account code. Use the Finder button if you do not know this. When you enter a code and press Tab the full name of the customer appears automatically in the Name box and details of any outstanding transactions on the account appear in the lower half of the screen.

The Tp column shows the type of transaction on each line:

(a) SI means sales invoice;
(b) SC means sales credit note;
(c) SA means sales payment on account.

1.5 Enter the Date of payment. By default this field will show today's date, as recorded in the computer system, but you can alter this. If you do so the new date will appear each time you start a fresh receipt until you close the window, so there is no need to change it every time.

1.6 Pressing Tab takes you to the Ref box. Here you can enter something like the customer's cheque number or the number of the customer's remittance advice or the number of the invoice being paid, or some other identifying reference. *Do not* leave this field blank: enter a unique reference of some kind.

Allocating receipts

1.7 When you reach the Amount box you have two options.

(a) If you can see at a glance that the amount of the cheque that you have received is the same as the amount of the outstanding invoice(s) shown in the lower half of the screen, leave the Amount box empty: just press Tab.

(b) If you are not sure what invoices are being paid it is safer to key in the amount of the cheque in the Amount box and press Tab. (A £ sign is not required.)

1.8 You must now allocate the receipt of the customer's payment to the outstanding invoice or invoices in the account, to indicate which invoice or invoices have been paid. The procedure is just like the procedure for allocating payments, as described in the previous chapter.

1.9 When you press Tab you will be taken to the **Receipt** box and an amount of 0.00 will be highlighted. If you click on the **Pay in Full** button this will change to the full amount of the invoice.

(a) If you left the Amount box blank this will also change to the amount of the invoice, as will the amount in the Analysis Total box. Press Tab again to move to the next line and repeat the procedure until the amount in the Amount box and the Analysis Total box equal the amount of your receipt. Click on **Save** and the screen will clear.

(b) If you did key in the amount of the receipt in the Amount box there are three possibilities.

(i) If the amount you entered was *less than* the amount of any invoice, it is a part payment by the customer. When you click on the **Pay in Full** button the amount you keyed in will appear in the Receipt box and in the Analysis Total box. There is no more money to allocate so you can just click on **Save**.

(ii) If the amount you keyed in was exactly the *same as* the amount of an invoice (or the same as the total of several invoices), then clicking on the **Pay in Full** button for the invoice or invoices will make an amount equal to the amount of the invoice(s) appear in the Receipt box and the Analysis Total box. Click on **Save** when there is no more money to allocate.

(iii) If the amount you keyed in was *greater than* the total of all the outstanding invoices you have received a payment on account. Click on the **Pay in Full** button each time you Tab to the next Receipt box until any outstanding invoices are paid. The total will accumulate in the Analysis Total box, but when you have finished the Amount box will still show a greater total than the Analysis Total box. Click on **Save** and you will get a message telling you that there is an unallocated cheque balance of £X, and asking if you want to post it as a payment on account. Assuming that this is what you want, click on Yes.

1.10 This might sound complicated, but it is not really when you start using the system. The following table summarises what we have said so far.

Amount received	Amount(s) outstanding	Action
£254.31	£254.31	Leave the Amount box blank and Tab to the Receipt box beside the invoice amount £254.31. Click on Pay in Full then Save.
£500	£200 £300	You can see at a glance that what you have received is the same as the amount outstanding. Proceed as in the previous example for the two invoice amounts.
£193.46	£247.82 £193.46	The customer is clearly paying the second of the two invoices. Leave the Amount box blank and Tab to the Receipt box beside the amount £193.46. Click on Pay in Full and then Save.
£752.57	£466.18 £286.39	Key in the amount £752.57 in the Amount box and press Tab. Click on Pay in Full for each of the two invoices. The total in the Analysis Box will show £466.18 the first time you do this and increase to £752.57 the second time. The two invoices have been paid in full. Click on Save.
£200 (Part payment)	£350	Key in the amount £200 in the Amount box and press Tab. Click on Pay in Full. The amount in the Receipt box will show £200, as will the total in the Analysis Box. Click on Save. When you next call up the account it will show that £150 is still outstanding.
£500 (Payment on account)	£350	Key in the amount £500 in the Amount box and press Tab. Click on Pay in Full. The amount in the Receipt box will show £350, as will the total in the Analysis Box. However the Amount box will still show £500. Click on Save and respond Yes when you get a message asking if you want to post a payment on account of £150.

Activity 7.1

Load Assignment 6 and find out the balances on the bank account and the debtors ledger control account.

Post the following receipts from customers, all dated 15/11/2000, following the procedures described above. Use the number of the first invoice that is being paid as your reference number.

ASPINA   £211.50
BRADLE   £500.00

DCSROO £200.00
ELITEC £941.11
ROSEAL £146.00

What are the balances on the bank account and the debtors ledger control account now?

Print out a report of the activity on the ELITEC account.

2 CREDIT NOTES AND CUSTOMER RECEIPTS

2.1 When a customer has been given a credit note, the details of the credit note should be recorded already in the customer's account. The customer will probably deduct the value of the credit note from his next payment of an invoice. The payment will therefore cover the invoice less the credit note value.

2.2 The best way of recording a receipt in the customer's account where a credit note is being used is as follows.

(a) Enter the *actual cheque amount* in the Amount box.

(b) Tab down to the Receipt box of the credit note transaction and click on **Pay in Full**.

(c) Tab to the Receipt box of the other outstanding invoice or invoices and click on **Pay in Full** until the total amount of the cheque is used up.

Activity 7.2

Load up Assignment 3.

You have received a cheque for £1,762.50 from Royal Properties Ltd. Post this receipt as you think appropriate.

---

3 DISCOUNTS

3.1 A customer might take advantage of an early settlement discount, when this is offered. When a customer takes a discount, you will need to be informed of the amount of discount that has been taken. (You might also be asked to check that the customer has calculated the discount correctly. You can do this with the calculator buttons if you like.)

3.2 Recording a receipt net of discount is similar to recording a payment to a supplier net of discount.

(a) In the Discount box type in the amount of the discount in pounds. Press Tab.

(b) The Receipt box will automatically show the reduced balanced due.

Activity 7.3

Load up Assignment 3.

You have decided to offer Harvey-Sagar Developments a settlement discount of 2% on all future invoices.

(a) Amend the record of this customer accordingly.

(b) Post an invoice to Harvey-Sagar Developments dated 15 November 2000 for £850 (net) for Office Cleaning. (Accept the default invoice number offered by Sage.)

(c) Post a receipt dated 20 November 2000 from Harvey-Sagar Developments for £2,694.28, following the instructions above.

---

4   RETURNED CHEQUES

4.1   Occasionally, a cheque received from a customer might be 'bounced' and returned by the bank marked 'Refer to Drawer'. The customer's bank is refusing to pay over the money because there are insufficient funds in the customer's bank account.

4.2   When a cheque bounces, the receipt will already have been recorded in the customer's account. This must now be corrected.

4.3   Click on **Tools** at the top of the main window and choose the option **Write Off, Refund, Return** from the menu that drops down.

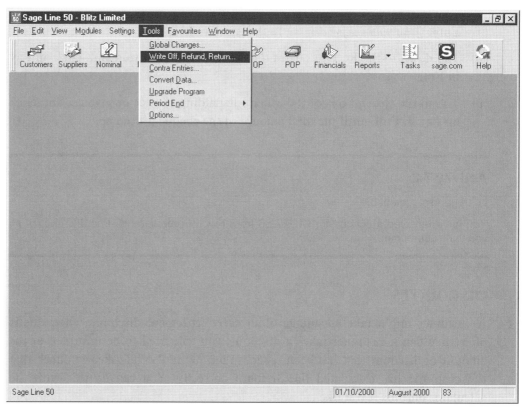

You are then asked to choose whether amendments will be made to the Sales ledger or the Purchase ledger (as shown on the following page). Choose the Sales Ledger option and click on **Next**.

4.4   You will see a list. This includes the item Customer Cheque Returns. Highlight this and click on the **Next** button at the foot of the window. A list of customer accounts will appear. Highlight the one you require and click on Next.

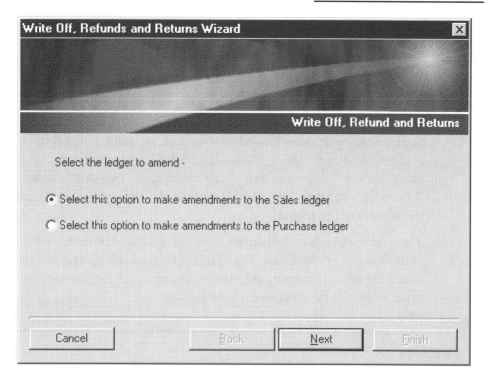

4.5 Next, select the cheque that has 'bounced', then click on Next. Enter the date of the transaction, which would usually be the date the cheque was dishonoured, and click Next. You will see a summary of what you are asking to be done. If you are happy with this, click on **Finish** to post the transaction. If not there is a **Back** option, allowing you to go back through these steps and change your decisions as necessary.

Activity 7.4

Load Assignment 6.

It is 31 October 2000. A cheque from A Wyche for £88.13 has bounced.

(a) What is the initial balance on A Wyche's account and on the bank account?

(b) Record the bounced cheque, following the instructions given above.

(c) What is the balance on the two accounts now?

(d) How is the transaction shown in A Wyche's customer's ledger account?

---

5 REFUNDING PAID INVOICES

5.1 To cancel an *unpaid* invoice, you should issue a credit note for the same amount.

5.2 However, when an invoice has been paid and it is subsequently decided that the customer should be given a refund in full, it is too late to issue a credit note and a different procedure is required to account for the refund.

5.3 Click on **Tools.** Then choose **Write Off, Refund, Return** and proceed exactly as described in the previous section, except that this time you choose **Customer Invoice Refunds**.

5.4 Details of all *fully-paid* invoices for the chosen customer will appear on screen. Click on the item to which the refund applies to highlight it and then click on the **Next** button. You are then asked which bank account you want to post the

ℬℙℙ
PUBLISHING

adjustment to. Choose 1200 for the case study. Then you get a summary of what you have said you want to do and are asked to confirm it by clicking on **Finish** (or Back if you are not happy).

5.5 The effect of this is as follows.

(a) A sales credit note is posted to the account in the Customers ledger, with the same reference as the refunded invoice, and showing 'Refund' in the details column. A dummy sales invoice is posted to the same account, and is automatically allocated in full to the credit note. The details column shows 'Allocation - Refund'. The sales turnover to date on the account is reduced by the amount of the refund.

(b) The appropriate Nominal ledger account for sales is reduced by (debited with) the amount refunded. The nominal ledger bank control account, out of which the refund is being paid, will be credited with the amount refunded (in other words the bank balance will be reduced).

Activity 7.5

Load Assignment 6.

What is the balance on the accounts for Bridgford and Co and Sales - Contract cleaning?

On 31 October 2000 it has been decided that Bridgford and Co should be given a refund for invoice number 10003.

Post this transaction. What is the new balance on Bridgford and Co's account and on the Sales - Contract cleaning account?

How does this transaction appear in Bridgford and Co's account?

Are any other accounts affected?

---

6 WRITING OFF SMALL AMOUNTS

6.1 It is quite common in practice for customers to mistakenly pay a few pence less than they owe. For example, a customer might remit a cheque for £76.00 to pay an invoice for £76.38.

6.2 When a company receives payments that are less than the invoiced amount, but only by a small amount, a decision might be taken to write-off the unpaid amount, because it is too small to worry about. It would cost too much (time-wise) to chase the customer for payment and the effort wouldn't be worthwhile.

6.3 Choose the **Tools** menu and then **Write Off, Refund, Return.** Pick the option *Write off Customer Transactions below a value* in the **Sales ledger** list.

6.4 A screen prompt asks you to 'Enter the value below which a transaction will be written off', and you must key in the amount below which the balance on any customer account will be written off as uncollectable. The value can be as little as 0.02 (ie. £0.02).

6.5 When you have keyed in this write-off and clicked on **Next,** the screen will automatically display every customer account and transaction for which the unpaid balance is currently less than the value you have entered.

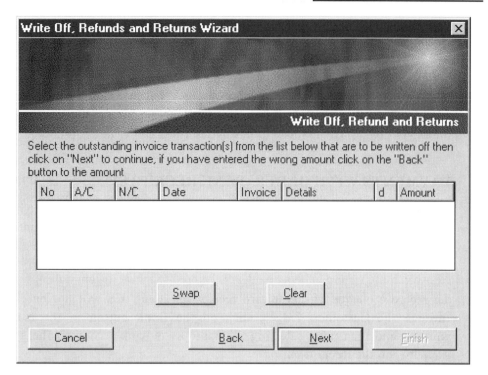

6.6 To write off the unpaid balance on an account firstly highlight the account by clicking on it. You will then see a list of transactions displayed in a box like that shown above. To highlight all transactions shown, click on the **Swap** button at the foot of the window.

6.7 When you have made your selection or selections, click on **Next.** A further screen will ask the date of the write off. Enter this, click **Next** and then **Finish**.

(a) The account(s) in the Customers ledger will be credited with the amount written off, with 'Bad Debt Write Off' shown as the details.

(b) In the Nominal ledger, the debtors control account (code 1100) will be credited with the amount written off, and the bad debt write off account (code 8100) is debited.

Activity 7.6

Load up Assignment 5.

It is 31/10/2000 (for the purpose of these exercises, whenever you are told 'it is .....' change the program date within Sage to that date) .

Post the following receipts from customers.

ASPINA   £105.00
CHADWI   £176.00
NORRIS   £1,087.27

Now, following the instructions above, write off any balances below £1.00.

What is the total amount written off?

Which nominal ledger accounts are affected?

---

7 ACCOUNT BALANCES

7.1 You might be asked to find out what is the unpaid balance on a customer's account. A customer might telephone, for example, and ask how much he owes. Or your supervisor might ask how much a particular customer still owes. The simplest way of finding the unpaid balance on an customer's account is to use the **Activity** button.

7.2   This gives a window similar to the Suppliers Ledger Activity window, which allows you to find the current unpaid balance on any supplier account in the Suppliers Ledger. Using this option was described earlier in Chapter 6.

8   PAYMENTS WITH ORDER (BANK RECEIPTS)

8.1   Customers might pay by cheque or credit card for goods or services when they make their order. The customer is not asking for credit; any may not want or need an account in the Customers Ledger. The transaction should be recorded as a sale and a bank receipt.

8.2   To record a cheque or credit card receipt for items that will not be processed through the Customers ledger, click on the **Bank** button in the main Sage window, and then (after selecting the appropriate bank account if there is more than one) on the **Receipt** button.

8.3   To enter the details of the receipt, you will need the following information:

(a)   The bank account to which the transaction will be posted (in the Blitz case study, this is the bank current account, code 1200).

(b)   The transaction date.

(c)   The reference number your company uses for cash sales transactions.

(d)   The nominal account to which the credit will be posted (ie the account code of the sales account or other income account in the nominal ledger to which the receipt should be posted as income).

(e)   The department code, if any.

(f)   A description of the item for which the payment has been received (also optional).

(g)   The net value of the item (excluding VAT).

(h)   The VAT code for the item.

Entering bank receipt details

8.4   When you click on the **Receipt** button, the following window will appear.

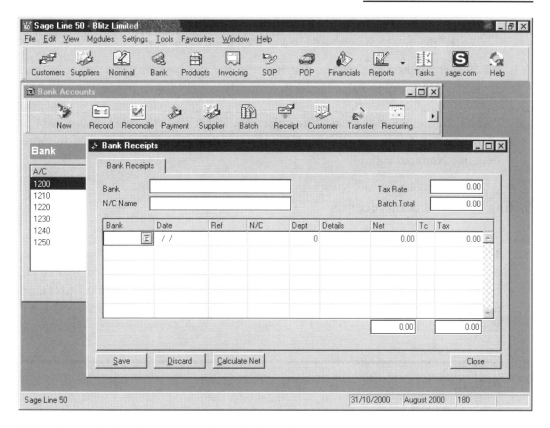

8.5 Enter the bank account code (1200 in Blitz) and the date as usual. For the **Ref** you can enter a reference for the transaction such as the customer's cheque number or your own paying-in slip number. Press Tab again.

8.6 Key in the code of the nominal ledger account (for sales or income) to which the receipt refers, then press Tab. In the Blitz case study, the code will be one of the following:

4000 Sales - contract cleaning
4001 Sales - window cleaning
4002 Sales - domestic services
4100 Sales - materials

8.7 When you key in the N/C code and press Tab, the N/C name will automatically appear in the N/C Name box at the top of the window.

8.8 In the Dept and Details boxes you can enter the code of the Department concerned if any and a description of the purpose of the payment from the customer.

8.9 You can enter either the net amount of the receipt (excluding VAT) or the gross amount (including VAT).

(a) If you enter the net amount, press Tab and the cursor will move to the T/c column. This may show a default code such as T1, but you can alter it if you wish. In the Blitz case study, the codes are:

T0 For zero-rated items
T1 For standard-rate items (currently taxed at the rate of 17.5%)

(b) If you key in the gross receipt in the Net column and click on **Calculate Net** (or press F9) this automatically deducts VAT at the standard rate (assuming tax code T1 applies). If you than press Tab you can change the tax code if you like and the amounts will be recalculated as appropriate. (If the code has to be altered from, say T0 to T1, you may need to Tab back to the Net box, re-enter the gross amount and click on Calculate net again.

8.10 Whichever method you choose for entering the net payment and tax code, the amount of VAT will be calculated automatically and displayed in the Tax column.

8.11 Press Tab to move to the next line on screen, where you can enter further details of the receipt if necessary (for example if a single receipt is being posted to more than one Nominal code).

Posting details of bank receipts

8.12 When you have entered all the details of a bank receipts click on the **Save** button. This will only be active if the amount in the Amount box is equal to the amount in the Analysis Total box. Once you have saved an entry the screen will clear, ready for the next entry. If you have finished all your entries click on **Close** or press Esc. (You will be asked if you are sure you wish to Exit. If you are, click on Yes.)

Activity 7.7

Load Assignment 1.

It is 8 October 2000. You have received the following amounts from non-sales ledger customers.

Gleamo Prize for shiny windows: £1,000 (N/C 4900; T/C T0)

D. Spenser, one-off payment for domestic services: £100 (gross)

Post these transactions using the paying-in slip reference 123478.

What is the balance on the bank account after you have done this? What nominal ledger accounts are affected besides those beginning with a 4?

9 REPORTS

9.1 You can produce reports for receipts of money from customers.

(a) A listing of receipts from customers in settlement of invoices (and payments on account) and of bank receipts that are not recorded in the sales ledger can be produced using the **Reports** button in the **Bank** window.

(b) A listing of bank transactions can be produced using the **Report** button in the Nominal Ledger window.

Only (a) is described here, since we saw how to produce a report of bank transactions in the previous chapter.

9.2 To get a report on receipts click on **Bank** in the main window, ensure that the account you want is highlighted (A/C 1200 is the case study) and then click on **Reports.** As we saw in the previous chapter a window appears offering you lots of options.

9.3 This time you want Day Books: Bank Receipts (Detailed). You would typically want to obtain a listing of receipts for a particular day (or week). In the Date section specify the date or dates of the transactions for listing. Then choose what sort of Output you want – Printer, Preview or File. If you choose to print the listing, the screen will give you prompts for producing the printout.

10 CONCLUSION

10.1 If you think you can follow the explanations in this chapter, you should now be ready to attempt **Assignment 4**.

Quick quiz

1 List the information you would need to post a receipt to the Customers ledger. (See paragraph 1.1)

2 Give one reason why a cheque may 'bounce'. (4.1)

3 What function in Sage is used to write off very small outstanding amounts? (6.3)

4 What Tax code is used in the Blitz case study for standard-rate items? (8.9)

5 How would you print a listing of bank receipts? (9.2 - 9.3)

Answers to activities

Answer 7.1

The opening balance on the bank account is £4,616.49 and the closing balance is £6,615.10. the opening balance on the Debtors ledger control account is £25,486.83 and the closing balance is £23,488.22.

The receipt from ELITEC is likely to have been the most difficult to deal with: it does match up precisely to existing invoice amounts, however. Note that ROSEAL has underpaid by a small amount. You should be left with a balance of £0.88 on this account.

Here are the sort of details that your report on ELITEC should have contained. (This is an extract from a Customer Activity (Detailed) report.)

No	Tp	Date	Refn	N/C	Details	T/C	Value	O/S	Debit	Credit
56	SI	22/09/2000	10021	4000	Kitchen cleaning	T1	756.70 p	556.70	756.70	
96	SI	08/10/2000	10043	4000	KITCHEN CLEANING	T1	756.70		756.70	
97	SI	08/10/2000	10043	4100	OVEN CLEANER	T1	71.68		71.68	
98	SI	08/10/2000	10043	4100	FLAME DETERGENT	T1	84.60		84.60	
99	SI	08/10/2000	10043	4100	BRUSHES	T1	28.13		28.13	
161	SR	10/10/2000	10021	1200	Sales Receipt	T9	200.00			200.00
196	SI	16/10/2000	10054	4000	Kitchen cleaning	T1	223.25 *	223.25	223.25	
246	SR	15/11/2000	10043	1200	Sales Receipt	T9	941.11			941.11
							779.95	779.95	1,921.06	1,141. 11

Answer 7.3

The customer should end up with £17 discount and a balance of £0.00 if you do all of this correctly.

Answer 7.4

(a) £0.00 and £4,616.49.

(c) £88.13 and £4,528.36.

(d) As follows. The cheque receipt on 10 October is now shown as a cancelled cheque and the invoice from 22 September is reinstated.

No	Tp	Date	Refn	Details	Amount	O/S	Debit	Credit
70	SI	22/09/2000	10035	Window cleaning	88.13		88.13	
150	SR	10/10/2000	CANCEL	Cancelled cheque	88.13			88.13
246	SI	31/10/2000	CANCEL	Cancelled cheque	88.13	88.13	88.13	

What other account in the nominal ledger is affected?

Answer 7.5 _____

The initial balances are £0.00 and £27,167.80.

The new balances are £0.00 and £26,752.80.

Here is the activity as recorded in Bridgford's account.

No	Tp	Date	Refn	Details	Amount O/S	Debit	Credit
38	SI	22/09/2000	10003	Office cleaning	487.63	487.63	
94	SI	08/10/2000	10041	Office cleaning at inv	493.50	493.50	
145	SR	10/10/2000	10003	Sales Receipt	981.13		981.13
246	SC	31/10/2000	REFUND	Refund - 10003	487.63		487.63
247	SI	31/10/2000	REFUND	Allocation - 10003	487.63	487.63	

The Bank account (1200) is affected and so is the Sales Tax Control (2200) account.

Answer 7.6 _____

The three amounts written off are £0.75, £0.43, and £0.25, a total of £1.43. This is debited to the Bad Debt Write Off account (8100) and credited to the Debtors Ledger Control account (1100). Check the activity on these accounts to see the transactions for yourself. (The memorandum accounts for the three customers are also credited, of course.)

Answer 7.7 _____

It should be £35,046.07 (debit). The bank account is the other nominal ledger account affected.

8 Other cash transactions

This chapter contains

1   Petty cash transactions

2   Journal entries and bank-cash transactions

3   Bank transactions not involving sales or purchases

4   Bank reconciliations

5   Conclusion

Learning objectives

On completion of this chapter you will be able to:

- Make the accounting entries for petty cash transactions

- Make the accounting entries for other cash transactions

- Use Sage to carry out a bank reconciliation

Knowledge and understanding

1   The relationship between different software packages.

2   The purpose and application of different software packages.

3   Types of data held on a computer system.

4   Location of information sources.

BPP
PUBLISHING

1   PETTY CASH TRANSACTIONS

1.1   A petty cash account is a record of relatively small cash payments and cash receipts. The balance on the petty cash account at any time should be the amount of cash (notes and coins) held within the business. Petty cash is commonly kept in a locked metal box, in a safe or locked drawer. The box will contain notes and coins, vouchers recording amounts of cash withdrawn (and the reasons for using the cash) and vouchers for petty cash receipts.

1.2   The accounting records for petty cash are often maintained in a book, or a spreadsheet. Transactions are recorded from the petty cash vouchers into the petty cash book.

1.3   A petty cash account must also be maintained in the nominal ledger. The person responsible for petty cash needs to ensure entries from the petty cash book are entered into the into 'main' accounting system. Requests for petty cash **must be authorised** in line with stated policy.

1.4   For payments of cash out of petty cash, details must be entered of

   (a)   The amount withdrawn.

   (b)   The purpose. This will be used to allocate the nominal ledger account to which the item of expense relates.

1.5   Similarly, for receipts of cash into petty cash, details must be entered of

   (a)   The amount received.

   (b)   The reason for the receipt - used to allocated the nominal ledger account.

Recording petty cash transactions

1.6   The information you need to record a cash payment or cash receipt is as follows.

   (a)   The code of the nominal ledger account to which the payment will be debited or the receipt credited.

   (b)   The transaction date.

   (c)   If appropriate, a reference number such as the petty cash voucher number.

   (d)   A description of the reason for the payment or receipt unless the nominal account code used means this is obvious.

   (e)   Either the net value of the item (excluding VAT), or the gross amount of the item (including VAT).

   (f)   The appropriate VAT code.

1.7   The petty cash account is included in the list in the Bank Accounts window. Just select this account (code 1230) instead of the main bank account (code 1230).

1.8   Transactions are posted **exactly as for Bank receipts and payments**, using the same buttons. Try the following Activity.

Activity 8.1

Load up Assignment 3.

Post the following transactions to the petty cash account. Transactions are numbered consecutively, beginning at PC013. VAT receipts have not been obtained, so no VAT applies.

25 Oct   Stationery: £5.26.
28 Oct   Refreshments: £4.45
24 Oct   Present for new baby: £27.99 (N/C 6202)
25 Oct   Loan (Joan Davies): £50 (N/C 9998)
31 Oct   Received from Joan Davies: £50.

What is the balance on the petty cash account and on account 7504 now?

2   JOURNAL ENTRIES AND BANK-CASH TRANSACTIONS

2.1   A journal is a 'book of prime entry' in an accounting system. Its purpose is to record transactions and accounting entries that will not be recorded in any other book of prime entry.

2.2   Although a journal can be thought of as a 'book' for recording transactions to be posted to the nominal ledger, it is common for journal transactions to be recorded on sheets of paper, known as journal vouchers.

2.3   Entries in the journal must subsequently be posted to the appropriate accounts in the nominal ledger. For every journal transaction, there will have to be:

(a)   A debit entry in one nominal ledger account.
(b)   A corresponding credit entry in another nominal ledger account.

2.4   In other words, there are two sides to every transaction, the debit entry and the credit entry.

2.5   A transaction recorded in the journal, for example, could relate to a transfer between accounts in the nominal ledger. In the Sage system, a journal entry is used, for example, to record transfers of petty cash from the bank account to the cash account.

2.6   Movements of money between the bank account and petty cash are known as bank-cash transactions.

Recording bank-cash transactions

2.7   To record a movement of money from the bank account to cash (that is, a cash withdrawal) or to record the payment of cash (notes and coin) into the bank, click on the **Nominal** button in the main Sage window and then on the **Journals** button in the Nominal Ledger window. The window shown below will be displayed.

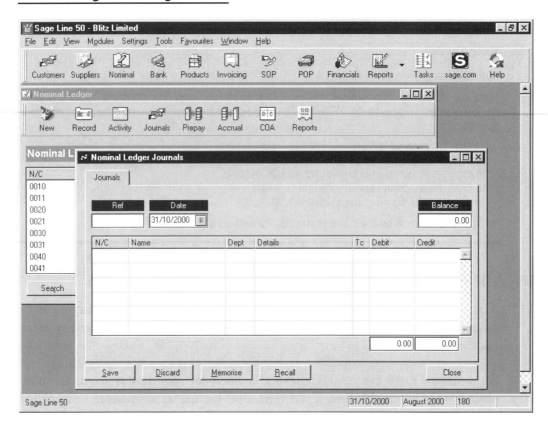

2.8   The cursor begins at the Ref box.

Ref

2.9   This is an optional item, which can be used to identify the transaction. The journal voucher number could be inserted here (up to a maximum of six characters).

Date

2.10 If necessary, enter the transaction date, as a six-digit code in the format DDMMYY or use the calendar button.

2.11 The cursor will now move past the box labelled Balance (which is updated automatically) straight down to the main part of the screen. Here, you must enter the details of the debit item and the credit item, one per line, for the transaction.

2.12 For a bank-cash transaction, the debit and credit entries are as follows.

(a) When *cash is withdrawn* from the bank.

		Nominal ledger code
DEBIT	Petty cash	1230
CREDIT	Bank current account	1200

(b) When *cash is paid into* the bank from petty cash.

		Nominal ledger code
DEBIT	Bank current account	1200
CREDIT	Petty cash	1230

N/C and Name

2.13 Enter the nominal ledger code of the bank account (1200) or the petty cash account (1230). It does not matter which code you enter on the first line. You will need to enter both, one per line, to complete the input details. When you enter the code, the account name will appear in the Name box automatically. (To find other codes you can use the Finder button in the normal way: click on it or press function key F4 when the cursor is in this box.)

Details

2.14 You can enter brief details of the transaction. For example:

N/C	Name	Description	T/c	Debit	Credit
1230	PETTY CASH	Received from bank a/c	T9	100.00	
1200	BANK CURRENT A/C	To petty cash float	T9		100.00

2.15 The description for one side of the entry should always indicate the other nominal ledger account to which the transaction relates. In the example above, the details for the withdrawal of £100 from the bank (the credit of 100.00 for N/C 1200) refer to petty cash which is the recipient of the money.

T/c (Tax Code)

2.16 A bank-cash transaction does not involve VAT. Enter tax code T9.

Debit/Credit

2.17 Enter the amount of the transaction, in the debit or the credit column, according to whether the nominal ledger account should be debited or credited.

2.18 Remember that there must be two entries for a bank-cash transaction, one a debit and one a matching credit, to complete a journal entry. In fact the system will not allow you to post your journal until Debits equal Credits and the amount shown in the Balance box is nil.

2.19 When you have completed the entry, Click on **Save** as usual and the nominal ledger accounts will be updated with the transaction details.

Activity 8.2

Load Assignment 6.

A payment of £1200 has been incorrectly analysed as Legal Fees. In fact £500 of this related to consultancy fees and £300 was advertising. All figures are stated net.

Post a journal to correct this (reference J23) dated 6 November 2000. What is the balance on the advertising account now?

---

3 BANK TRANSACTIONS NOT INVOLVING SALES OR PURCHASES

3.1 A business will occasionally receive or make payments by cheque (that is, through its bank account, not in cash) that do not involve sales or purchases, receipts from customers or payments to suppliers. These cash payments or receipts should be recorded using the **Payment** and **Receipt** buttons in the Bank window. These options are described in Chapter 6 (payments) and Chapter 7 (receipts).

3.2 Examples of transactions you could be expected to record are suggested below.

    (a) Payment of PAYE income tax to the Inland Revenue authorities
    (b) Payment of a court fine (eg a parking ticket fine)
    (c) Payment for a road vehicle licence (car tax)
    (d) The receipt of a loan

4 BANK RECONCILIATIONS

4.1 Sage includes a facility for making a bank reconciliation - ie checking the bank account records in the nominal ledger against a bank statement sent by the bank.

4.2 If a transaction is the same in both the bank statement and the nominal ledger account it is said to be 'reconciled'. The reconciliation process therefore involves checking every item on the bank statement against the transactions listed in the nominal ledger bank account and matching the transactions. Any differences should then be identified, to complete the reconciliation.

Note that you always work *from* the bank statement *to* the nominal ledger account. *Unreconciled* (also called *uncleared*) items are those that have *not yet appeared in the bank statement*, even though they have been recorded in the nominal ledger account.

Documents for checking

4.3 You will obviously need a bank statement from the bank to carry out a reconciliation. Paying in slips will also probably be needed, as we shall see. You will also need a list of transactions in the nominal ledger bank account.

4.4 To produce a print-out of the bank transactions, you can click on the **Bank Statement** button (the simpler option), or else (in all versions) click on the **Nominal** button in the main Sage window and select the bank account (account 1200) by scrolling down to it and clicking on it to highlight it. Then click on the **Report** button in the Nominal Ledger window. The reason why you need this report is explained in a moment.

4.5 Four standard reports are listed – Day Books: Nominal Ledger, Nominal Activity, Nominal Balances and Nominal List. You want the one called *Nominal Activity*, so click on this to highlight it. If possible the Output option to choose is Printer, but if you do not have access to a printer, choose Preview. Then click on Run. Specify account code 1200 in the Report Criteria or Additional Report Filter window. You don't actually need to do this if you highlighted account 1200 before clicking on **Reports,** but it is good practice to do so.

4.6 If you are printing the report a series of windows will give you printing options and instructions.

Starting the bank reconciliation

4.7   Click on the **Bank** button in the main Sage window and (having highlighted the account you want to reconcile, if there is more than one account) then on the **Reconcile** button in the Bank Accounts window.

4.8   The program will display the window shown below.

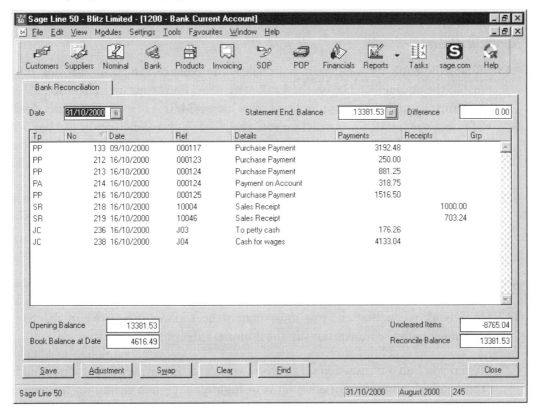

4.9   Key in the date of the *bank statement* and the closing balance shown at the end of the bank statement.

4.10   You can use the scroll bar or the cursor direction keys ↓ and ↑ to look through the list, and the Page Up, Page Down, Home and End keys to speed up the process.

4.11   Four boxes on the screen need some explanation.

Opening Balance

4.12   This is the bank Reconcile Balance brought forward from the last time a bank reconciliation was done using the Sage software. It should reflect the opening balance on the bank statement. If there has not been a previous bank statement, or if the procedure has never been carried out before, the balance brought forward will be 0.00.

Uncleared items

4.13   This is the net total (debits plus credits) of all items or receipts that are left unreconciled on the screen. Each time you reconcile an item listed in the bank statement with an item on the screen, you will find that the balance in this box changes.

Book Balance (at Date)

4.14 This is the current account balance for the bank account in the nominal ledger. The main reason why this balance is different to the bank Reconcile Balance is because, unlike the bank statement, it takes into account any receipts or payments that were in the process of clearing through the banking system when the bank statement was produced.

Reconcile Balance

4.15 When the bank reconciliation is finished, the balance shown in this box must match the ending balance on the bank statement. Each time an item is identified as being reconciled, the total in this box is increased (if it is a receipt) or decreased (if it is a payment). The first time you ever do a bank reconciliation the box will show 0.00; subsequently it will show the same amount as the Opening Balance box when you begin.

4.16 You will find that the Reconcile Balance plus the value of uncleared items is always equal to the book balance.

Reconcile Balance + Uncleared Items = Book Balance

Reconciliation procedures

4.17 In a bank reconciliation, you must match the transactions listed in the bank statement with the transactions in the nominal ledger bank account.

4.18 When you find a transaction on the bank statement is matched by a transaction in the nominal bank account click on it to highlight the transaction on the screen. The figures in the Reconcile Balance box and the Uncleared Items box will change by the amount of the transaction that you just highlighted.

4.19 If you make a mistake, and want to de-select a transaction, just click on it again.

Items made up of several transactions

4.20 You may have a problem in matching items because there may be some that are the total of several smaller transactions. This happens on both the bank statement and on the screen listing.

(a) If several receipts were paid into the bank on a single paying-in slip the bank statement will probably only show the total. You need to consult the paying-in slips to see how these items are made up, and match individual receipts.

(b) The reconciliation screen will lump together any transactions of the same type (eg five customer receipts) that were posted one after the other and had the same date, unless they were given a unique *reference* number when they were posted. A single total will then be shown for all of these individual transactions, making matching far more difficult. The details will just say 'Customer Deposit'.

You may remember that we emphasised the importance of giving receipts a unique reference number when we were describing how they should be posted. This is the reason why.

(A possible solution, that would make a *virtue* of these 'problems', would be to post receipts from paying-in slips, giving each batch of receipts the same reference as the paying-in slip number. In fact this would make it *easier* to match items on the bank statement and the reconciliation screen.)

Items in the bank statement but not in the ledger account

4.21   There could be some items in the bank statement that have not been entered in the nominal ledger bank account. For example, there could be some bank charges that have not yet been recorded in the account.

4.22   You can make an adjustment, and post the receipt or payment to the bank account in the nominal ledger. To do this click on the **Adjustment** button at the foot of the window. A new window will appear, as shown below.

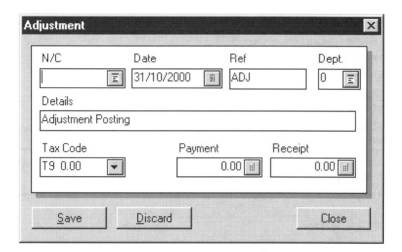

4.23   The entries to make are as follows.

(a)   *N/C (Nominal Code).* Enter the nominal ledger code for the account to which the item of income or expense relates. In the Blitz case study, for example, a deduction of bank interest would be coded 7900 and a deduction of bank charges would be coded 7901.

(b)   *Date.* Enter the date of the receipt or payment.

(c)   *Details.* By default this says 'Adjustment Posting but it is better to enter your own brief narrative details of the item.

(d)   *Tax Code.* The VAT code would be T9 for bank charges, but for other items (for example, some direct debits) it would be T1. Check with your supervisor if you are not sure.

(e)   *Payment / Receipt.* Enter the gross value of the receipt or payment, in the appropriate box. (The other box is left as 0.00.)

4.24   Click on **Save** when you are satisfied that your adjustment details are correct. The transaction will be posted in the appropriate nominal ledger accounts.

Completing the reconciliation

4.25   When you have checked the items in the bank statement against the nominal bank account, the value in the Reconcile Balance box should equal the balance on the bank statement itself. If it does not, you have made a mistake. Consult your supervisor.

4.26 If it does reconcile, click on the **Save** button. This will clear the reconciled transactions (ie the transactions that you have matched and highlighted in the nominal bank account and the bank statement). The unreconciled items will be displayed on screen the next time you do a bank reconciliation. The reconciled transactions will not be listed next time, provided you have cleared them.

4.27 To get a list of unreconciled payments and receipts use the Bank Reports option and find these reports in the list that appears.

Activity 8.3

Load Assignment 6. On 20 October you receive the following bank statement.

Date	Details		Withdrawals	Deposits	Balance
10-Oct-2000	Balance from sheet 5				13,381.53
11-Oct-2000		000117	3,192.48		10,189.05
14-Oct-2000	BGC			1,000.00	11,189.05
18-Oct-2000		000124	1,200.00		
18-Oct-2000		000125	1,516.50		8,472.55
20-Oct-2000	BACS		4,133.04		4,339.51
20-Oct-2000	Bank interest		74.50		4265.01

Perform a bank reconciliation as at 20 October 2000, following the procedures explained in the preceding section. What are the outstanding items, if any?

5 CONCLUSION

5.1 You may want more practice with a bank reconciliation. This is included in **Assignment 5**, which you can now attempt.

Quick quiz

1 How is petty cash usually stored? (See paragraph 1.1)

2 No record of petty cash is required to be kept in the nominal ledger. TRUE or FALSE? (1.3)

3 As petty cash amounts are small, there is no need to know the purpose of the funds. TRUE or FALSE? (1.4)

4 What are journal entries used for? (2.1)

5 How do you access the bank reconciliation function in Sage? (4.7)

Answers to activities

Answer 8.1

You should get £262.30 (Dr) for petty cash and £415.10 (Dr) for account 7504.

Answer 8.2

The balance on the advertising account should be £3050.00

(Cr Legal Fees (7600) £800; Dr Consultancy (7602) £500, Dr Advertising (6201) £300.)

Answer 8.3

If you have ever performed a manual bank reconciliation you should find the computerised method much easier.

The outstanding items are as follows.

Cheque 000123	250.00
Cheque 000126	176.26
Receipt	(703.24)
Total	(276.98)

9 Other credit transactions

This chapter contains

1   Contra entries

2   Exceeding a credit limit

3   Writing off bad debts

4   Chasing customers for overdue payments

5   Correcting errors

6   Conclusion

Learning objectives

On completion of this chapter you will be able to:

- Process contra entries

- Act when customers exceed their credit limit

- Write off bad debts

- Chase customers for payment, using an aged debtors list

- Correct errors in computerised accounting entries

Knowledge and understanding

1   The relationship between different software packages.

2   The purpose and application of different software packages.

3   Types of data held on a computer system.

4   Location of information sources.

BPP PUBLISHING

1   CONTRA ENTRIES

1.1   *Contra* is an accounting term that means against, or on the opposite side. A contra entry is made in the accounts of a business when a debit entry can be matched with a credit entry so that one cancels out the other. A common type of contra entry occurs when a supplier is also a customer. The amount owed as a supplier and the amount owing as a customer can be offset, to leave just a net amount owed or owing.

2   For example, suppose that ABC Limited is both a customer of your business, currently owing £1,000, and a supplier to your business who is currently owed £700. ABC Ltd pays £300 to settle the debt. The £700 owed has been offset against the £1,000 owing, and ABC Limited has simply paid the net debt of £300. This would be recorded in the accounts as a

(a)   A cash receipt of £300; and

(b)   A contra entry for £700, to cancel the debt to ABC as a supplier and the remaining £700 owed by ABC as a customer.

1.3   The accounting entries done for contra transactions are as follows.

(a)   In the sales ledger, the customer's account is credited with the amount of the contra entry. This reduces the customer's outstanding debt.

(b)   In the purchase ledger, the supplier's account is debited with the same amount.

(c)   In the nominal ledger, the double entry transactions are:

CREDIT   Debtors Control Account (code 1100)
DEBIT   Bank Current Account (code 1200)
            (or any other specified bank account)

DEBIT   Creditors Control Account (code 2100)
CREDIT   Bank Current Account (code 1200)
            (or any other specified bank account)

Posting a contra entry

Post the payment or receipt first

1.4   Before you post a contra entry, you should record the actual cash payment (or receipt) in the purchase ledger (or sales ledger). For example, suppose that your company owes ABC Ltd £700, ABC Ltd owes your company £1,000 and ABC Ltd sends you a cheque for £300 to settle the difference. Your first step should be to record the £300 received as a part payment of an invoice in the account for ABC Ltd in the sales ledger. This will make the outstanding balance on the customer account (£700) equal to the outstanding balance on the supplier account (£700).

1.5   You can find out the balances on the two accounts by looking at them in the windows that appear when you click on the **Customers** button and the **Suppliers** button. Subtract one from the other to find out the amount due.

1.6   In Sage it is *not* essential that there are equal amounts owed and owing before you post a contra entry, but it is good accounting practice, so always post the payment (and/or) receipt that brings this about *first*.

Making the contra

1.7 Click on the word **Tools** at the top of the screen. A menu will appear from which you should select **Contra Entries**. A window will be displayed, for entering the details.

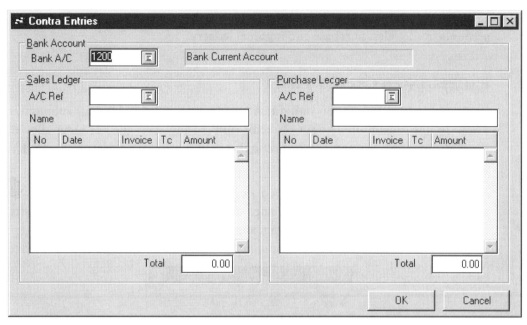

Check the correct Bank account is displayed, then Tab into the Sales A/C box, which will be blank.

Sales Ledger A/C (Customer Account)

1.8 Enter the customer's account reference code if you know it (or use the Finder button or press function key F4 if not). When you press Tab the customer's name will be displayed automatically, and a list of outstanding invoices on that customer's account will appear in the left-hand box below. (Credit notes and payments on account are not listed.)

Purchase Ledger A/C (Supplier Account)

1.9 Enter the supplier's account reference code. This would normally be the same as the customer's code, but not necessarily so – for instance, a customer might trade under a different name when making supplies. When the code is entered, pressing Tab brings up the supplier's name and a list of outstanding invoices appears in the right hand box below it. (Again, credit notes and payments on account are not listed.)

1.10 Now that the two accounts are shown side-by-side, you should be able to identify the matching transactions for which you want to make the contra entry.

1.11 To make the contra entry, select the appropriate transaction (sales invoice) in the customer account, by clicking on it. The amount in the Total box for sales invoices at the bottom of the screen is increased by the value of the transaction. (Note: you can de-select an invoice by clicking on it again.)

1.12 When you have selected the appropriate sales invoice find the appropriate purchase invoice in the other box, and select it by clicking. The amount in the

Total box for purchase invoices at the bottom of the screen is increased by the value of the transaction you have selected.

1.13 So long as you first posted any payment that was due or receipt that had been received the two totals will now be equal.

1.14 Click on OK to save the transaction, which will be posted to the appropriate accounts in the sales, purchase and nominal ledgers.

2 EXCEEDING A CREDIT LIMIT

2.1 Credit limits can be set for individual customers (or by individual suppliers). These fix the maximum amount of credit (unpaid invoices) the customer should have at any time. In some organisations credit limits are not always strictly observed.

2.2 A warning message will be displayed on screen whenever an invoice you are processing takes the outstanding balance on the account above its current credit limit. This is the warning you see if you are using the **Invoicing** option.

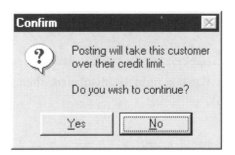

2.3 You should be aware of your organisation's policy regarding credit limits. You should ask your supervisor what to do whenever you are not sure.

2.4 If you know that you should proceed, perhaps on instructions from your supervisor, you can select the **Yes** option. The program will then allow you to continue with the entry, despite the warning.

2.5 If your supervisor instructs you to increase the customer's credit limit, click on **No** and then (without closing the current **Invoice** window) click on the **Customers** button, select the Customer's account from the list and then click on **Record.** Activate the Credit Control Tab and click into the Credit Limit box, key in the new limit and then click on **Save.** Then press Esc twice to get back to the invoice window. The invoice will now be accepted without the warning.

2.6 A customer who is over his credit limit is listed *in red* in the main Customers window.

Activity 9.1

Load Assignment 3.

Post an invoice for £400 (net) to School of Dance. The invoice is for Window cleaning, is numbered 21785, and is dated 14 November 2000.

By how much is School of Dance over its credit limit and what is the new balance on the Sales – Window Cleaning account?

3 WRITING OFF BAD DEBTS

3.1 Occasionally, a customer who has been invoiced will fail to pay, and the debt must eventually be 'written off' as uncollectable. There are various reasons why a debt could become a 'bad debt'. Three common reasons are:

(a) The customer proves unreliable and is unlikely to pay.

(b) The customer goes out of business.

(c) There is a dispute with the customer about whether a particular invoice should be paid, and it is eventually decided to write off the individual transaction as a bad debt.

3.2 When a debt is written off as uncollectable, one of two possible situations could apply.

(a) The customer will not be granted credit ever again. The customer's entire debt is written off, and the customer's account will eventually be deleted from the sales ledger.

(b) An individual transaction is written off, but the company will continue to sell on credit to the customer. A dispute about one transaction is not allowed to affect the long-term relationship with the customer.

Writing off an account

3.3 To write off all the outstanding debts in a customer's account, click on the word **Tools** at the top of the screen and then on **Write Off, Refund, Return**.

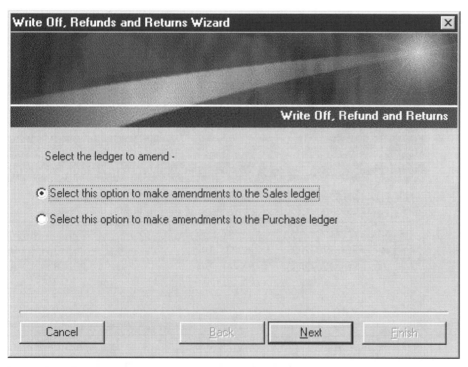

3.4 The option for amendments to the Sales ledger is selected when this window loads. You can click in the white circle and make amendments to the Purchase ledger if you like. If you accidentally pick the wrong option now or later you can click on the **Back** button to take you back to the previous step.

3.5 When you have this screen click on **Next** and another window will appear.

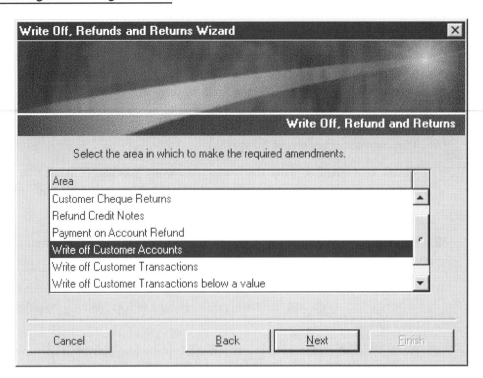

3.6 This gives you a number of options (a similar list appears if you select the Purchase ledger). The one we want on this occasion is **Write Off Customer Accounts**. Select this and then click on **Next.** A window appears very much like the one that drops down when you click on the Finder button or press F4 – you get a list of account names that you can scroll through. Select the account you want and then click on **Next.**

3.7 As this option writes off Customer Accounts rather than individual transactions, clicking on **Next** will write off *all* the transactions listed.

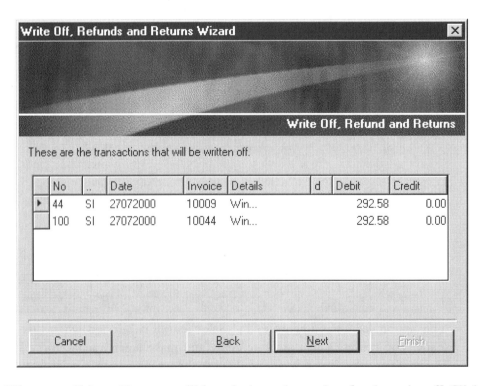

3.8 When you click on Next you will be asked to select a date for the write off. Click Next again and you will see the following.

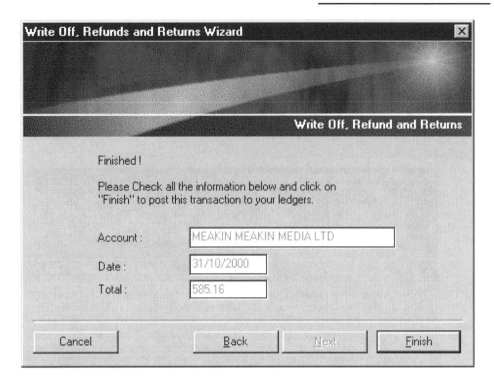

3.9   Click on **Finish** and you are returned to the main screen. The effect of all this is as follows.

   (a)   The customer's account in the Customers ledger will be updated automatically when you select the Yes option to write off the outstanding debts on the account. The account will remain, however, in the sales ledger and will not be deleted.

   (b)   The appropriate accounts in the nominal ledger will also be updated automatically:

   CREDIT   Debtors control account (N/C code 1100)
   DEBIT   Bad debt write off account (N/C code 8100)

   If you check the Customers account and Nominal accounts Activity records you will see the entry that has been made.

Removing the account from the ledger

3.10   You might think that, having chosen the option **Write off Account,** the account will no longer appear in the ledger. Actually, however the customer record will not be completely removed. This is because it is needed for record keeping and auditing purposes. Since there have been some transactions with the customer during the year (even if the only 'transaction' has been your write-off of all outstanding amounts), the record must be kept on the system.

Activity 9.2

Load up Assignment 2,

It is 15 November 2000. Write off the account of the customer named Vice Versa.

What entries are shown in the customer's Activity record once you have done this?

What accounts are affected in the nominal ledger?

Writing off a transaction

3.11 To write off a single outstanding invoice click on the word **Tools** at the top of the screen, then on **Write Off, Refund, Return** and select the Sales ledger option. The amendment you want this time is **Write Off Customer Transactions.** Select this, click on Next, then select the account. Clicking on Next brings you this screen and instructions.

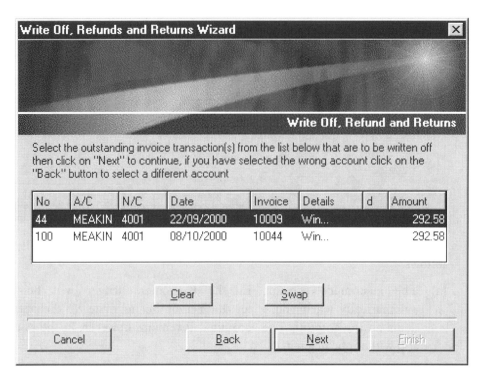

3.12 To write off Invoice 10009 click on this to select it, then click on Next and then Finish.

Activity 9.3

Load Assignment 5.

It is 20 November 2000. Write off invoice number 10025, following the instructions above as appropriate.

What is the amount of the write off and the new balance on the Debtors Control account?

---

4 CHASING CUSTOMERS FOR OVERDUE PAYMENTS

4.1 It is an unfortunate fact of business life that many customers delay payment of invoices. They will pay eventually, and there will not be a bad debt. However, unless a determined effort is made to collect the unpaid invoice or invoices, the customer might continue to delay payment for as long as possible. In most businesses, there are procedures for:

(a) Producing a regular list of unpaid invoices, analysing the length of time for which each invoice has been outstanding (an 'aged debtors list').

(b) Producing statements of unpaid invoices for individual customers, for sending out to the customer as a reminder.

(c) Producing and sending reminder letters to customers whose invoices are overdue for payment.

Aged debtors list

4.2 To produce a list of unpaid debts, analysed by age, print out an Aged debtors analysis (Detailed) using the **Reports** option in the Customers window. The procedures for producing an aged debtors list have already been described in Chapter 7.

Statements

4.3 A statement of account is a printed statement of the amounts of unpaid invoices currently owed by a customer. Statements are sent to customers to assist with debt collection.

4.4 For the case study in this book, a standard layout provided by Sage (Statement With Tear Off Remit Advice) is used. This shows the following details.

(a) Customer name, address and account code.

(b) The statement date.

(c) Brought forward figures at the beginning of the period covered by the statement.

(d) Details of transactions in the period covered by the statement (date, invoice number, description, amount).

(e) An analysis of outstanding amounts by age.

(f) A total of the amounts outstanding.

4.5 To produce statements, as you might guess, you use the **Statement** button in the **Customers** window. The following window will appear.

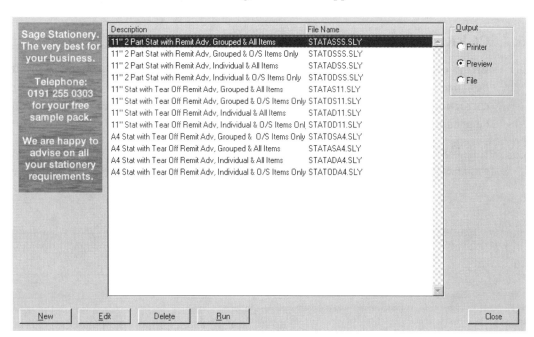

BPP
PUBLISHING

4.6 Clicking on run will bring up a the **Criteria** window which requires you to:

    (a) Specify an Account Range, or accept the defaults to print a statement for all accounts.

    (b) Specify a date range.

4.7 Note that the dates you specify affect how the information is shown in the statement. If you specify, say 01/01/1980 as the Beginning Date and leave the Ending Date as the end of the current month you will get full details of all transactions in that period. If you leave the dates as the first and last day of the current month, all transaction dated before the first day of the current month will be lumped together in a single brought forward figure.

4.8 Clicking on **OK** will produce the statements.

Reminder letters

4.9 Reminder letters can be sent to customers to urge them to settle invoices that are overdue for payment. The Sage package includes standard letters and also allows users to create their own.

4.10 The Letters function is accessed through the **Letters** button in the Customers window. We will not be explaining this feature further as it is not included in the guidelines for AAT Unit 20. However, you may wish to experiment with the function yourself.

Activity 9.4

Load Assignment 3. It is 31 December 2000 (change the Program Date to 31/12/2000).

Print out a statement and as stern a reminder letter as you can for Townend Angus Ltd.

How many days overdue is payment of the invoice?

5 CORRECTING ERRORS

5.1 Errors can easily be input to an accounts system, and spotted only after the input has been posted. They must be corrected. The appropriate procedure for correcting errors in the data on file depends on the nature of the error. Errors can be grouped into two types:

- Non-accounting errors
- Accounting errors

Non-accounting errors	*Accounting errors*
Errors in descriptive items, not affecting account code or money amounts	
	Errors in
Date	Account - ie input of the wrong account code
Reference items	Amount - ie the amount or value of a
Transaction details	transaction, such as entering £1,100
Department number	instead of £1,000
Tax code (provided correcting the error does not affect the amount of VAT payable, eg. using tax code T0 instead of T2)	

5.2   Whichever type you are correcting, it will save time if you can note down the number of transaction concerned when you first become aware of the error. This may involve you looking through a list of sales invoices (call up the **Activity** of the Debtors Ledger Control Account or the Creditors Ledger Control Account), or looking through a particular customer or supplier account (again using the **Activity** option).

5.3   With an accounting error you will need to get full details of the transaction and it is best to do this before you start the correction procedure. Locate the transaction in the appropriate ledger and, if possible, select the relevant account and print out an Activity report for that account. If you cannot get a print-out, note down the:

- Transaction number
- Date
- Account codes concerned (customer/supplier and nominal accounts)
- Invoice number or other reference number
- Details
- Amount (net and VAT)

Correcting non-accounting errors

5.4   To correct a non-accounting error, first close any windows that are currently open until you have only the main Sage window in front of you.

5.5   At the top of the screen you will see the word **File.** Click on this and a menu appears. The item you want is **Maintenance.** If you click on this the following appears.

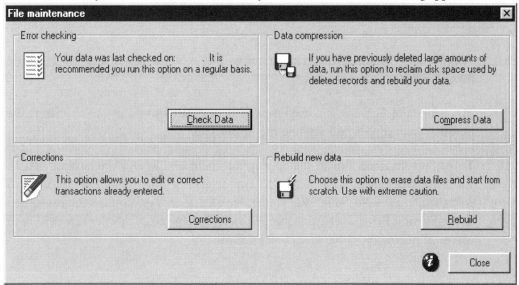

BPP
PUBLISHING

Posting error corrections

5.6 You only need use the **Corrections** button. If you click on this the following screen will appear. This lists all the transactions currently on the system, in transaction number order.

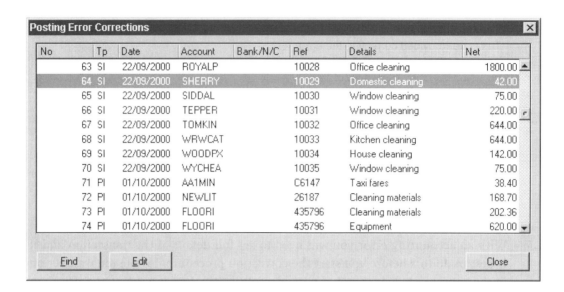

5.7 Your first job is to locate the transaction. If you noted down the transaction number this should be easy enough. Highlight the transaction and click on the **Edit** button. A new window will appear.

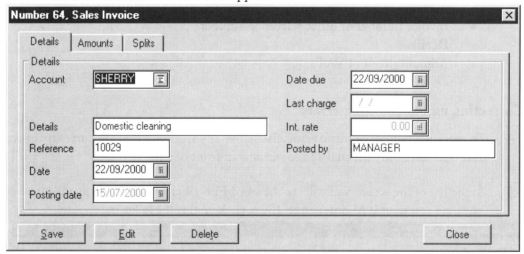

5.8 The **Details** section of the transaction will now be on screen and are available for editing.

5.9 To change the Amount you need to activate the **Amounts** Tab and to change the nominal code you should activate the **Splits** Tab.

5.10 To correct an error Tab to the appropriate field and key in the correct details. Then click on **Save**. A message will appear asking you if you 'Do you wish to post these changes?' . So long as you *are* sure click on Yes. You are then returned to the Posting Error Corrections screen and you can select another transaction to correct if necessary. Otherwise click on Close.

5.11 In the **Amounts** Tab you may correct the Net and Tax fields only if the Paid in Full flag box does is not ticked.

Correcting errors in account code or amount

5.12 You may only correct an *accounting* error using the **Maintenance** option if the transaction has not already been settled: in other words if a receipt or payment relating to the invoice has not yet been recorded on the system.

5.13 Journal entries will be required to correct errors in transactions that have been recorded as being paid. Two entries would be required, a reversing entry to cancel out the existing entry and another to input the transaction correctly.

5.14 This is a test of your accounting skills and your understanding of debits and credits. These concepts are covered in AAT Foundation Units 1 and 2.

Activity 9.5

Load the data for Assignment 3.

The details for a purchase invoice from the Ironcliffe Group posted on 26 August 2000 should have read 'Rent to 31 October 2000'.

Correct the details, as described above.

---

6 CONCLUSION

6.1 You should now be ready to attempt **Assignment 6**.

Activity 9.6

Still with Assignment 3 loaded, find the balance on each of the sales accounts. Then alter the amount of invoice number 10018 to £1000 plus VAT, and alter the details and nominal code to that for Window Cleaning.

What appears in the Activity record of the relevant customer's account after you have done this?

How have the balances on the sales accounts changed?

Quick quiz

1 What is a contra entry? (See paragraph 1.1)

2 How do you access the contra entries facility in Sage? (1.7)

3 How would you increase a customer's credit limit? (2.9)

4 List three reasons why a customer may not pay an invoice. (3.1)

5 Give two examples of accounting errors. (5.1)

Answers to activities

Answer 9.1

School of Dance is £163.75 over the limit. The new balance on the Sales – Window Cleaning account is £2,920.40.

Answer 9.2

Here is what you should see in Vice Versa's account.

No	Tp	Date	Refn	Details	Amount	O/S	Debit	Credit
58	SI	22/09/2000	10035	Window cleaning	52.88		52.88	
84	SC	15/11/2000	BADDBT	Bad Debt Write Off	52.88			52.88

The write off affects the Debtors control account (1100) and the Bad Debt Write Off account (8100).

Answer 9.3

The write off is for £2,714.25. The new balance on the Debtors Control account is £17,235.19.

Answer 9.4

More than 90 days.

Answer 9.6

You should see the following activity.

No	Tp	Date	Refn	Details	Amount	O/S	Debit	Credit
53	SI	22/09/2000	10018	Window cleaning	1175.00	1175.00	1175.00	
107	SI	22/09/2000	10018	Deleted – see tran 53	940.00			

The balances change as follows.

Account	Before £	After £	Change £
4000	20,807.80	20,007.80	800.00
4001	2,520.40	3,520.40	1,000.00
4002	853.10	853.10	None
4100	980.14	980.14	None

Part C
Information technology and security

10 Security issues

This chapter contains

1   The identification of risks

2   Risks to the computer users

3   Risks to hardware

4   Controlling access to buildings

5   Controls over staff

6   Risks to disks and tapes

7   Risks to data

8   Back-up procedures

9   The Data Protection Act

Learning objectives

On completion of this chapter you will:

- Understand the main risks to information and equipment

- Be aware of the requirements of the Data Protection Act

Knowledge and understanding

1   Organisational security policies.

2   Organisation procedures for changing passwords and making back ups.

3   Location of hardware, software and back up copies.

4   Location of information sources.

BPP PUBLISHING

1 THE IDENTIFICATION OF RISKS

1.1 Information technology has brought many changes to working practices and procedures in the office. Much information processing is now **faster, more accurate** and **more reliable** than was ever possible using manual processing methods.

1.2 Computers are used widely. Many organisations **depend** on computer systems to support their day-to-day operation of the business.

1.3 Because we now rely so much on computers, there are risks if computer systems **fail**. If users do not put adequate security measures and procedures into place, computer failure can result in the **loss of much valuable data**.

1.4 **Security** involves the prevention of unauthorised modification, disclosure or destruction of data and the maintenance of uninterrupted computing services.

1.5 Security measures can only be successfully implemented if computer users are aware of the **risks**. There are many different risks, for instance, accidentally deleting files, the risk of fire, the risk of system breakdown. A useful classification identifies seven types of risk, as follows.

- Human error
- Technical error
- Natural disasters
- Deliberate actions
- Commercial espionage
- Malicious damage
- Industrial action

Activity 10.1

See if you can think of examples of risks, in the context of your use of computers, one for each of these categories.

1.6 The risk that actually occurs most often is probably **human error**.

1.7 One other area of risk in the information technology environment to which increasing attention has been paid in recent years are risks to you, the **computer user**.

2 RISKS TO THE COMPUTER USER

2.1 Risks to the computer user can be placed in one of two categories.

(a) The first category includes all those **hazards** to which **any office worker** is exposed, whether or not he or she is using a computer.

(b) The second category covers those risks which arise from using a **keyboard** (or mouse) and **screen**.

General risks

2.2 As an employee, you are legally obliged to take reasonable care to **avoid injury to yourself and others**. Employers also have a number of duties imposed on them by legislation; **employers' duties** include the provision of certain minimum acceptable standards for the working environment.

- Cleanliness
- Ventilation
- Temperature
- Lighting
- Seating

2.3 Now consider the **workstation** itself. When drivers get into a car that was last driven by someone else, they might check the driving seat position, the angle of the backrest, the tilt of the seat, the angle of the steering column and the positioning of the mirrors. This ensures that they will be **comfortable** and maintain a **good posture**.

2.4 However, many people do not think about posture and comfort in the office, even though they may spend far longer at a desk than in a car. Your chair should have adjustable height settings and an adjustable back support.

Computer-related risks

2.5 If you have ever worked for long periods at a computer, you may have experienced some **discomfort**. This might have been caused by your use of the **screen** or the **keyboard**. Look at the workstation which you normally use when working with a computer and consider the sources of risk.

The VDU

2.6 If a screen is too bright, it can cause **eye strain**. There are two common ways of dealing with this problem. The first is to turn the brightness down; all monitors have a brightness and a contrast switch. The second is to fit some kind of anti-glare filter.

2.7 Medical evidence now suggests that working with a VDU does not cause eye defects. It can, however, lead to **sore eyes**, **headaches** or discomfort in the **neck, shoulders and arms**.

2.8 The **position** of the VDU is important in preventing discomfort. Most VDUs are mounted on some kind of **pedestal** and, depending on the desk space available, they may be sited on the surface of the desk itself or may be perched on the base unit of a desktop computer. Health and Safety regulations on 'display screen equipment' require that all VDUs have to have a **swivel and tilt** capability.

The keyboard

2.9 Poor positioning of a keyboard can lead to **postural problems**. The angle of keyboards should be adjustable and the workspace in front of them should be of sufficient width for a user to rest his or her forearms. The **angle of typing** can be made more comfortable by placing the wrists on a narrow raised platform in front of the keyboard.

2.10   The most widely discussed keyboard-related complaint is RSI, or **repetitive strain injury**. This is a disorder which affects the upper limbs particularly the forearms and hands. Although there is legal and medical dispute about whether RSI is a genuine condition (because employers tend to settle claims for injury out of court), it seems to arise from poorly designed equipment, environment and posture, which leads to muscles being starved of oxygen, the build up of waste products in the body and the compression of nerves.

Other computer equipment

2.11   There are a number of other potential problems which you may encounter if you use computers, or indeed any other **electrical equipment**. These are really self-explanatory, but you should bear them in mind when you assess the safety of your working environment. The principal risks are injury from **electric shock**, attraction of **static electricity** and the hazard of loose or badly-routed computer **cabling**.

Minimising risks to the person

2.12   Positive steps can be taken to reduce most of the risks described above. If you are in a job where your remuneration depends on the number of keystrokes you achieve in the working day, you may feel a certain reluctance to adopt some of these measures.

(a)   Ensure that your place of work is **comfortable** and conducive to maintaining a **good posture**.

(b)   Ensure that the **layout** of the workstation will not necessitate **awkward posture** or movements. (You should not need to balance the keyboard on your knees, nor should you need to move you head to be able to see the screen.)

(c)   Take **occasional breaks,** or as a minimum change your posture from time to time to prevent muscle strain.

(d)   Try out different ways of positioning the **keyboard, VDU and input documents** to find one that suits you.

(e)   Reduce the **glare** from your screen in one of the ways described above. Focus should be **sharp**, characters should **not flicker** and there should be **no reflections**.

3   RISKS TO HARDWARE

3.1   The risks to computer hardware vary depending upon the **type of hardware**. You may feel that the risks in a mainframe environment are not your concern, as minimisation of the risk of fire and flooding should have been addressed when the system was installed.

3.2   This may be so, but **you can help** by, for example, observing standard fire regulations in such an environment. It is not just your PC which you must protect; you must be conscious of risks to the **whole IT environment**.

Physical threats

3.3 Physical security comprises two sorts of control.

(a) Protection against **natural and man made disasters,** such as fire, flood or sabotage.

(b) Protection against **intruders** obtaining physical access to the system.

Fire

3.4 Fire is the **most serious hazard** to computer systems. Destruction of data can be even more costly than the destruction of hardware.

3.5 A proper fire safety plan is an essential feature of security procedures, in order to prevent fire, detect fire and put out the fire. Fire safety includes:

(a) **Site preparation** (for example, appropriate building **materials,** fire doors).

(b) **Detection** (for example, **smoke detectors**).

(c) **Extinguishing** (for example, **sprinklers**).

(d) Training for staff in observing **fire safety procedures** (for example, **no smoking** in computer room).

Water

3.6 Water is a serious hazard. **Flooding** and water damage are often encountered following **firefighting** activities elsewhere in a building.

3.7 This problem can be countered by the use of **waterproof ceilings and floors** together with the provision of **adequate drainage**.

3.8 In some areas **flooding** is a natural risk, for example in parts of central London and many other towns and cities near rivers or coasts. **Basements** are therefore generally not regarded as appropriate sites for computer installation!

Weather

3.9 Wind, rain and storms can all cause substantial **damage to buildings**.

3.10 **Cutbacks in maintenance** expenditure may lead to leaking roofs or dripping pipes, which can invite problems of this type, and maintenance should be kept up if at all possible.

3.11 **Lightning** and electrical storms can play havoc with **power supplies,** causing power **failures** or power **surges** which effect computer processing operations.

3.12 One way of combating this is by the use of **uninterrupted (protected) power supplies.** This will protect equipment from fluctuations in the supply. Power failure can be protected against by the use of a **separate generator**.

Terrorist activity

3.13 The threat of bombs planted by **political terrorists** has beset UK organisations for many years. Other parts of the world such as the Middle East, central Europe and the US have been equally or worse afflicted. Political terrorism is the main risk, but there are also threats from individuals with **grudges.**

3.14 In some cases there is very little that an organisation can do: its buildings may just happen to **be in the wrong place** and bear the brunt of an attack aimed at another organisation or intended to cause general disruption.

3.15 There are some avoidance measures that should be taken, however.

(a) **Physical access** to buildings should be controlled (see the next section).

(b) Activities likely to give rise to terrorism such as **exploitation** of workers or **cruelty** to animals should be stopped.

(c) The organisation should consult with police and fire authorities about potential risks, and **co-operate** with their efforts to avoid them.

Accidental damage

3.16 **People** are a physical threat to computer installations because they can be **careless and clumsy**: there can be few of us who have not at some time spilt a cup of coffee over a desk covered with papers.

3.17 Combating accidental damage is a matter of:

- Sensible **attitudes** to office behaviour
- Good office **layout**

Computer theft

3.18 A problem which is related to the problem of physical access control is that of equipment theft. As computer equipment becomes **smaller** and **more portable**, it can be 'smuggled' out of buildings with greater ease.

3.19 A **log of all equipment** should be maintained. This may already exist in basic form as a part of the fixed asset register. Anyone taking any equipment off-site should book it out and book it back in.

3.20 Computer theft may be carried out by persons who have official access to equipment. It may equally be carried out by those who do not. **Burglar alarms** should be installed.

3.21 **Smaller items** of equipment, such as laptop computers and floppy disks, should always be **locked securely away**. Larger items cannot be moved with ease and one approach adopted is the use of **bolts** to secure them to desks. This discourages 'opportunity' thieves. Larger organisations may also employ site security guards and install closed circuit camera systems.

Activity 10.2

Your department is located in an open-plan office, has five networked desktop PCs, a laser printer and a dot matrix printer.

You have just read an article suggesting that the best form of security is to lock hardware away in fireproof cabinets, but you feel that this is impracticable. Make a note of any alternative security measures which you could adopt to protect the hardware.

4   CONTROLLING ACCESS TO BUILDINGS

4.1   The way to minimise many of the risks discussed in the above section is to introduce a series of **access** controls, to prevent intruders getting near the computer **equipment** or storage media. Methods of controlling human access include:

- Personnel (security guards)
- Mechanical devices (eg keys, whose issue is recorded)
- Electronic identification devices (eg card-swipe systems)

4.2   It may not be cost effective or convenient to have the **same type** of access controls around the **whole building** all of the time. Instead, the various security requirements of different departments should be estimated, and appropriate boundaries drawn. Some areas will be **very restricted**, whereas others will be **relatively open**.

4.3   Guidelines for data security which should be applied within the office are as follows.

(a)   **Fireproof cabinets** should be used to store files, or lockable metal boxes for floppy disks. If files contain confidential data, they should be kept in a **safe**.

(b)   Computers with **lockable keyboards** are sometimes used. Computer terminals should be **sited carefully**, to minimise the risk of unauthorised use.

(c)   If a computer printout is likely to include confidential data, it should be **shredded** before it is eventually thrown away after use.

(d)   **Disks** containing valuable data should not be left lying around an office. They can get lost or stolen. More likely still, they can get damaged, by spilling **tea or coffee** over them, or allowing the disks to gather **dust**, which can make them unreadable.

(e)   The computer's **environment** (humidity, temperature, dust) should be properly controlled. This is not so important with modern systems as in the past, but any extreme temperature or conditions should be avoided.

Personal identification numbers (PINs)

4.4   In some systems, the user might have a special **personal identification number**, or PIN, which identifies him or her to the system. According to what the user's PIN is, the user will be **allowed access** to certain data and parts of the system, but **forbidden access** to other parts.

Door locks

4.5   Conventional door locks are of value in certain circumstances, particularly where users are only required to pass through the door a **couple of times a day**. If the number of people using the door increases and the frequency of use is high, it will be difficult to persuade staff to lock a door every time they pass through it.

4.6   If this approach is adopted, a 'good' lock must be accompanied by a **strong door**, otherwise an intruder may simply bypass the lock. Similarly, other points of entry into the room/complex must be as well protected, otherwise the intruder will simply use a **window** to gain access.

171

4.7 One difficulty with conventional locks is the matter of **key control**. Inevitably, each person authorised to use the door will have a key and there will also be a master key maintained by security. Cleaners and other contractors might be issued with keys. Practices such as lending out keys or taking duplicate keys may be difficult to prevent.

4.8 One approach to this is the installation of **combination locks,** where a numbered keypad is located outside the door and access allowed only after the correct 'code', or sequence of digits has been entered. This will only be effective if users keep the combination **secret** and the combination is **changed** frequently.

Card entry systems

4.9 There is a range of card entry systems available. This is a more sophisticated means of control than the use of locks, as **cards can be programmed** to allow access to certain parts of a building only.

4.10 These allow a high degree of monitoring of staff movements; they can for example be used instead of clock cards to record details of time spent on site. Such cards can be incorporated into **identity cards**, which also carry the photograph and signature of the user.

5 CONTROLS OVER STAFF

Staff selection

5.1 The vast majority of employees are **honest** and have good intentions. The damage that people can do to computer systems are best overcome by proper **training**.

5.2 However, a small minority of employees may inflict **deliberate damage** on a system.

5.3 Controls related to personnel include the following.

   (a) Checks and balances so that a security violation must **pass through several steps** before being implemented.

   (b) **Segregation of duties** (division of responsibilities).

   (c) **Job rotation,** so that employees change duties regularly, making it uncertain that an individual will be able to set up a breach of security in the time available.

   (d) Enforced **vacations**.

   (e) Access to information granted not on rank in the management hierarchy or precedent, but on a **need-to-know** basis.

   (f) Careful **selection** of personnel.

Division of responsibilities

5.4 Some employees have to be in a **position of trust** although a well-designed security system puts as few people in this powerful position as possible.

5.5 Dividing up responsibilities, as far as **security** is concerned, has two purposes.

(a) To assign the **responsibility** for certain tasks to specific jobs and individuals. A person in a given job has the responsibility for ensuring that certain controls are applied

(b) To prevent **deliberate error**. It is easier for a person to commit fraud if he can input data, write programs and operate the computer all by himself. By dividing up the work, it is more difficult to commit fraud.

5.6 Desirable as such controls may be, especially where accounting systems are concerned, they conflict with modern ideas about **multi-skilled employees** and widespread **sharing of information**.

Fraud

5.7 Computer frauds come from disgruntled employees, outside criminals (who may bribe an employee to breach the organisation's defences) and hackers.

5.8 Two **types** of frauds can be identified.

(a) Single **large scale frauds**, usually the purloining of large amounts of money.

(b) Small-scale, but **long term frauds**. If an organisation has 20,000 employees, then five pence sliced off the monthly salary cheque for each employee (the 'salami' technique) would net the fraudster £1,000 per month.

5.9 Examples of **methods** of fraud are given below.

(a) Creation of **fictitious supplier accounts** and submission of false invoices, usually for services rather than goods, so that payments are sent to the fictitious supplier.

(b) Abuse of corporate **credit card facilities**, for example to purchase more fuel than is used in the employee's company car.

(c) Corruption and bribery, particularly where individuals are in a position of authority as regards selecting suppliers.

(d) Theft of incoming cheques.

(e) **Theft** of portable fixed assets.

(f) Giving **unauthorised discounts** to customers.

(g) **Stock losses**.

(h) **Fictitious staff** on the payroll.

6 RISKS TO DISKS AND TAPES

6.1 We have examined some of the more common risks to computer **hardware** and the computer environment. Some of these risks can also affect the **physical things** on which data and software are held. The most widely used forms of storage medium are **disks and tapes**.

BPP PUBLISHING

Handling floppy disks, CDs and tapes

6.2 Floppy **disks** are not so floppy these days and CDs are fairly sturdy. However, both should be handled with care, just as you would treat a valuable music CD with care.

    (a) They will break or be seriously damaged if you are strong enough to **bend them,** or if you **tread on them** or **run them over** with the castors of your chair.

    (b) They do not take kindly to having **hot drinks** spilled over them or to being left on sunny windowsills.

    (c) CDs in particular should be protected from **dust** and **scratches** and **finger prints**: hold them along the outer edge or by the centre hole. *Never* touch the surface of the disk inside a floppy disk's casing.

    (d) For floppy disks write on the label **before** you stick it on to the disk and write only with a **felt tip pen**, never a ball point. If you write on a CD you should only write on the 'label' side - again only with a felt-tip pen.

    (e) Floppy disks are 'magnetic' disks so they are affected by **magnets**. (CDs are optical disks so magnets are not a problem.)

6.3 **Tapes** can be snipped with scissors, or get knotted up, and they can also be damaged by magnets and heat and liquid. Treat them with the same care you would give to a much-loved audio tape or video tape.

7 RISKS TO DATA

7.1 Risks to **data** can be in the form of deliberate or accidental:

- Destruction
- Theft
- Unauthorised disclosure

7.2 Data can be protected from the risk of theft or unauthorised disclosure by suitable controls. There are two forms of access control; the first (as described earlier) prevents **physical** access to the hardware and the second prevents access from the hardware to the software. This is known as **logical** access control.

7.3 In its commonest form, logical access control consists of a password system. Data destruction can be protected against by taking **back-ups** and the risk of alteration of data minimised by a variety of basic precautions.

Passwords

7.4 **Passwords** are a set of characters which may be allocated to a person, a terminal or a facility which are required to be keyed into the system before further access is permitted. Passwords can be applied to data files, program files and to parts of a program.

    (a) One password may be required to **read a file,** but another to **write new data** to it.

(b) The terminal user can be **restricted** to the use of certain files and programs (eg in a banking system, junior grades of staff are only allowed to access certain routine programs).

7.5 In order to access a system the user needs first to enter a string of characters. If what is entered **matches** a password issued to an authorised user or valid for that particular terminal the system permits access. Otherwise the system **shuts down** and may record the attempted unauthorised access.

7.6 Passwords ought to be effective in keeping out unauthorised users, but they are by no means foolproof.

(a) By **experimenting** with possible passwords, an unauthorised person can gain access to a program or file by **guessing** the correct password. This is not as difficult as it may seem when too many computer users specify 'obvious' passwords for their files or programs. In addition **computer programs** are available that run through millions of possible combinations at lightning speed until the correct one is found.

(b) Someone who is authorised to access a data or program file may **tell an unauthorised person** what the password is, perhaps through carelessness.

(c) Many password systems come with **standard passwords** as part of the system, such as LETMEIN. It is essential for these to be removed if the system is to be at all secure. Such common passwords become widely known to people in the industry using similar packages.

(d) Password systems they rely upon users to use them **conscientiously**. Users can be sloppy with their security control. Passwords are often left in plain view or 'hidden' beneath keyboards or inside desk drawers where others could find them.

BPP - Best Password Practice

Here is a checklist of points to be observed by computer users to whom passwords have been allocated.

- **Keep your password secret**. Do *not* reveal it to anyone else.

- **Do *not* write it down**. The second easiest way of revealing a password is to write it on an adhesive label and stick this to the VDU, the desk beneath the keyboard, the inside of a desk drawer or the underside of an overhead filing cabinet.

- **Change your password regularly.**

- Change and use your password **discreetly**. Even though a password does not show up on screen, it is easy for onlookers to see which keys are being used. (FRED is a popular password for this reason; the relevant keys are close together on a QWERTY keyboard.)

- **Do not use an obvious password**. (FRED is an obvious password. Your name or nickname is another)

- **Change** your password if you **suspect** that anyone else knows it.

7.7 In a logical access system, data and software, or individual computer systems, will be **classified** according to the **sensitivity** and **confidentiality** of data.

(a) Thus **payroll** data or details of the draft corporate budget for the coming year may be perceived as highly sensitive and made available to identified individuals only.

(b) Other financial information may be made **available to certain groups** of staff only, for example members of the finance function or a certain grade of management.

(c) Other data may be **unrestricted.**

7.8 A logical access system performs three operations when access is requested and a password entered.

- **Identification** of the user.
- **Authentication** of user identity.
- Check on user **authority.**

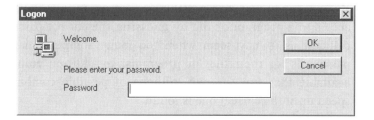

Telecommunications dangers

7.9 When data is transmitted over a network or **telecommunications link** (especially the **Internet**) there are numerous security dangers.

(a) Corruptions such as **viruses** on a single computer can spread through the network to all of the organisation's computers. (Viruses are described at greater length later in this chapter.)

(b) Staff can do damage through their own computer to data stored on other computers. For example, they may try to transfer a file from their own hard disk to a colleague's hard disk without realising that their colleague has a file with the same name. Unless care is exercised it is easy to **overwrite somebody else's data.**

(c) Disaffected employees have much greater potential to do **deliberate damage** to valuable corporate data or systems because the network could give them access to parts of the system that they are not really authorised to use.

(d) If the organisation is linked to an external network, persons outside the company (**hackers**) may be able to get into the company's internal network, either to steal data or to damage the system.

Systems can have **firewalls** (which disable part of the telecoms technology) to prevent unwelcome intrusions into company systems, but a determined hacker may well be able to bypass even these. (There is more on hackers below.)

(e) Employees may **download inaccurate information** or imperfect or **virus-ridden software** from an external network. For example 'beta' (free trial) versions of forthcoming new editions of many major packages are often available on the Internet, but the whole point about a beta version is that it is not fully tested and may contain bugs that could disrupt an entire system.

(f) Information transmitted from one part of an organisation to another may be **intercepted.** Data can be 'encrypted' (scrambled) in an attempt to make it unintelligible to eavesdroppers, but there is not yet any entirely satisfactory method of doing this. (See below. The problem is being worked upon by those with a vested interest, such as credit card companies, and will no doubt be resolved in time.)

(g) The **communications link itself may break down or distort data**. The worldwide telecommunications infrastructure is improving thanks to the use of new technologies, and there are communications 'protocols' governing the format of data and signals transferred. At present, however, transmitted data is only as secure as the medium through which it is transmitted, no matter what controls are operated at either end.

Encryption and other safety measures

7.10 **Encryption** involves scrambling the data at one end of the line, transmitting the scrambled data, and unscrambling it at the receiver's end of the line. Encryption aims to prevent unauthorised people intercepting and reading communications.

7.11 **Authentication** is a technique of making sure that a message has come from an authorised sender. Authentication involves adding extra data which has previously been agreed between the senders and recipients.

7.12 **Dial-back security** operates by requiring the person wanting access to the network to dial into it and identify themselves first. The system then dials the person back on their authorised number before allowing them access.

7.13 All attempted **violations of security** should be automatically **logged** and the log checked regularly. In a multi-user system, the terminal attempting the violation may be automatically disconnected.

Hacking

7.14 A hacker is a **person who attempts to invade the privacy of a system**.

7.15 Hackers normally have some **programming** knowledge, but do not need to be experts to cause extensive damage. Hackers, in the past, have mainly been concerned to **copy** information, but a recent trend has been their desire to **corrupt it**.

7.16 The **Computer Misuse Act 1990** makes hacking an offence, but clearly this does not **prevent** it.

Viruses

7.17 A **virus** is a small program which replicates itself, and aims to damage computer systems.

7.18 Viruses need an **opportunity to spread**. The programmers of viruses therefore place viruses in the kind of software which is most likely to be copied. This includes:

(a) **Free software** (for example from the Internet).

(b) **Pirated software** (cheaper than original versions).

(c) **Games software** (wide appeal).

(d) **E-mail attachments** (often with instructions to send the message on to others).

7.19 The problem has been exacerbated by the **portability of computers and disks** and the **increased availability and use of e-mail**.

7.20 It is consequently very difficult to keep control over **what disks** are inserted into an organisation's computers and similarly **what** files are received via e-mail.

7.21 An activated virus can **show itself** in a number of ways.

(a) The **Jerusalem** virus **slows down** the operation of the infected machine so much that it becomes virtually unusable, then deletes files.

(b) **Cascade** causes letters on the **screen** to 'fall' to the bottom of the screen and may reformat the hard disk.

(c) **Casino** displays a one-armed bandit game on screen; if you fail to win the jackpot, your **hard disk is wiped**.

(d) The **Melissa** virus corrupts Microsoft Office documents.

(e) The **Love-bug** virus deletes various files from the operating system, and corrupts other files. It also sends itself on to all addresses held in the users address book.

7.22 The most serious type of virus is one which **infects an operating system** as this governs the whole execution of a program.

7.23 Viruses can spread via data disk, but have been known to copy themselves over whole **networks**.

Type of virus	Explanation
File viruses	File viruses infect program files. When you run an infected program the virus copies itself to another file.
Boot sector viruses	The boot sector is the part of every hard disk and diskette which is read by the computer when it starts up. If the boot sector of a diskette is infected, the virus runs when you attempt to boot from the diskette, and infects the hard disk.
Worms	A worm is a program which spreads (usually) over network connections.
Dropper	A dropper is a program, not a virus itself, that installs a virus on the PC while performing another function.
Macro viruses	A macro virus is written in an application's 'macro' language, which is intended to allow users to automate commonly performed tasks. Many applications have macro capabilities including all the programs in **Microsoft Office**. The distinguishing factor which makes it possible to create a virus with a macro is the existence of **auto-execute events**. Auto-execute events are opening a file, closing a file, and starting an application. Once a macro is running, it can copy itself to other documents, delete files, and create general havoc in a system. The well- known Melissa virus was a form of macro virus.

Case example

Love bug virus creates worldwide chaos

A computer virus which exploits office workers' yearnings for love shut down computer systems from Hong Kong to the Houses of Parliament yesterday and caused untold millions of pounds worth of delays and damage to stored files across the world.

The virus, nicknamed 'the love bug' is **carried in an email** with the heading 'ILOVEYOU'. The text of the message reads: 'Kindly check the attached love letter from me!' A **click on the attached file launches the virus**, which promptly spreads by sending itself to everyone in the recipient's email address book, overloading email systems.

Once embedded in a host computer, the virus can download more dangerous software from a remote website, rename files and redirect Internet browsers. 'It's a very effective virus. It's one of the most aggressive and nastiest I've ever seen,' said Kieran Fitzsimmons of MessageLabs, which screens millions of company emails for viruses. 'It manifests itself almost everywhere in the computer.'

IT specialists described the love bug as '**a visual basic worm**' far more dangerous and fast-spreading than the similar **Melissa virus, which also replicated itself by email**. Melissa infected about a million computers and caused £50m of damage.

ILOVEYOU is eight times bigger, sends itself to everyone in a recipient's address book instead of just the first 50 (and then deletes the address book), and, unlike Melissa, **tampers with operating systems**.

Adapted from The Guardian May 5, 2000

Bugs

7.24 A **bug** is an **unintentional fault** in a program, and can be misinterpreted as a virus. Virtually all complex software contains bugs. Minor bugs merely cause inconvenience, while major bugs can cause catastrophic data loss.

Jokes and hoaxes

7.25 Some programs claim to be doing something destructive to your computer, but are actually 'harmless' jokes.

7.26 There are a number of common hoaxes. The most common is **Good Times**. This hoax has been around for a couple of years, and usually takes the form of a virus warning about viruses contained in e-mail. People pass along the warning because they are trying to be helpful, not realising they are wasting the time of all concerned.

Identification of a virus

7.27 There are two ways of identifying a virus. The first is to identify it before it does any damage. The second is to identify it when it is activated.

7.28 It is difficult for the typical user to identify the presence of a virus. There are sometimes **tell-tale signs,** such as slight changes in file lengths as displayed in the directory, or additional disk activity before a program is run, but **more sophisticated controls** than this are needed.

(a) **Anti-virus software** such as Dr Solomon's is capable of detecting and eradicating a vast number of viruses before they do any damage. Upgrades are released regularly to deal with new viruses.

(b) Organisations must have **procedures** to guard against the downloading of unauthorised files to their systems. Many viruses and trojans have been spread as files attached to e-mails (eg Melissa, Love-bug).

(c) Organisations, as a matter of routine, should **ensure that any file received from outside,** (whether on disk or attached to an e-mail), **is virus-free** before the file is downloaded.

(d) Any **flaws in a widely used program** should be rectified as soon as they come to light.

8   BACK-UP PROCEDURES

8.1   **Back-up** means to make a copy that can be used if the computer system or files become unusable in future. A back-up copy of a file is a duplicate copy kept separately from the main system and only used if the original fails.

8.2   The **purpose of backing up data** is to ensure that the most recent usable copy of the data can be recovered and restored in the event of loss or corruption on the system.

8.3   A related concept is that of **archiving.** Archiving data is the process of moving (by copying) data from primary storage, such as a hard disk, to tape or other portable media for long-term storage.

8.4   Archiving provides a legally acceptable **business history**, while freeing up **hard disk space**.

8.5   In a well-planned data back-up scheme, a copy of backed up data is delivered (preferably daily) to a secure **off-site** storage facility.

8.6   A tape **rotation scheme** can provide a restorable history from one day to several years, depending on the needs of the business.

8.7   A well-planned **back-up and archive strategy** should include:

(a) A plan and schedule for the regular back-up of critical data.
(b) Archive plans.
(c) A disaster recovery plan that includes off-site storage.

8.8   Regular tests should be undertaken to **verify that data backed up can be successfully restored**.

8.9   The **intervals** at which back-ups are performed must be decided. Most organisations back up their data daily.

8.10 A **rotation scheme** that provides an appropriate data history must be selected. The **Grandfather, Father, Son** scheme uses twelve tapes - allowing recovery of three months data.

Grandfather, Father, Son back-up rotation scheme

Tape No.	Tape name	When written to	Overwritten
Tape 1	Son 1	Every Monday	Weekly
Tape 2	Son 2	Every Tuesday	Weekly
Tape 3	Son 3	Every Wednesday	Weekly
Tape 4	Son 4	Every Thursday	Weekly
Tape 5	**Father** week 1	**First** Friday	**Monthly**
Tape 6	Father week 2	Second Friday	Monthly
Tape 7	Father week 3	Third Friday	Monthly
Tape 8	Father week 4	Fourth Friday	Monthly
Tape 9	Father week 5 (if needed)	Fifth Friday	Monthly
Tape 10	**Grandfather** month 1	**Last business day** month 1	**Quarterly**
Tape 11	Grandfather month 2	Last business day month 2	Quarterly
Tape 12	Grandfather month 3	Last business day month 3	Quarterly

8.11 Even with a well planned back-up strategy some re-inputting may be required. For example, if after three hours work on a Wednesday a file becomes corrupt, the Tuesday version can be restored – but Wednesday's work will need to be re-input.

Activity 10.3

You have a PC which you use primarily to create and edit your own spreadsheets. You save these to the computer's hard disk. The machine is sometimes used by colleagues and much of your work is confidential. What precautions should you take to ensure the security of the data in your spreadsheets?

9   THE DATA PROTECTION ACT

Why is privacy an important issue?

9.1 In recent years, there has been a growing popular fear that **information** about individuals which was stored on computer files and processed by computer could be **misused**.

9.2 In particular, it was felt that an individual could easily be harmed by the existence of computerised data about him or her which was inaccurate or misleading and which could be **transferred to unauthorised third parties** at high speed and little cost.

9.3 In the UK the current legislation is the **Data Protection Act 1998**. This Act replaced the earlier Data Protection Act 1984.

The Data Protection Act 1998

9.4 The Data Protection Act 1998 is an attempt to protect the **individual**.

Definitions of terms used in the Act

9.5   In order to understand the Act it is necessary to know some of the technical terms used in it.

(a) **Personal data** is information about a living individual, including expressions of opinion about him or her. Data about other organisations (eg supplier or customer companies) is not personal data, unless it contains data about individuals who belong to those other organisations.

(b) **Data users** are organisations or individuals who control the contents of files of personal data and the use of personal data which is processed (or intended to be processed) automatically - ie who use personal data which is covered by the terms of the Act.

(c) A **data subject** is an individual who is the subject of personal data.

The data protection principles

9.6   Data users must comply with the Data Protection Principles contained in the Act. These are shown in the following table.

DATA PROTECTION PRINCIPLES

1   Personal data shall be processed fairly and lawfully and, in particular, shall not be processed unless:

(a)   At least one of the conditions in Schedule 2 is met. (See paragraph 9.9(c) of this Chapter.)

(b)   In the case of sensitive personal data, at least one of the conditions in Schedule 3 is also met. (See paragraph 9.9(d) of this Chapter.)

2   Personal data shall be obtained only for one or more specified and lawful purposes, and shall not be further processed in any manner incompatible with that purpose or those purposes.

3   Personal data shall be adequate, relevant and not excessive in relation to the purpose or purposes for which they are processed.

4   Personal data shall be accurate and, where necessary, kept up to date.

5   Personal data processed for any purpose or purposes shall not be kept for longer than is necessary for that purpose or those purposes.

6   Personal data shall be processed in accordance with the rights of data subjects under this Act.

7   Appropriate technical and organisational measures shall be taken against unauthorised or unlawful processing of personal data and against accidental loss or destruction of, or damage to, personal data.

8   Personal data shall not be transferred to a country or territory outside the European Economic Area unless that country or territory ensures an adequate level of protection for the rights and freedoms of data subjects in relation to the processing of personal data.

The coverage of the Act

9.7   Key points of the Act can be summarised as follows.

(a) With certain exceptions, all **data users** and all computer bureaux have had to **register** under the Act with the **Data Protection Registrar**.

(b) **Individuals** (data subjects) are awarded certain **legal rights**.

(c) **Data holders** must adhere to the **data protection principles**.

Registration under the Act

9.8 The Data Protection Registrar keeps a Register of all data users. Each entry in the Register relates to a data user or computer bureau. Unless a data user has an entry in the Register he may not hold personal data. Even if the data user is registered, he must only hold data and use data for the **purposes** which are registered. A data user must apply to be registered.

9.9 Features of the 1998 legislation are:

(a) Everyone now has the right to go to court to seek redress for **any breach** of data protection law, rather than just for certain aspects of it.

(b) Filing systems that are structured so as to facilitate access to information about a particular person now fall within the legislation. This includes systems that are **paper-based** or on **microfilm** or **microfiche**. Personnel records meet this classification.

(c) Processing of personal data is **forbidden** except in the following circumstances.

    (i)   With the **consent** of the subject (person).
    (ii)   As a result of a **contractual arrangement**.
    (iii) Because of a **legal obligation**.
    (iv) To **protect the vital interests** of the subject.
    (v)   Where processing is in the **public interest**.
    (vi) Where processing is required to exercise **official authority**.

(d) The processing of 'sensitive data' is forbidden, unless express consent has been obtained or there are conflicting obligations under employment law. Sensitive data includes data relating to **racial origin**, **political opinions**, **religious beliefs**, physical or mental **health, sexual proclivities** and **trade union** membership.

(e) Data subjects have the right to a **copy of data** held about them and also the right to know **why** the data are being processed.

Quick quiz

1   List five types of risk in a computerised environment. (See paragraph 1.5)

2   What responsibilities do employers have regarding the working environment? (2.2)

3   What does RSI stand for? (2.10)

4   List three methods of controlling human access to buildings. (4.1)

5   In the UK, what Act deals with the privacy issues related to information held about people? (9.3)

Answers to activities

Answer 10.1

Examples might be as follows.

(a) *Human error*. Entering data in the wrong period, using the wrong data or getting up from your desk leaving the computer in edit mode.

(b) *Technical error*. Computer not reading a disk properly, bugs in a software package or failed communications links between computers.

(c) *Natural disasters*. Fire, flooding or lightning.

(d) *Deliberate actions*. Fraud, perhaps involving electronic transfer of funds to private accounts or alterations to salary data on the payroll master file.

(e) *Commercial espionage*. Certain financial institutions in the City of London have coated their windows with a reflective substance so that their screens cannot be seen from neighbouring buildings.

(f) *Malicious damage*. There are well documented cases of disgruntled employees destroying data or introducing viruses just before leaving an organisation.

(g) *Industrial action*. Loss of use of the processing function, even for a short time, can cause severe disruption.

Answer 10.2

(a) 'Postcode' all pieces of hardware. Invisible ink postcoding is popular, but visible marking is a better deterrent. Soldering irons are ideal for writing on plastic casing.

(b) Mark the equipment in other ways. Some organisations spray their hardware with permanent paint, perhaps in a particular colour (bright red is popular) or using stencilled shapes.

(c) Hardware can be bolted to desks. If bolts are passed through the desk and through the bottom of the hardware casing, the equipment can be rendered immobile.

(d) Ensure that the organisation's standard security procedures (magnetic passes, keypad access to offices, signing-in of visitors etc) are followed.

Answer 10.3

You should Password protect each spreadsheet file. If you don't know how to do this, look it up in the Help facility of your spreadsheet program.

You should also take regular back-ups of all work you produce and store the back-up disks in a secure location. If your department does not have procedures for storage of disks used for individual projects, you will need to consider how this can best be achieved.

Part D
Assignments

Assignment 1: Supplier invoices and credit notes

ASSIGNMENT 1: SUPPLIER INVOICES AND CREDIT NOTES

Loading and carrying out the assignment

For instructions on how to load the data for assignments refer to Section 7 of Chapter 2. Check with your tutor in case special instructions apply to your college's system.

If you need to break off from this assignment part-way through, back-up your entries so far on a floppy disk, following the instructions given on screen when you quit the Sage program. You can then restore your entries when you start work again. (See Appendix 3)

If you want to keep a permanent copy of your finished work, back it up and save the back-up file in a separate suitably named sub-directory on your floppy disk.

Purpose

Assignment 1 tests your ability to set up accounts for new suppliers in the purchase ledger, to process invoices and credit notes from suppliers, to post the entries to the appropriate accounts in the suppliers and nominal ledgers, to produce reports and to check the current balance on the creditors control account.

The **Tasks** for this assignment will be found following the **Information.** Read the information and all the tasks *before* commencing work.

Information

Your supervisor asks you to process eight invoices and two credit notes received from suppliers. Today's date is 2 October 2000. Details are as follows.

Invoices from existing suppliers

Invoice No	Supplier	A/C Ref	Details	Nominal ledger account		Net amount (excluding VAT)
					£	£
C6147	AA1 Mini Cabs	AA1MIN	Taxi fares	Travelling		38.40
26187	Newlite Cleaning Fluids	NEWLIT	Cleaning materials	Materials purchases		168.70
435796	Flooring Supplies Ltd	FLOORI	Cleaning materials	Materials purchases	202.36	
			Equipment	Plant and machinery	620.00	
						822.36
4821	First Steps Ladder Hire	FIRSTS	Ladder hire	Equipment hire		126.75

All these invoices are subject to VAT at the standard rate of 17.5%. All invoices are dated 1 October 2000.

Invoices from new suppliers (Inv no = invoice number. Inv date = invoice date)

(a)   Samurai Insurance Brokers
        15 Osnabruck Street
        London EC3 5JG
        Tel: 020-7488 1066

A/C ref	Inv no	Inv date	Nominal ledger account	Net amount £	VAT
SAMURA	02381	1 Oct 2000	Premises insurance	1,650.00	
			Vehicle insurance	1,125.00	
			Miscellaneous insurance	430.00	
				3,205.00	

This invoice has a Post-It note attached by your supervisor saying 'NB - insurance is exempt from VAT - code T2.'

(b)   3D Technical Bookshops
        116 Albert Road
        Wood Green
        London N22 7RB
        Tel: 020-8889 3539
        Contact: Adrian

A/C ref	Inv no	Inv date	Nominal ledger account	Net amount £	VAT
3DTECH	001462	30 Sep 2000	Books	179.95	0%

(c)   Thames Water
      Umbrella House
      Weather Street
      London WC1 9JK
      Tel: 020-7837 4411

A/C ref	Inv no	Inv date	Nominal ledger account	Net amount £	VAT
THAMES	132157	1 Oct 2000	Water rates	420.00	0%

(d)   ANS Newspaper Group
      19 Cecil Road
      London NW10 4PP
      Tel: 020-8453 2926
      Contact: Mandy Walker

A/C ref	Inv no	Inv date	Nominal ledger account	Net amount £	VAT
ANSNEW	621014	29 Sep 2000	Advertising	750.00	17.5%

For all invoices, you have been given details of the item purchased, and you have been instructed to allocate each item to an appropriate nominal ledger account. Refer to the nominal ledger codes in Appendix 1 of this book if necessary.

Credit Notes from Suppliers

Credit note no	Supplier	A/C ref	Net amount £	VAT
K0320	B L Office Furnishing	BLOFFI	150.00	17.5%
C0259	Trojan Secretarial Service	TROJAN	60.00	17.5%

Both credit notes are dated 1 October 2000.

The credit note from B L Office Furnishing is for the return of office furniture supplied in damaged condition. The credit note from the Trojan Secretarial Service is for overcharging; a temporary secretary had been employed for two days, but Trojan, the agency supplying the secretary, had charged for three days.

Your supervisor has asked you to identify the nominal ledger accounts for the credit note transactions, but has told you that the credit note for B L Office Furnishing relates to fixed assets (furniture and fixtures) and the credit note for Trojan Secretarial Service relates to casual wages.

Tasks

(a)   Enter these transactions in the Suppliers Ledger and post the details. Use the tax code T0 for items with 0% VAT.

(b)   Print a detailed suppliers invoices day book listing and suppliers credits day books listing covering *only* the transactions you have posted. If you do not have access to a printer, you should display these listings (one at a time) on your screen. Check that the number of entries in the system so far is 83. What is the total amount of transactions in each day book listing?

(c)   Obtain the balance on the Creditors Control Account, after all the entries have been posted. (This is the total amount currently owed to suppliers for goods or services obtained on credit.) The nominal ledger code for this account is 2100.

You can obtain the balance on the account either by looking at an appropriate screen display or by printing a copy of the Activity for the account.

Assignment 2: Customer invoices and credit notes

ASSIGNMENT 2: CUSTOMER INVOICES AND CREDIT NOTES

Loading and carrying out the assignment

For instructions on how to load the data for assignments refer to Section 7 of Chapter 2. Check with your tutor in case special instructions apply to your college's system.

If you need to break off from this assignment part-way through, back-up your entries so far on a floppy disk, following the instructions given on screen when you quit the Sage program. You can then restore your entries when you start work again. (See Appendix 3)

If you want to keep a permanent copy of your finished work, back it up and save the back-up file in a separate suitably named sub-directory on your floppy disk.

Purpose

Assignment 2 tests your ability to set up accounts for new customers in the customers ledger, to process invoices and credit notes to customers, to post the entries to the appropriate accounts in the customers and nominal ledgers, to produce listings and to answer queries from customers by searching the ledger files. If you have access to a printer, the assignment also tests your ability to produce invoices and credit notes.

The **Tasks** for this assignment will be found following the **Information.** Read the information and all the tasks *before* commencing work.

Information

It is now 8 October 2000. You have been asked to process a batch of invoices and credit notes, using the Sage Invoicing option from the main menu.

Invoices

The invoice details for processing are as follows. All invoices are subject to VAT at the standard rate (17.5%): code T1.

(1)	*Customer Name*	R P Marwood	
	New Customer?	Yes	
	Address	17 Eton Villas	
		Harrow Road	
		London NW3 0JS	
	Telephone	020-7722 4488	
	Contact	Mr Marwood	
	Credit Limit?	No	
	Details		*Net Amount*
	Domestic services		£66.00

(2)	*Customer Name*	School of Dance	
	New Customer?	Yes	
	Address	10 Underwood Street	
		London N1 6SD	
	Telephone	020-7490 2449	
	Contact	Bernice	
	Credit Limit?	Yes, £600	
	Details		*Net Amount*
	Cleaning school property		£250.00

(3)	*Customer Name*	B & T Fashions Ltd	
	New Customer?	Yes	
	Address	8 Green Lanes	
		London N16 4LM	
	Telephone	020-7226 2703	
	Contact	Peter Bruce	
	Credit Limit?	No	
	Details		*Net Amount*
	Window cleaning		£144.00

(4)   *Customer Name*   The Keith Group
       New Customer?   Yes
       Address   3 Sheringham Avenue
                              London N14 2TT
       Telephone   020-8360 7723
       Contact   Pat Walker
       Credit Limit?   Yes, £2,500

       Details   *Net Amount*
       Office cleaning at Grants Parade   £1,420.00
       London N14 and Spur House, Watford

(5)   *Customer Name*   Rapid Pizzas
       New Customer?   Yes
       Address   90 Upper Street
                              London N10 4ZX
       Telephone   020-8444 4136
       Contact   Luciano Palmarozza
       Credit Limit?   No
       Settlement discount 5%

       Details
       5 cases of Flame detergent at £12 per case
       3 boxes of Bream cleaner at £30.40 per box
       50 pairs of cleaning gloves at £0.84 per pair

(6)   *Customer Name*   Bridgford & Co
       New Customer?   No

       Details   *Net Amount*
       Office cleaning at   £420.00
       invoice address

(7)   *Customer Name*   D J Hargreaves
       New Customer?   No

       Details   *Net Amount*
       Domestic services   £43.50

(8)   *Customer Name*   Elite Caterers
       New Customer?   No

       Details   *Net Amount*
       Kitchen cleaning   £644.00
       In addition, supply of materials
       10 boxes of oven cleaner at £6.10 per box
       6 cases of Flame detergent at £12 per case
       7 brushes at £3.42 each

(9)   *Customer Name*   Meakin Media Services
                              Ltd
       New Customer?   No

       Details   *Net Amount*
       Window cleaning   £249.00

BPP
PUBLISHING

(10)	*Customer Name*	A Rose Ltd	
	New Customer?	Not sure	
	Address	8 Mill Mead Road	
		London N17 7HP	
	Telephone	020-8808 4204	
	Credit Limit?	No	

Details	*Net Amount*
Window cleaning	£125.00

(11)	*Customer Name*	Gardeners Delight
	New Customer?	Not sure
	Invoice Address	212 Spa Road
		London NW3 3DQ
	Delivery Address	Gardeners Delight
		Centre
		Buckmans Road
		London NW3
	Telephone	020-8368 2115
	Contact	Joe Grundy
	Credit Limit?	No
	Settlement discount	5%

Details
30 cases of window cleaning fluid at £21.00 per case

(12)	*Customer Name*	Payne Properties Ltd	
	New Customer?	Yes	
	Address	18 Caledonian Road	
		London N1 9PN	
	Telephone	020-7837 3442	
	Contact	Carl Megson	
	Credit Limit?	Yes, £2,500	
	Settlement discount	5%	

Details	*Net Amount*
Office cleaning at invoice address and 8 Richardson Street	£1,210.00

(13)	*Customer Name*	T P Paul	
	New Customer?	Yes	
	Address	1 Arcola Street	
		London N8 1QB	
	Telephone	020-8348 5453	
	Contact	Mrs Paul	
	Credit Limit?	No	

Details	*Net Amount*
Domestic services	£60.00

(14)	*Customer Name*	Siddall Wallis
	New Customer?	No

Details	*Net Amount*
Window cleaning	£182.00

(15)	*Customer Name*	Norris Hydraulics Ltd
	New Customer?	No

Details	*Net Amount*
Factory and office cleaning	£816.40

Credit Notes

The following service credit notes are to be produced. Make sure these are numbered 1, 2 and 3, and all dated 8 October 2000.

(1)   *Customer*   Gelling Private Bank

       Details   Credit note for £250 (plus VAT), following a customer complaint about the poor quality of cleaning at one of the office premises.

(2)   *Customer*   Royal Properties Ltd

       Details   Credit note for £300 (plus VAT), following an agreement with the customer that the scale of the office cleaning service provided was less than originally anticipated.

(3)   *Customer*   DCS Roofing

       Details   Credit note for £150.00 (plus VAT), after customer complaint about a window broken by a Blitz window cleaner.

Tasks

(a)   Use the Service and Service Credit options in the Invoicing window to enter the invoice and credit note details in the system. Make sure that the first invoice in the series is numbered 10036. Where appropriate, establish new customer accounts.

       Check the nominal ledger accounts used by Blitz Limited to account for sales. These are included in the list in Appendix 1.

(b)   Print (or Preview) the invoices and credit notes. If you can, back-up your work *before* posting the invoices, so that you can correct any errors discovered later without re-entering all the data.

(c)   Post the invoice and credit note details to the appropriate accounts in the customers ledger and nominal ledger.

(d)   Produce day book listings of customer invoices and customer credits for these transactions. Print the listings if you have access to a printer. Otherwise, display each listing on screen.

(e)   Your supervisor wants to know the current balance on the Debtors Control Account in the nominal ledger. Find out what this is. If you have access to a printer, print out the details of this account.

(f)   Your supervisor also wants to know the current debit, credit and net total balances on each of the four sales accounts (codes 4000, 4001, 4002 and 4100 in the nominal ledger). After you have entered the invoice and credit note details, find out what these balances are.

(g) *This task can only be carried out if you have access to a printer.*

The invoice you have produced for the School of Dance has been damaged accidentally. Coffee has been spilled over it. Produce another invoice for sending to the customer.

(h) You receive a telephone call from your contact at CCC Engineering Limited. They have not yet received an invoice for factory cleaning services, but need to know what the cost will be, for a management meeting that afternoon. Find out the amount of the invoice.

(i) *Word-processing exercise*

Unload the Word and Excel exercises from the CD-ROM onto a blank floppy disk. (see Chapter 2 for more detailed instructions). (If you have not done Exercise 5 in Chapter 2, do this first.)

Without closing Sage switch to the word processing application on your computer (Microsoft Word or whatever). Open the document A2FAX which will now be on your floppy disk and *save* it with another appropriate name.

Prepare a fax to send to CCC Engineering in time for their management meeting this afternoon. The fax number is 01923 354071. Other details can be found from CCC Engineering's customer record or from an audit trail report. Copy from Sage and Paste into your word processing document if you wish to, and can work out how.

Note. To switch between applications use Alt + Tab.

(j) *Word-processing exercise*

For the purpose of this exercise we will assume that the missing invoice was one of an early batch that was prepared manually, not using the Sage system.

Open the document A2INV and prepare a duplicate invoice for CCC Engineering. The details are those you found for the previous task.

Mention the duplicate invoice in your fax produced for the previous task. (Alter it if you have saved and closed it already.)

If you have access to a printer, print out the fax and the duplicate invoice.

Assignment 3: Payments to suppliers

ASSIGNMENT 3: PAYMENTS TO SUPPLIERS

Loading and carrying out the assignment

For instructions on how to load the data for assignments, refer to Section 7 of Chapter 2. Check with your tutor in case special instructions apply to your college's system.

If you need to break off from this assignment part-way through, back-up your entries so far on a floppy disk, following the instructions given on screen when you quit the Sage program. You can then restore your entries when you start work again. (See Appendix 3)

If you want to keep a permanent copy of your finished work, back it up and save the back-up file in a separate suitably named sub-directory on your floppy disk.

Purpose

Assignment 3 tests your ability to process payments to suppliers, to post the transactions to the appropriate accounts in the purchase ledger and nominal ledger, to deal with part payments, credit notes, settlement discounts and payments in advance, to deal with payments for cheque requisitions, to produce reports for payments, and to check the current balance on the bank account and creditors control account in the nominal ledger. If you have access to a printer, the Assignment also tests your ability to produce remittance advices.

The **Tasks** for this assignment will be found following the **Information.** Read the information and all the tasks *before* commencing work.

Information

(Read this information now, but don't post any transactions until attempting the tasks on the following page.)

It is now 9 October 2000. You have been asked to process a batch of payments.

(1)   Your supervisor has asked you to record the following payment transactions.

Supplier	Ref code	Amount	Cheque no
AA1 Mini Cabs	AA1MIN	£117.50	000100
British Telecom plc	BTELEC	£540.50	000101
Capital Radiopaging	CAPITA	£376.00	000102
B L Office Furnishing	BLOFFI	£1,493.78	000103
First Steps Ladder Hire	FIRSTS	£332.23	000104
Samurai Insurance Brokers	SAMURA	£3,205.00	000105
3D Technical Bookshops	3DTECH	£179.95	000106
The Ironcliffe Group	IRONCL	£3,000.00	000107
Trojan Secretarial Services	TROJAN	£141.00	000108
Muswell Hill Council	MUSWEL	£1,240.00	000109
North London Advertiser	NORTHL	£1,175.00	000110
Sterling Supplies	STERLI	£642.37	000111
Uniform Workerwear	UNIFOR	£763.75	000112
Van Centre	VANCEN	£19,059.44	000113

The payments to B L Office Furnishing and Trojan Secretarial Services are net of credit notes outstanding on these accounts.

(2)   You have also been asked to process a newly-received credit note of £235 (£200 plus VAT of £35) from the Chieftain Newspaper Group (because of an error in an advertisement printed in a newspaper), and a cheque (number 000114) to this supplier for the balance outstanding on the account of £1,175. The credit note number is SC0108. The nominal account code is 6201.

(3)   You have been given the following note by your supervisor.

We have received full credit notes and revised invoices from three suppliers because they offered us early settlement discounts over the phone but did not reflect this on their original invoices, which have already been posted.

The suppliers and the relevant Nominal Codes are:

Floorsanders (Equipment) (FLOORS)   0020
Harrow Cleaning Supplies (HARROW)   5000
Matthias Scaffolding (MATTHI)   0020

Please proceed as follows.

(a)   Post the credit notes, which are each for the full amount currently shown as outstanding on these accounts. Use the reference 'Disc'.

(b)   Post the revised invoices shown below. Use code T3 and post VAT manually.

(c)   Pay the invoices taking advantage of the discounts.

(d)   We are still negotiating long-term terms, so hold off making any changes to the suppliers record settlement discount % until terms are finalised.

The revised invoice details are as follows.

Supplier	Invoice no	Gross	VAT	Net
FLOORS	34005	1,005.31	143.31	862.00
HARROW	HC1213	2,840.62	412.22	2,428.40
MATTHI	63041	3,335.48	475.48	2,860.00

(4) Blitz Limited will be purchasing more equipment from Highpile Cleaning Supplies (code HIGHPI). It has been agreed with the supplier that Blitz should make a payment of £3,500, to settle its outstanding debt and as a payment in advance for future purchases. You have been asked to record the payment. The cheque number is 000118.

(5) You have also been asked to prepare cheques and record the payments for the following cheque requisitions. The supplier names will be filled in manually.

Cheque no	Amount	Purpose	Nominal code
000119	£258.50 (inc VAT at 17.5%)	Training course	8203
000120	£105.50 (no VAT)	Train ticket	7400
000121	£98.70 (inc VAT at 17.5%)	Refreshments	8205

Tasks

(a) Print a remittance advice for Samurai Insurance Brokers and B L Office Furnishing. (You need access to a printer to do this.) Do this *before* you post the payment transactions.

(b) Post the transactions listed on the previous page to the appropriate ledger accounts.

(c) Print a report for the payments to suppliers and the bank transaction payments. If you do not have access to a printer, produce a screen display for the report. What is the total amount of payments?

(d) Print a copy of the bank account transactions (nominal ledger code 1200) to date (9 October 2000), and establish how much money, according to the records, is remaining in this account. If you do not have access to a printer, obtain a screen display of the account to establish the remaining cash balance.

(e) Establish the current balance on the creditors control account (nominal ledger account code 2100).

(f) *Spreadsheet exercise*

To do this exercise you require access to Microsoft Excel.

If you have not already done so, unload the Word and Excel exercises onto a floppy disk, as explained in Chapter 2. Then start up your spreadsheet package, and open the spreadsheet file named A3SPRSHT which will now be on the floppy disk, and save it with a new name.

Your supervisor has manually keyed some information from Sage into a spreadsheet.

(i) Explain the meaning of the numbers in the columns headed No. and Ref.

(ii) Your supervisor cannot understand why the totals do not match those shown in your payments report. Can you work out why? Alter the spreadsheet so that it produces the correct totals. The *totals* are calculated automatically, but you can alter the other amounts.

(iii) Use the skills you have acquired in working with word processors to improve the appearance of this document. (If you are using both Word and Excel you will see strong similarities in the features available.)

(iv) If you have access to a printer, print out your revised version of the spreadsheet.

BPP
PUBLISHING

Assignment 4: Receipts from customers

ASSIGNMENT 4: RECEIPTS FROM CUSTOMERS

Loading and carrying out the assignment

For instructions on how to load the data for assignments, refer to Section 7 of Chapter 2. Check with your tutor in case special instructions apply to your college's system.

If you need to break off from this assignment part-way through, back-up your entries so far on a floppy disk, following the instructions given on screen when you quit the Sage program. You can restore your entries when you start work again. (See Appendix 3)

If you want to keep a permanent copy of your finished work, back it up and save the back-up file in a separate, suitably named sub-directory on your floppy.

Purpose

The purpose of this assignment is to test your ability to enter details of payments received from customers and to post these details to the appropriate ledgers. The transactions include payments in full and part payments, receipts with a deduction for a credit note, receipts with a deduction for an early settlement discount, payments on account, payments with order, writing off small unpaid balances on a customer account and a customer refund. The completeness and accuracy of your input will be checked by a further test of your ability to produce reports and listings, and to find the current balance on the bank current account and the debtors control account.

The **Tasks** for this assignment will be found following the **Information.** Read the information and all the tasks *before* commencing work.

Information

You are asked by your supervisor to process the following transactions. The transactions are for processing on 12 October 2000, unless otherwise indicated.

(1)   You have been given the following two customer invoices to process. You have been asked to enter and post the invoice details. If you have access to a printer, you should also produce invoices for these customers, as well as posting the invoice details to the ledgers.

Customer name	Bradley Fashions Ltd
A/C Reference Code	BRADLE
New Customer?	Yes
Address	18 Hospital Bridge Road
	St Albans, Herts
	SA5 9QT
Telephone	01727 532678
Credit Limit?	Yes, £2,500
Contact	Lee

Details

For contract cleaning services, £820 plus VAT at the standard rate

Customer name	A Rathod
A/C Reference Code	RATHOD
New Customer?	Yes
Address	200 West Road
	London N17 4GN
Telephone	020-8808 7814
Credit Limit?	No

Details

For domestic services, £75 plus VAT at the standard rate

(2)   The following payments have been received from existing customers. You have been asked to post the details to the ledgers. Your supervisor instructs you that you must use the relevant invoice number as the reference (or the first invoice number if several are being paid).

Customer	*A/C ref code*	*Amount* £
E T Adams	ADAMSE	143.35
Farrar Air Tools Ltd	FARRAR	940.00
D J Hargreaves	HARGRE	51.11
A Rose Ltd	ROSEAL	141.00
CCC Engineering	CCCENG	1527.50
Bridgford and Co	BRIDGF	981.13
Goodman Brickworks Ltd	GOODMA	141.47
Townend Angus Ltd	TOWNEN	1087.70
P Wood	WOODPX	166.85
P Leyser & Co	LEYSER	96.59
A Wyche	WYCHEA	88.13
D C Sherry	SHERRY	49.35

(3)   You have been asked to cancel an invoice of £70.50 for T P Paul. This was an invoice for domestic cleaning services, nominal account code 4002.

(4)   You have also been asked to post details of the following payments from customers, for which each customer has taken advantage of an early settlement discount of 5%.

Customer	A/C ref code	Cheque amount £	Discount taken £
Payne Properties	PAYNEP	1350.66	60.50
Rapid Pizzas	RAPIDP	215.66	9.66

(5)   The following payments have been received, where the customer has reduced the payment to allow for a credit note.

Customer	A/C ref code	Amount paid(cheque amount) £
Gelling Private Bank	GELLIN	1727.25
DCS Roofing	DCSROO	82.25

Note. It may be advisable to take a back -up at this point, if you are happy with all the entries you have made, in case you make an error in posting the remaining transactions.

(6)   The following part-payments have been received:

Customer	A/C ref code	Amount paid (cheque amount) £
Elite Caterers	ELITEC	200.00
Campbell Consultants	CAMPBE	70.00

(7)   You have been asked to enter and post details of a payment of £828.75 by Clough and Partners. This payment is partly to settle an outstanding invoice and partly a payment in advance for services not yet provided by Blitz Limited.

(8)   A payment on account has been received from the following new customer.

Customer name	M Zakis Ltd
A/C Reference Code	MZAKIS
Address	43 Ballards Lane
	London N12 0DG
Telephone	020-8445 2993
Credit Limit?	No
Amount of payment on account:	£500

(9)   The following payments have been received:

Customer	A/C ref code	Amount paid(cheque amount) £
A T Haslam	HASLAM	42.00
R P Marwood	MARWOO	77.50

In each case, the customer has not paid the full invoice amount, but it has been decided to write off the small unpaid amount in each case. Post the details of the amounts to be written off. (Hint. Take a note of the unpaid amount in each case. If you forget to do this, can you think of a way of searching for this information in the Customers ledger?)

(10)   Immediate payments have been received (by cheque) for the following items, without a requirement to supply an invoice or give credit to the customer. Payments *include* VAT at the standard rate of 17.5% in each case.

Item	Amount received £	Paying-in slip number
Window cleaning	47.00	500000
Domestic services	101.05	500001
Domestic services	61.10	500002
Materials sales	117.50	500003
Window cleaning	86.95	500004

These receipts must be entered and posted to the appropriate accounts.

Tasks

(a)   Enter and post the transactions as described in information items (1) to (10) above. Make all the necessary entries, including the set up of new customer accounts where appropriate.

(b)   Produce a report for:

   (i)   Amounts received from credit customers on 12 October 2000.

   (ii)   Bank receipts (ie amounts received from sources other than credit customers) on 12 October 2000.

   Print the report if you have access to a printer; otherwise produce a screen display. What is the total amount received?

(c)   After you have printed these reports, you are asked to process a refund of £96.59 to P Leyser for a payment already received. The refund has been agreed by the chief accountant with the customer.

(d)   As at the end of processing, establish the total debits, credits and overall balances on the following accounts in the nominal ledger

	Account Code
Bank current account	1200
Debtors control account	1100

(e)   Your supervisor wants to know how much is still owed by the customer Elite Caterers. What is the outstanding balance on this account?

Assignment 5: Other cash transactions

ASSIGNMENT 5: OTHER CASH TRANSACTIONS

Loading and carrying out the assignment

For instructions on how to load the data for assignments, refer to Section 7 of Chapter 2. Check with your tutor in case special instructions apply to your college's system.

If you need to break off from this assignment part-way through, back-up your entries so far on a floppy disk, following the instructions given on screen when you quit the Sage program. You can restore your entries when you start work again. (See Appendix 3)

If you want to keep a permanent copy of your finished work, back it up and save the back-up file in a separate, suitably named sub-directory on your floppy disk.

Purpose

The purpose of Assignment 5 is to test your ability to post entries for petty cash in the nominal ledger and to make a small number of journal entries, and to carry out a bank reconciliation. In addition, the assignment includes a further test of your ability to post transactions for customer and supplier invoices, and customer and supplier payments.

The **Tasks** for this assignment will be found following the **Information**. Read the information and all the tasks *before* commencing work.

Information

(1)   On 13 October 2000, Blitz Limited's directors decided to set up a petty cash system with a float of £300. A cheque (number 000122) for £300 in cash was drawn on the company's bank account that day.

(2)   The following invoices have been received from suppliers.

Supplier	New supplier	Invoice number	Date	Details	Net amount £	VAT £
Hardin & Nobbs Chapel Place White Hart Lane London N17 4HA 020-8801 1907 A/C Ref HARDIN	Yes	2641	12 Oct 2000	Legal fees (N/C 7600)	1200.00	210.00
Flooring Supplies Ltd	No	435850	8 Oct 2000	Cleaning materials (N/C 5000)	762.00	133.35
Trojan Secretarial Services	No	03012	12 Oct 2000	Casual labour (N/C 7005)	210.00	36.75
AA1 Mini Cabs	No	C6281	15 Oct 2000	Taxis (N/C 7401)	134.70	23.57
Great North Hotel 75 Park Road Ealing London W5 6RU 020-8997 6005 A/C Ref GREATN	Yes	6601	7 Oct 2000	Hotel room (N/C 7402)	110.00	19.25
				Hotel meal (N/C 7406)	26.00	4.55
				Hotel telephone (N/C 7502)	3.40	0.60
				Total	139.40	24.40
Lerwick Cleaning Co Ryelands Road Norwich, NH7 4DB 01603 590624	Yes	S4031	14 Oct 2000	Cleaning materials (N/C 5000)	1400.00	245.00
				Carriage (N/C 5100)	20.00	3.50
A/C Ref LERWIC				Total	1420.00	248.50
First Steps Ladder Hire	No	5024	8 Oct 2000	Ladder hire (N/C 7700)	81.00	14.18
Prairie Couriers Ltd	No	T34228	14 Oct 2000	Couriers (N/C 7501)	92.50	16.19
Amin Launderers 16 Southey Road London N15 3AK 020-8802 2541 A/C Ref AMINLA	Yes	0877	8 Oct 2000	Laundry (N/C 7802)	145.00	25.38

(3) The following invoices are to be sent out to customers, all dated 16 October
2000, with VAT charged at the standard rate.

Customer	New customer?	Invoice number	Details	Net amount £
Aspinall & Co	No	10053	Window cleaning	90.00
Elite Caterers	No	10054	Kitchen cleaning	190.00
S T Chana 78 Katherine Road London N9 8UL 020-8803 0147 No credit limit A/C Ref CHANAS	Yes	10055	Domestic services	135.00
L Haynes & Co 14 Millmead Road London N17 2XD 020-8885 3731 No credit limit A/C Ref HAYNES	Yes	10056	Window cleaning Materials sales Total	82.00 45.20 127.20
Brookes Acoustics Ltd	No	10057	Warehouse cleaning	670.00
CCC Engineering	No	10058	Factory cleaning	850.00
Tek Systems 115 Cricklewood Broadway London NW2 5ES 020-8452 9442 Credit limit £2,000 A/C Ref TEKSYS	Yes	10059	Contract cleaning Materials sales Total	450.00 63.00 513.00
Telefilm Latinamerica 100 Tower Bridge Road London SE1 6FJ 020-7403 2144 Credit limit £2,500 A/C Ref TELEFI	Yes	10060	Contract cleaning	830.00
GHH Commercial Bank	No	10061	Contract cleaning	950.00
The Keith Group	No	10062	Office cleaning	850.00
Owen of London 19 Piccadilly London W1 9CD 020-7734 2043 Credit limit £3,000 A/C Ref OWENLO	Yes	10063	Contract cleaning Window cleaning Materials sales Total	750.00 130.00 55.40 935.40
Biophysica Orbit Court 33 Fairfax Road London NW6 4LL 020-7624 2002 No credit limit A/C Ref BIOPHY	Yes	10064	Window cleaning Domestic services Total	63.00 45.00 108.00

(4) The following payments to suppliers were made on 16 October 2000.

Date	Supplier	Cheque number	Amount £	Details
16 Oct 2000	Ace Telephone Answering	000123	250.00	Part payment of invoice
16 Oct 2000	ANS Newspaper Group	000124	1200.00	Payment of invoice plus payment on account
16 Oct 2000	Wells Business Systems	000125	1516.50	Payment of invoice, net of credit note CN4245 for £387 (gross) dated 14/10/2000. Nominal code 0030.

(5)   The following payments have been received from customers.

Date	Supplier	Amount £	Details
14 Oct 2000	Campbell Consultants	70.00	Part payment of invoice
15 Oct 2000	Brookes Acoustics Ltd	1000.00	Part payment of invoice
16 Oct 2000	Gardeners Delight	703.24	Payment of invoice, discount of £31.50 taken

(6)   The company has received a cheque from Mr V J Richardson, a relative of one of the directors, for £10,000. The money was banked on 12 October 2000. It represents a loan from Mr Richardson to the company. A journal voucher has been prepared as follows:

JOURNAL VOUCHER			J02
	N/C	Debit £	Credit £
Cash	1200	10,000	
Loan account	2300		10,000

Loan from Mr V J Richardson

(7)   In the period to 16 October 2000, petty cash vouchers for expenditure items were as follows. (VAT is only shown where the company has obtained a valid VAT invoice.)

Ref	Date	Item	N/C code	Net amount £	VAT £	Gross amount £
PC001	13/10/2000	Postage stamps	7501	24.00	0	24.00
PC002	13/10/2000	Biscuits, coffee	8205	32.49	0	32.49
PC003	13/10/2000	Milk	8205	15.20	0	15.20
PC004	13/10/2000	Taxis	7400	25.00	0	25.00
PC005	14/10/2000	Train fares	7400	9.20	0	9.20
PC006	14/10/2000	Washing up liquid	8205	1.75	0	1.75
PC007	14/10/2000	Photocopying	7500	24.00	4.20	28.20
PC008	15/10/2000	Stationery	7504	37.24	6.52	43.76
PC009	15/10/2000	Taxis	7400	15.00	0	15.00
PC010	16/10/2000	Sandwiches, cakes	8205	38.26	0	38.26
PC011	16/10/2000	Parking	7304	7.00	0	7.00
PC012	16/10/2000	Train fares	7400	8.40	0	8.40

Notes and coin totalling £72.00 were paid into petty cash on 16 October. This was money received for various small window cleaning jobs, for which VAT should be recorded at the standard rate.

(8) Blitz Limited has not yet set up a computerised payroll system. Wages were paid by bank transfer on 16 October 2000, and the following transactions need to be accounted for.

	Code	Debit £	Credit £
Bank account	1200		4133.04
PAYE	2210		2217.96
National Insurance	2211		975.20
Directors salaries	7001	1350.80	
Staff salaries	7003	475.75	
Wages – regular	6000	4859.65	
Employers NI	7006	640.00	
		7326.20	7326.20

(9) On 19 October 2000, the following bank statement was received from the company's bank.

Account 11765444

BLITZ LIMITED
25 APPLE ROAD
LONDON N12 3PP

Centre Bank
Apple Road Branch
38 Apple Road
London N22

Particulars	Date	Withdrawn £	Paid in £	Balance £
BGC	21 AUG		20000.00	
BGC	21 AUG		20000.00	40000.00
BAC	16 SEP	6053.93		
				33946.07
000100	12 OCT	117.50		
000103	12 OCT	1493.78		
000104	12 OCT	332.23		
000105	12 OCT	3205.00		
000107	12 OCT	3000.00		
000111	12 OCT	642.37		
000113	12 OCT	19059.44		
000114	12 OCT	1175.00		4920.75
000101	13 OCT	540.50		
000102	13 OCT	376.00		
000106	13 OCT	179.95		
000108	13 OCT	141.00		
000109	13 OCT	1240.00		
000112	13 OCT	763.75		
000116	13 OCT	2767.77		1088.22DR
BGC	13 OCT		143.35	
BGC	13 OCT		51.11	
BGC	13 OCT		1527.50	
BGC	13 OCT		981.13	
BGC	13 OCT		940.00	
BGC	13 OCT		1087.70	
BGC	13 OCT		88.13	
BGC	13 OCT		141.00	
BGC	13 OCT		141.47	
BGC	13 OCT		166.85	
BGC	13 OCT		49.35	
BGC	13 OCT		96.59	
BGC	13 OCT		1350.66	
BGC	13 OCT		215.66	

BPP PUBLISHING

Particulars	Date	Withdrawn £	Paid in £	Balance £
BGC	13 OCT		1727.25	
BGC	13 OCT		200.00	
BGC	13 OCT		70.00	
BGC	13 OCT		828.75	
BGC	13 OCT		82.25	
BGC	13 OCT		101.05	
BGC	13 OCT		42.00	
BGC	13 OCT		500.00	
BGC	13 OCT		47.00	
BGC	13 OCT		77.50	
BGC	13 OCT		86.95	
BGC	13 OCT		61.10	
BGC	13 OCT		117.50	9833.63
000110	13 OCT	1175.00		
000115	13 OCT	962.21		
000118	13 OCT	3500.00		
000119	13 OCT	258.50		
000120	13 OCT	105.50		
000121	13 OCT	98.70		
CASH WITHDRAWAL	16 OCT	300.00		
TRANSFER-LEYSER	16 OCT	96.59		3337.13
BGC	16 OCT		70.00	
BGC	16 OCT		10000.00	13407.13
BANK CHARGES	16 OCT	25.60		13381.53

Tasks

(a) Post the transaction for withdrawing cash from the company's bank account to set up a petty cash system. Use the cheque number as a reference for the transaction (information item [1]).

(b) Post the transactions for invoices received from suppliers (information item [2]).

(c) Post the transactions for invoices sent out to customers (information item [3]).

(d) Post the payments to suppliers (information item [4]).

(e) Post the receipts from customers (information item [5]).

(f) Post the receipt of the money as a loan from Mr V J Richardson, using the journal voucher as your source document. The transaction reference should be the journal voucher number. The tax reference code should be T9.

(g) Post the petty cash transactions to the nominal ledger, for both expenditure and income items. Enter the income items as a single transaction, with reference PCR001. Produce a listing for the petty cash payments. Print the listing if you have access to a printer.

(h) The company uses an imprest system for petty cash. On 16 October 2000, the money in petty cash should be topped up to £300. A cheque (number 000126) is to be drawn on the bank account to withdraw cash.

    (i) What should be the cheque amount?

    (ii) Assume that a cheque for this amount is drawn, and petty cash is restored to £300. Post this cash withdrawal transaction. Give it a reference code 000126 and a tax code T9.

(i)   Post the wages and salaries transactions, shown in information item (8), to the appropriate nominal ledger accounts. Post the transactions by means of a journal entry. Give the transaction a reference of J04. Use tax code T9.

(j)   Your supervisor wishes to know the balances on the following nominal ledger accounts after you have dealt with tasks (a) to (i).

	Nominal ledger account code
Debtors control account	1100
Bank - current account	1200
Creditors control account	2100
Staff salaries	7003
Travelling	7400
Equipment hire	7700
Sales - contract cleaning	4000
Sales - window cleaning	4001
Sales - domestic services	4002
Sales - materials	4100
Petty cash	1230
Discounts allowed	4009

Report the balances on these accounts.

(k)   Carry out a bank reconciliation on 19 October 2000, after you have completed tasks (a) to (j). How many unreconciled transactions are there and what are the amounts for:

(i)   Statement balance.

(ii)   Uncleared items.

(iii)   Trial balance?

A word of advice - your supervisor has advised that an error was made when posting cheque 000118. The cheque was for £3,500.00, but was mistakenly entered into Line 50 as £2,364.69. A correcting entry has been made for £1,135.31. You should match these two entries from your nominal account listing of account 1200 against the £3,500.00 that will show on the bank statement for cheque 000118.

BPP PUBLISHING

Assignment 6: Other credit transactions

ASSIGNMENT 6: OTHER CREDIT TRANSACTIONS

Loading and carrying out the assignment

For instructions on how to load the data for assignments, refer to Section 7 of Chapter 2. Check with your tutor in case special instructions apply to your college's system.

If you need to break off from this assignment part-way through, back-up your entries so far on a floppy disk, following the instructions given on screen when you quit the Sage program. You can restore your entries when you start work again. (See Appendix 3)

If you want to keep a permanent copy of your finished work, back it up and save the back-up file in a separate, suitably named sub-directory on your floppy disk.

Purpose

This assignment tests your ability to post contra entries and write-offs for bad debts and to correct errors. It also tests your ability to deal with a variety of customer problems: customers who exceed their credit limit and late payers, and chasing customers for payment by producing an aged debtors list, statements and reminder letters.

The **Tasks** for this assignment will be found following the **Information.** Read the information and all the tasks *before* commencing work.

Information

Tim Nicholas and Maria Green, the directors of Blitz Limited, are quite pleased with the first few months of trading by the company. They are very aware, however, that the company must continue to win more sales if it is to be successful. This could mean having to take the risk of selling services to customers who might not be creditworthy. In addition, cash flow could be a problem. The company has already borrowed £10,000 from Mr V Richardson, and has used a bank overdraft facility. The directors have therefore recognised a need to collect money from debtors efficiently, to make sure that cash keeps coming into the business.

(1)   Credit limits have been set for some of Blitz Limited's customers. If a customer exceeds his credit limit, however, the company's policy from now onwards will be to supply the goods or services and increase the customer's credit limit by £1,000. However, the directors wish to be informed of any such change.

(2)   On 21 October 2000, you have been asked to process the following transactions. All sales are subject to VAT at the standard rate.

Credit Sales

Customer	New customer?	Invoice number	Details	Net amount £
ANS Newspaper Group 19 Cecil Road London NW10 5CD 020-8453 2926 No credit limit A/C code ANSNEW	Yes	10065	Window cleaning	150.00
Brookes Acoustics Ltd	No	10066	Window cleaning	120.00
CCC Engineering Ltd	No	10067	Contract cleaning	630.00
R C Chadwick	No	10068	Domestic services	50.00
South Sea Airtours Girton House 62 Appendale Road London N17 1RA 020-8885 5553 Credit limit £2,500 A/C code SOUTHS	Yes	10069	Contract cleaning Materials sales Total	480.00 75.00 555.00
Clough & Partners	No	10070	Window cleaning	70.00
GHH Commercial Bank	No	10071	Contract cleaning	500.00
The Keith Group	No	10072	Contract cleaning Window cleaning Total	350.00 140.00 490.00
D J Hargreaves	No	10073	Domestic services	60.00
Meakin Media	No	10074	Window cleaning	100.00
Norris Hydraulics Ltd	No	10075	Contract cleaning	620.00
K Ogden Property Co	No	10076	Contract cleaning	480.00
Owen of London	No	10077	Window cleaning	150.00
School of Dance	No	10078	Contract cleaning	320.00

R I Tepper	No	10079	Contract cleaning	250.00
B Walton & Co	No	10080	Window cleaning	150.00
WRW Catering	No	10081	Contract cleaning	370.00
The Lapsley Agency	Yes	10082	Window cleaning	144.00
105 Thetford Road			Domestic services	105.00
London N9 0PB			Total	249.00
020-8803 0147				
No credit limit				
A/C code LAPSLE				

Cash sales

The following amounts were received from cash sales to customers.

Date	Details	Gross amount (including VAT) £	Method of payment	Paying in slip
21 October 2000	Domestic services	51.70	Cheque	500005
21 October 2000	Domestic services	44.00	Cheque	500006
21 October 2000	Materials sales	37.60	Cheque	500007
22 October 2000	Materials sales	25.38	Notes and coin	
23 October 2000	Domestic services	35.25	Notes and coin	
23 October 2000	Materials sales	52.88	Cheque	500008

The cheque payments were banked on 23 October 2000. The two receipts in notes and coin were put into petty cash (with reference codes PCR002 and PCR003 respectively).

Invoices from suppliers

The following invoices were received from suppliers. All three suppliers are also credit customers of the company.

Supplier	New supplier?	Invoice number	Date	Details	Net amount £	VAT £
ANS Newspaper Group	No	621347	20 Oct 2000	Advertising (N/C 6201)	471.28	82.47
Elite Caterers 85B Crowland Road London N15 9KW 020-8800 2069 A/C ref ELITEC	Yes	2046	20 Oct 2000	Catering (N/C 7403)	250.00	43.75
Meakin Media Ltd 4 Nursery Road Ashford Middlesex, AF8 5TS 01784 358452 A/C ref MEAKIN	Yes	10035	20 Oct 2000	Advertising (N/C 6201)	200.00	35.00

Receipts from customers

The following receipts from customers were obtained on 22 October 2000.

Customer	A/C ref	Amount £	Details
A Rathod	RATHOD	88.13	
A Rose Ltd	ROSEAL	146.88	
S T Chanas	CHANAS	158.00	
Biophysica	BIOPHY	52.88	To settle a part of an invoice relating to domestic services
Aspinall & Co	ASPINA	105.75	
Elite Caterers	ELITEC	1427.31	
Meakin Media Ltd	MEAKIN	350.16	

Tasks

(a) Post the credit sales transactions using the Service invoice option from the Invoicing menu.

   (i) Prepare a list of customers who have exceeded their current credit limit.
   (ii) Increase the credit limit for each of these customers by £1,000 each.

(b) Post the cash sales transactions (both the bank transactions and the petty cash transactions).

(c) Post the three invoices received from suppliers.

(d) Post the receipts from customers. The accounts of Elite Caterers and Meakin Media should be settled by means of *contra entries*.

(e) A cheque is being prepared to settle the account with ANS Newspaper group (cheque number 000127, dated 22 October 2000). The amount owed by ANS Newspaper Group should be offset against amounts owed to ANS, and the amount of the cheque should be for the difference.

   (i) What is the amount of the cheque?

   (ii) Post this cheque, and settle the accounts in the Suppliers and Customers ledgers by means of a contra entry.

(f) On 23 October 2000, you are instructed to write off small unpaid balances in any customer's account. Unpaid balances of £1 or less should be written off.

   (i) Write off these small unpaid balances.
   (ii) What is the total amount of bad debts written off in this exercise?

(g) Information has been received that the following customers have gone out of business.

Name	A/C ref
E T Adams	ADAMSE
L Haynes & Co	HAYNES

   You are instructed that if there are any unpaid debts outstanding on the account of E T Adams or L Haynes & Co, the debts should be written off.

(h) A credit note (reference 004) was issued to Owen of London on 22 October 2000 for £150 (plus VAT). Post this transaction, giving it a N/C code of 4000. (You are not required to produce the credit note itself.) Preview on screen a statement showing all transactions to date for GHH Commercial Bank.

(i)   An invoice from AA1 Mini Cabs for £158.27 in October was entered in the accounts with a nominal ledger account code of 7401. Your supervisor tells you that the code should have been 7400. You are required to alter the code.

(j)   A badly printed invoice from Newlite Cleaning Fluids dated 12 September was entered in the accounts incorrectly as £473.91 including VAT. The net amount, which is all that can be seen on the invoice, was actually £403. You are required to correct the error. What is the corrected figure?

(k)   What are the current balances on the following nominal ledger accounts?

	Code
Bank current account	1200
Debtors control account	1100
Creditors control account	2100
Bad debt write off account	8100
Advertising account	6201
Sales - contract cleaning	4000
Sales - window cleaning	4001
Sales - domestic services	4002
Sales - materials	4100

(l)   *Spreadsheet exercise: Aged Debtors Analysis*

Suppose that no more payments are received from customers before 5 November 2000. On 5 November, it is decided to review the current state of debtors, and take action to chase late payers.

However, due to a small fire which affected some of Blitz's computer hardware, it proves impossible to use the Sage system on 5 November.

Fortunately, the data from a print-out of an aged debtors analysis dated 4 November has been copied by your supervisor into a spreadsheet. If you still have the floppy disk onto which you unloaded the Word and Excel exercises earlier you will find a file named A6AGED. (If you don't have the disk you used earlier, unload a fresh copy of the Word and Excel exercises - see Chapter 2.)

(i)   Open A6AGED.XLS using your spreadsheet program and save it with a new name.

(ii)   Check that the total value of debtors outstanding agrees with the value on your Sage system now that you have posted all the transactions for this assignment.

(iii)   Sort the data in order of value of overall balance: largest first. Which five customers owe the largest amounts? (See the note below if you don't know how to sort the data.)

(iv)   Sort the data in order of largest balance outstanding for over 30 days. Make a list of customers with a balance of over £1,000 that has been outstanding for more than 30 days.

(v)   Resort the data into customer account code order.

(*Hint.* In Microsoft Excel you can sort data by clicking on the word **Data** at the top of the screen and then on **Sort** in the menu that drops down.)

Part E
Solutions

SOLUTION TO ASSIGNMENT 1: SUPPLIER INVOICES AND CREDIT NOTES

You can enter the new supplier accounts in the Suppliers Ledger using either the Invoices button or the Record button.

If you use the Record button, as suggested in Chapter 4, you should set up accounts for the four new suppliers before entering any invoice details. Having set up the new accounts, you can switch to the Invoices window to process the 8 invoices.

Having processed and posted the invoice details, you should then close the Invoices window and open the Credits window to process and post the details of the 2 credit notes.

Points to check

You should check the following points.

Date

For each invoice (or credit note) you should enter the actual date of the invoice (or credit note), rather than simply using today's date.

Nominal ledger codes

Carefully check transaction details shown below in the two listings. These list the entry details for the transactions. Make sure that you have specified the correct nominal ledger code for each transaction. To find the correct N/C codes for the credit notes, you should have looked for the account codes for Furniture and Fixtures (0040) and Wages - Casual (7005).

When an invoice is for purchases or items of expense for more than one nominal ledger account, you should enter each part of the invoice separately. This means that you should have entered:

(a)   2 lines of details for the invoice from Flooring Supplies Ltd, one for the purchase of cleaning materials (code 5000) and one for the purchase of plant and machinery (code 0020); and

(b)   3 lines of details for the invoice from Samurai Insurance Brokers, one for the premises insurance (code 7104), one for the vehicle insurance (code 7303) and one for miscellaneous items of insurance (code 8204).

Listings

When you have entered and posted the details of the invoices and credit notes, you can print the 'day book' listings.

Use the Reports button in the *Suppliers ledger* window and select Day Books: Supplier Invoices (detailed) and then Day Books: Supplier Credits (detailed).

You should specify the date ranges 29/09/2000 to 02/10/2000 for supplier invoices and 01/10/2000 to 01/10/2000 for credit notes.

The printouts should appear as follows, with 11 entries in the purchases day book and 2 entries in the purchases returns day book. (However, the sequence of transactions and the transaction numbers can vary, according to the order in which you entered them in the system.) The gross value of transactions is shown at the bottom of each listing.

Blitz Limited

Day Books : Supplier Invoices (Detailed)

Date from: 29/09/2000 **Supplier From:**
Date to: 02/10/2000 **Supplier To:**
ZZZZZZZZ

Trans From: 1 **N/C From:**
Trans To: 83 **N/C To:** 99999999

Dept From: 0
Dept To: 999

No	Tp	A/c	N/C	Date	Ref.	Details	Net	T/C	VAT	Total
71	PI	AA1MIN	7400	01102000	C6147	Taxi fares	38.40	T1	6.72	45.12
72	PI	NEWLIT	5000	01102000	26187	Cleaning materials	168.70	T1	29.52	198.22
73	PI	FLOORI	5000	01102000	435796	Cleaning materials	202.36	T1	35.41	237.77
74	PI	FLOORI	0020	01102000	435796	Equipment	620.00	T1	108.50	728.50
75	PI	FIRSTS	7700	01102000	4821	Ladder hire	126.75	T1	22.18	148.93
76	PI	SAMURA	7104	01102000	02381	Premises insurance	1650.00	T2	0.00	1650.00
77	PI	SAMURA	7303	01102000	02381	Vehicle insurance	1125.00	T2	0.00	1125.00
78	PI	SAMURA	8204	01102000	02381	Misc insurance	430.00	T2	0.00	430.00
79	PI	3DTECH	7505	30092000	001462	Books	179.95	T0	0.00	179.95
80	PI	THAMES	7102	01102000	132157	Water rates	420.00	T0	0.00	420.00
81	PI	ANSNEW	6201	29092000	621014	Advertising	750.00	T1	131.25	881.25
						Totals	5711.16		333.58	6044.74

Blitz Limited

Day Books : Supplier Credits (Detailed)

Date from: 01/10/2000 **Supplier From:**
Date to: 01/10/2000 **Supplier To:**
ZZZZZZZZ

Trans From: 1 **N/C From:**
Trans To: 83 **N/C To:** 99999999

Dept From: 0
Dept To: 999

No	Tp	A/c	N/C	Date	Ref.	Details				
82	PC	BLOFFI	0040	01102000	K0320	Damaged furniture	150.00	T1	26.25	176.25
83	PC	TROJAN	7005	01102000	C0259	Temp overcharge	60.00	T1	10.50	70.50
						Totals :	210.00		36.75	246.75

Creditors control account

The balance on the creditors control account is £50,517.10.

	£
Total credits (invoices)	50,763.85
Total debits (credit notes)	246.75
Balance	50,517.10

This can be obtained by Escaping from the Suppliers Ledger to the main screen, and clicking on the Nominal Ledger button. In the Nominal Ledger window, click on Clear to ensure that no accounts are selected, then scroll down to account 2100 and select it by clicking on it. Then click on the Activity button and accept the defaults you are offered. At the bottom of the screen you will find the total balances.

SOLUTION TO ASSIGNMENT 2: CUSTOMER INVOICES AND CREDIT NOTES

The solution here is written on the assumption that you have access to a printer and are producing invoices using the **Service** and **SrvCredit** options in the *Invoicing* window).

Invoices

When using the Invoicing window options, you should *save* each transaction when you have input the details, print the invoices in batches, and then update the ledgers.

Make sure you specify the nominal account code correctly for each item in each invoice.

Code	Account
4000	Sales - contract cleaning
4001	Sales - window cleaning
4002	Sales - domestic services
4100	Sales - materials

Where appropriate, enter new customer details, following the screen prompts. The default tax code is T1 if you choose to set this (we recommend you do). The suggested reference codes to use are as follows:

Customer	Ref code
R P Marwood	MARWOO
School of Dance	SCHOOL
B & T Fashions Ltd	BTFASH
The Keith Group	KEITHG
Rapid Pizzas	RAPIDP
Gardeners Delight	GARDEN
Payne Properties	PAYNEP
T P Paul	PAULTP

You must decide whether invoices (or credit notes) should be entered using the Product button or the Service button. You may prefer to use the Service option for materials sales this is ok as long as you ensure the invoice is posted to the correct nominal ledger sales account. (A business that sold mainly products rather than services would obviously use the Product Invoice.)

Order details

You should insert order details into an invoice where appropriate. Clicking on the Order Details index tab will give you a pop-up window for adding information about the delivery address. In this assignment, you need to add order details for the invoice to Gardeners Delight - ie you need to add details of the delivery address, which is different from the invoice address.

Details

You should add details for the invoice, based on the information given in the assignment. If you prepared a Service invoice that includes materials (the Elite Caterers invoice), you should have calculated yourself the amount payable (net of VAT) for materials, and entered this amount in the invoice.

225

Use tax code T1 for every invoice. The VAT and total amount payable are calculated automatically.

Footer

There is no requirement on any invoice for footer details, and you will not need to use the Footer index tab (or button).

Printing

To print the invoices, you must first select the invoices and then click on the Print Invoices button in the Invoicing window. Ensure you select the correct layout and paper-size for your printer.

Posting

When you use the Invoicing window options, you must post the transactions to the ledgers using the Update Ledgers button. Select all of the items listed in the Invoicing window: you can do this by clicking on Clear and then on Swap. Decide whether you want a print-out when the Update Ledgers window appears, and then simply click on OK. Follow the screen prompt for printing. A part of a printed listing of the invoices that might be produced is shown below. The invoice numbers may not be the same as yours, depending on the order in which you entered the data. Columns for Stock Code and Quantity have been omitted for lack of space.

Blitz Limited

Update Ledgers Report

Inv/Crd	Audit	Date	A/C	N/C	Details	Net	VAT	Total
2	85	08102000	ROYALP	4000	Revised scale of cleaning	−300.00	−52.50	−352.50
					Invoice Totals:	−300.00	−52.50	−352.50
10041	94	08102000	BRIDGF	4000	Office cleaning	420.00	73.50	493.50
					Invoice Totals:	420.00	73.50	493.50
10042	95	08102000	HARGRE	4002	Domestic services	43.50	7.61	51.11
					Invoice Totals:	43.50	7.61	51.11
10043	96	08102000	ELITEC	4000	KITCHEN CLEANING	644.00	112.70	756.70
	97			4100	10 BOXES OF OVEN CLEANER	61.00	10.68	71.68
	98			4100	6 CASES OF FLAME DETERGENT	72.00	12.60	84.60
	99			4100	7 BRUSHES	23.94	4.19	28.13
					Invoice Totals:	800.94	140.17	941.11
10044	100	08102000	MEAKIN	4001	Window cleaning	249.00	43.58	292.58
					Invoice Totals:	249.00	43.58	292.58

Credit notes

Use the SrvCredit option and process the credit notes just like the service invoices.

Listings

Click on the reports button in the *Customers* window.

(a)   Use the Day Books: Customer Invoices (Detailed) option to preview or print the sales day book listing for invoices.

(b)   Use the Day Books: Customer Credits (Detailed) option to preview or print the sales day book listing for credit notes.

In selecting the items for listing, you can specify the date range from 08/10/2000 to 08/10/2000.

Extracts from the listings are shown below. (The Dept column is omitted.)Check the totals shown. You should have obtained these same *totals* yourself (invoice numbers for particular customers may be different: it depends on the order in which you post the details.)

Blitz Limited

Day Books : Customer Invoices (Detailed)

Date from: 08/10/2000   **Supplier From:**
Date to: 08/10/2000   **Supplier To:**
ZZZZZZZZ

Trans From: 1   **N/C From:**
Trans To: 106   **N/C To:** 99999999

Dept From: 0
Dept To: 999

No.	Tp	A/c	N/C	Date	Refn.	Details	Net	VAT	T/c	Total
87	SI	MARWOO	4002	08102000	10036	Domestic services	66.00	11.55	T1	77.55
88	SI	SCHOOL	4000	08102000	10037	Cleaning school	250.00	43.75	T1	293.75
89	SI	BTFASH	4001	08102000	10038	Window cleaning	144.00	25.20	T1	169.20
90	SI	KEITHG	4000	08102000	10039	Office cleaning	1420.00	248.50	T1	1668.50
91	SI	RAPIDP	4100	08102000	10040	FLAME DETERGENT	60.00	9.98	T1	69.98
92	SI	RAPIDP	4100	08102000	10040	BREAM CLEANER	91.20	15.16	T1	106.36
93	SI	RAPIDP	4100	08102000	10040	CLEANING GLOVES	42.00	6.98	T1	48.98
94	SI	BRIDGF	4000	08102000	10041	Office cleaning	420.00	73.50	T1	493.50
95	SI	HARGRE	4002	08102000	10042	Domestic services	43.50	7.61	T1	51.11
96	SI	ELITEC	4000	08102000	10043	KITCHEN CLEANING	644.00	112.70	T1	756.70
97	SI	ELITEC	4100	08102000	10043	OVEN CLEANER	61.00	10.68	T1	71.68
98	SI	ELITEC	4100	08102000	10043	FLAME DETERGENT	72.00	12.60	T1	84.60
99	SI	ELITEC	4100	08102000	10043	BRUSHES	23.94	4.19	T1	28.13
100	SI	MEAKIN	4001	08102000	10044	Window cleaning	249.00	43.58	T1	292.58
101	SI	ROSEAL	4001	08102000	10045	Window cleaning	125.00	21.88	T1	146.88
102	SI	GARDEN	4100	08102000	10046	WIND. CLEAN FLUID	630.00	104.74	T1	734.74
103	SI	PAYNEP	4000	08102000	10047	Office cleaning	1210.00	201.16	T1	1411.16
104	SI	PAULTP	4002	08102000	10050	Domestic services	60.00	10.50	T1	70.50
105	SI	SIDDAL	4001	08102000	10048	Window cleaning	182.00	31.85	T1	213.85
106	SI	NORRIS	4000	08102000	10049	Factory and office	816.40	142.87	T1	959.27
:						Totals	6610.04	1138.98		7749.02

Blitz Limited

Day Books : Customer Credits (Detailed)

Date from: 08/10/2000   **Supplier From:**
Date to: 08/10/2000   **Supplier To:**
ZZZZZZZZ

Trans From: 1   **N/C From:**
Trans To: 106   **N/C To:** 99999999

Dept From: 0
Dept To: 999

No.	Tp	A/c	N/C	Date	Refn.	Details	Net	VAT	T/c	Total
84	SC	GELLIN	4000	08102000	1	Poor quality cleaning	250.00	43.75	T1	293.75
85	SC	ROYALP	4000	08102000	2	Revised scale of cleaning	300.00	52.50	T1	352.50
86	SC	DCSROO	4001	08102000	3	Broken window	150.00	26.25	T1	176.25
	:					Totals	700.00	122.50		822.50

Balance on the debtors control account

Escape to the main window, and click on the Nominal Ledger button. Then select the Debtors Control Account (code 1100) and click on Activity. Accept the default transaction range you are offered. If you check the totals at the foot of the account, you should find that they are as follows.

	Debit	Credit
Totals:	30369.45	822.50
Balance:	29546.95	

Sales accounts

You can find the balances for each sales account using the Nominal Ledger Activity window. Click on the Nominal Ledger button, scroll down to the accounts concerned and highlight them, then click on Activity. Accept the defaults you are offered. Use the < and > buttons at the bottom of the screen to move from one account to the next.

The current balances shown in the box at the foot of each account's Activity window should be as follows:

Account		Debit	Credit	Balance
		£	£	£
4000	Sales - contract cleaning	550.00	21,357.80	20,807.80
4001	Sales - window cleaning	150.00	2,670.40	2,520.40
4002	Sales - domestic services	0.00	853.10	853.10
4100	Sales – materials	0.00	980.14	980.14

School of Dance

(a)   One method is to use the Search button in the Invoicing window where the Account Reference field Is Equal to SCHOOL. If you click on Apply and Close this will give you a window that includes only the relevant invoice.

(b)   Select this invoice and click on the Print button in the Invoicing window.

CCC Engineering

Click on Customers and select the CCCENG account. Then click on the Activity button. You can find the amount currently owed by the customer, but not whether an invoice has been printed. The invoice amount is £1,527.50.

Windows exercises

The next two pages show suggested solutions to the two Windows exercises in this assignment. Your versions will probably look different, especially if you used a word processor other than Word.

For your duplicate invoice you will need to know the original invoice details including the VAT. An audit trail report for transaction number 40 is the best source. Use the Reports button in the main window and specify a transaction range 40 to 40 (and a date range ending on or after 8/10/2000). Alternatively you can look at CCC Engineering's transaction history and calculate the VAT manually.

To copy from one application to the other, select (highlight) the item press Ctrl + C to copy, switch to the other application and position your cursor, then press Ctrl + V. (This is probably more trouble than it is worth in this example, but it is a very useful trick to know.)

Blitz Limited

25 Apple Road
London N12 3PP

Fax Cover Sheet

DATE:	October 8, 2000	**TIME:**	11:15
TO:	V Cockcroft CCC Engineering Ltd	**PHONE:** **FAX:**	01923 354022 01923 354071
FROM:	Your name Blitz Limited	**PHONE:** **FAX:**	020 8912 2013 020 8912 6387
RE:	Invoice number 10005		

Number of pages including cover sheet: Two

Message

This is in response to your telephone call earlier this morning.

The amount due is £1,527.50 (including VAT of £227.50). For your reference a copy of the invoice accompanies this cover note. Payment is due within 30 days of the date of the invoice.

Blitz Limited

25 Apple Road
London
N12 3PP
Tel: 020 8912 2013
Fax: 020 8912 6387

INVOICE

INVOICE NO: 10005
DATE: 22 September, 2000

To:

CCC Engineering Limited
28 Gardener Road
Watford
WF3 7GH

Deliver To:

Invoice address

QUANTITY	DESCRIPTION	UNIT PRICE	AMOUNT
	Factory cleaning	N/A	1300.00
		SUBTOTAL	1300.00
		VAT	227.50
		SHIPPING & HANDLING	-
		TOTAL DUE	1527.50

Make all cheques payable to: Blitz Limited
If you have any questions concerning this invoice, call: Your name, 020 8912 2013

THANK YOU FOR YOUR BUSINESS!

SOLUTION TO ASSIGNMENT 3: PAYMENTS TO SUPPLIERS

Remittance advice notes

If you intend to print the remittance advice notes (Task (b) of the assignment), you *must* produce the remittance advice notes before you save the payments in question.

Payments to suppliers

You should now process the payment transactions for the 14 payments shown in paragraph (1) in Assignment 3. Click on Bank in the main Sage window and then on the Supplier button. Follow the procedures described in Chapter 6.

It is simpler to use the Pay in Full button for these payments, rather than typing in the amount of the cheque (though it is worth trying both methods to see the difference). In the former case, press Tab when you reach the £ sign box. Click on Pay in Full when the cursor is in the Payment boxes until the £ sign box shows the correct amount.

Save each transaction after you have printed a remittance advice if required.

Chieftain Newspaper Group

To process the payment to the Chieftain Newspaper group, you must first post the credit note transaction to the relevant account in the Suppliers Ledger. There is no need to close down the Bank option and return to the main Sage window if you do not want to. Just click on Suppliers and then Credit to input the credit note details – as explained in Chapter 4.

When you have entered and posted the credit note transaction, press Esc to return to the Supplier payments window (or open it up again if you closed it). You can then process the payment to the supplier.

Credit notes and early settlement discounts

You will first need to find out the amount of the credit notes by looking at the Activity for each of the accounts mentioned. The amounts you should have posted are as follows.

Account	Gross	VAT	Net
FLOORS	1,012.85	150.85	862.00
HARROW	2,853.37	424.97	2,428.40
MATTHI	3,360.50	500.50	2,860.00

Post the new invoices as you have done in previous assignments except that instead of accepting tax code T1 and letting the program calculate VAT at 17.5% on the full amount, use code T3 and type in the amount of VAT shown on the invoice.

To pay the new invoices, you will have to calculate the discount to establish what the amount of each cheque payment should be. You should have produced the following results:

Supplier code	Gross amount £	Net amount £	Discount %	Discount £	Cheque payment (gross less discount) £
FLOORS	1,005.31	862.00	5%	43.10	962.21
HARROW	2,840.62	2,428.40	3%	72.85	2767.77
MATTHI	3,335.48	2,860.00	5%	143.00	3192.48

To enter the payment details, Tab past the £ sign box and click on Pay in Full when you reach the Payment box. Then type in the amount of the discount in the Discount box.

Highpile Cleaning Supplies

Here, you are paying an invoice and also making a payment on account for invoices not yet received. Type 3500 in the £ sign box and then when you reach the Payment box click on Pay in Full.

Now click on Save. You will be told that there is an unallocated cheque balance of £1,135.31. Click on Yes to post it as a payment on account.

Bank transaction payments

To make the payments for the cheque requisitions, from the Bank Accounts window and click on Payment. For each payment that includes VAT (cheques 000119 and 000121) you can enter the gross payment in the Net column and then click on Calc Net. The VAT will be calculated automatically, and the Net amount adjusted to exclude VAT. The tax code for the train ticket (cheque 000120) should be T0.

Listing

You have processed payments to suppliers (Suppliers Ledger) and for three bank transactions (Nominal Ledger). There are several ways of doing this in Line 50. We suggest that you click on Reports in the Bank accounts window and select:

(a)   Day Books: Bank Payments (Summary); and also
(b)   Day Books: Supplier Payments (Summary).

Enter 09/10/2000 as the date in both date boxes, when making your specifications for the listing.

The output in printed form should be as follows. (Check that your totals match the totals shown here.)

Blitz Limited
Day Books: Supplier Payments (Summary)

Date from: 09/10/2000   Bank From:
Date to: 09/10/2000   Bank To: 99999999

Transaction From: 1   **Supplier From:**
Transaction To: 136   **Supplier To:**
ZZZZZZZZ :

No.	Bank	A/c	Date	Refn.	Details	Net	VAT	Total
107	1200	AA1MIN	09102000	000100 Purchase Payment	117.50	0.00	117.50
108	1200	BTELEC	09102000	000101 Purchase Payment	540.50	0.00	540.50
109	1200	CAPITA	09102000	000102 Purchase Payment	376.00	0.00	376.00
110	1200	BLOFFI	09102000	000103 Purchase Payment	1493.78	0.00	1493.78
111	1200	FIRSTS	09102000	000104 Purchase Payment	332.23	0.00	332.23
112	1200	SAMURA	09102000	000105 Purchase Payment	3205.00	0.00	3205.00
113	1200	3DTECH	09102000	000106 Purchase Payment	179.95	0.00	179.95
114	1200	IRONCL	09102000	000107 Purchase Payment	3000.00	0.00	3000.00
115	1200	TROJAN	09102000	000108 Purchase Payment	141.00	0.00	141.00
116	1200	MUSWEL	09102000	000109 Purchase Payment	1240.00	0.00	1240.00
117	1200	NORTHL	09102000	000110 Purchase Payment	1175.00	0.00	1175.00
118	1200	STERLI	09102000	000111 Purchase Payment	642.37	0.00	642.37
119	1200	UNIFOR	09102000	000112 Purchase Payment	763.75	0.00	763.75
120	1200	VANCEN	09102000	000113 Purchase Payment	19059.44	0.00	19059.44
122	1200	CHIEFT	09102000	000114 Purchase Payment	1175.00	0.00	1175.00
129	1200	FLOORS	09102000	000115 Purchase Payment	962.21	0.00	962.21
131	1200	HARROW	09102000	000116 Purchase Payment	2767.77	0.00	2767.77
133	1200	MATTHI	09102000	000117 Purchase Payment	3192.48	0.00	3192.48
135	1200	HIGHPI	09102000	000118 Purchase Payment	2364.69	0.00	2364.69
136	1200	HIGHPI	09102000	000118 Payment on Account	1135.31	0.00	1135.31

| | **Totals** | : | | | | 43,863.98 | 0.00 | 43,863.98 |

Blitz Limited

Day Books: Bank Payments (Summary)

Date from: 09/10/2000	Bank From:
Date to: 09/10/2000	Bank To: 99999999

Transaction From: 1	N/C **From:**
Transaction To: 133	N/C **To:** ZZZZZZZ :

Dept From: 0
Dept To: 999

No	Tp	A/C	Date	Chq. No	Details	Net	VAT	T/c	
137	BP	8203	09102000	000119	Training course	220.00	38.50	T1	258.50
138	BP	7400	09102000	000120	Train ticket	105.50	0.00	T0	105.50
139	BP	8205	09102000	000121	Refreshments	84.00	14.70	T1	98.70
					Totals	409.50	53.20		462.70

Bank balance

You can print or display the Activity on the bank current account by selecting it in the Nominal Ledger (code 1200). Accept the default 'From' date and specify a 'To' date of 09/10/2000. You should get a credit balance of £10,380.61.

(Note: the Tp column indicates bank receipt [BR], purchase payment [PP], payment on account [PA], or bank payment [BP]).

Nominal Activity

Date from: 09/10/2000
Date to: 09/10/2000

N/C **1200**
N/C **To: 1200**

Transaction From: 1
Transaction To: 133

No.	Tp	Date	Refn	Details	Value	Debit	Credit
1	BR	19082000		M Green - shares	20000.00	20000.00	
2	BR	19082000		T Nicholas - shares	20000.00	20000.00	
8	JC	16092000	xxxxx	Wages and salaries	6053.93		6053.93
107	PP	09102000	100	Purchase Payment	117.50		117.50
108	PP	09102000	101	Purchase Payment	540.50		540.50
109	PP	09102000	100102	Purchase Payment	376.00		376.00
110	PP	09102000	103	Purchase Payment	1493.78		1493.78
111	PP	09102000	104	Purchase Payment	332.23		332.23
112	PP	09102000	105	Purchase Payment	3205.00		3205.00
113	PP	09102000	106	Purchase Payment	179.95		179.95
114	PP	09102000	107	Purchase Payment	3000.00		3000.00
115	PP	09102000	108	Purchase Payment	141.00		141.00
116	PP	09102000	109	Purchase Payment	1240.00		1240.00
117	PP	09102000	110	Purchase Payment	1175.00		1175.00
118	PP	09102000	111	Purchase Payment	642.37		642.37
119	PP	09102000	112	Purchase Payment	763.75		763.75
120	PP	09102000	113	Purchase Payment	19059.44		19059.44
122	PP	09102000	114	Purchase Payment	1175.00		1175.00
129	PP	09102000	115	Purchase Payment	962.21		962.21
131	PP	09102000	116	Purchase Payment	2767.77		2767.77
133	PP	09102000	117	Purchase Payment	3192.48		3192.48
135	PP	09102000	118	Purchase Payment	2364.69		2364.69
136	PA	09102000	118	Payment on Account	1135.31		1135.31
137	BP	09102000	119	Training course	258.50		258.50
138	BP	09102000	120	Train ticket	105.50		105.50
139	BP	09102000	121	Refreshments	98.70		98.70

Totals : 40000.00 50380.61

History Balance : 10380.61

Balance on the creditors control account

You should repeat the same exercise but this time select the creditors control account - account code 2100. The balance on the account is now £6,113.86.

Spreadsheet

If you did this exercise you should fairly easily have been able to explain that the No. column lists the number of the transaction – the number allocated by the Sage package to each consecutive transaction that you post. The Ref column shows either the cheque number or the credit note number or, in the case of discounts, the original invoice number.

The problem with the totals is that some items have been included that should not have been included and one item has been omitted. To put things right you should have deleted the amounts shown in boxes ('cells') 16, 19, 21 and 23 in columns G and I, and you should have entered the amount 1,135.31 in cell I25.

As part of your tidying up exercise you could have changed the lines in capitals to small letters, made the headings italic, given the spreadsheet a title, and so on. No 'answer' is shown because many 'answers' are acceptable, although they will be different in appearance.

SOLUTION TO ASSIGNMENT 4: RECEIPTS FROM CUSTOMERS

The assignment requires you to process a variety of transactions.

Posting new invoices

The procedures for entering details of new customer accounts and producing invoices were described in Chapter 5. You should use the Invoicing option in the main window, and:

(a)   The Service window to produce the invoice.

(b)   The Print Invoices button to print the invoices.

(c)   The Update Ledgers button to post the transactions to the ledgers.

The nominal account code should be 4000 for the invoice to Bradley Fashions (contract cleaning) and 4002 for the invoice to A Rathod (domestic services).

One of the two invoices is reproduced on the next page. If you have forgotten how to produce invoices, look again at Chapter 5.

Receipts - payment in full for invoices

Posting the 12 receipts transactions listed in item (2) in the information for the assignment should not present any difficulties. Click on the Bank button and then on the Customer button.

These are all payments in full for one or more outstanding invoices. In every case, you can use the Pay in Full button for allocating the receipt to an invoice. Make sure you include references for each receipt.

Click on Save when you have posted the details for each customer and move on to the next customer.

In the case of two customers (D J Hargreaves and A Rose Ltd) the amount received is in payment for just one invoice, when there are two outstanding invoices on the account. In cases where it is not clear what is being paid you should either allocate the payment to the earliest invoices on the account or record the payment as a payment on account - until it can be established which invoices are being paid.

Invoice   Page 1
10051
12/10/2000

BLITZ LTD

25 APPLE ROAD

LONDON

N12 3PP

BRADLEY FASHIONS LTD
18 HOSPITAL BRIDGE
ROAD
ST ALBANS
HERTS

BRADLE

Quantity Details	Disc%	Disc Amount	Net Amount	VAT Amount
Contract cleaning services	0.00	0.00	820.00	143.50

Total Net	820.00
Total VAT	143.50
Carriage	0.00
Invoice Total	963.50

T P Paul

The invoice of £70.50 for T P Paul can be cancelled by creating a credit note for £70.50. You can do this by using the SrvCredit option in the Invoicing window.

Discounts

Begin by checking that the discount has been correctly calculated. If you disagree with the customer's calculation, you would have to speak to your supervisor or (if authorised to do so) telephone the customer to query the mistake.

To check the calculation you first need to find out the transaction number(s) by looking up the customers' Activity and then the net amount due by looking at these transactions in the Financials listing.

The transactions are numbers 103 and numbers 91, 92 and 93. In the case of Rapid Pizzas, the discount of £9.66 must be divided into three chunks.

Transaction no	Net amount	Discount (5%)
103	1210.00	60.50
91	60.00	3.00
92	91.20	4.56
93	42.00	2.10
		9.66

Post this by returning to the Bank Customer receipts window and entering the relevant account code. In each case (Payne Properties and Rapid Pizzas) you should remember to follow these procedures.

(a)   Make sure you enter a reference for the invoice being paid.

(b)   Tab through the Amount box leaving it blank.

(c)   Tab through the Receipt box leaving it blank.

(d)   Enter the amount of the discount in the appropriate box and press Tab. The amount in the Receipt box will automatically be calculated.

(e)   Click on Save.

Deductions for credit notes

Stay in the Bank Customer window. For each customer account, enter the invoice as the reference number. Leave the Amount box blank and Tab to the Receipt box. Click on Pay in Full in each case.

Part payments

The part payments by Elite Caterers and Campbell Consultants should be processed either:

(a)   By *keying in* the amount of the payment in the Amount box, and then Tabbing to the Receipt box of the first invoice listed and clicking on Pay in Full; *or*

(b)   By Tabbing through the Amount box and then *keying in* the amount of the payment in the first Receipt box you come to. Then you can just click on Save.

Clough and Partners

This payment of an invoice plus a payment on account must be processed by *typing* the amount received in the Amount box. When you click on Save after entering the receipt details, accept the Post as a Payment on Account message.

M Zakis Ltd

Before you process the receipt from M Zakis, you must set up an account for the (new) customer in the Customers ledger. Type in the code MZAKIS and press Tab. Click on **New** when the Customer Account window appears.

When you have set up and saved the account, return to the Bank Customer window and process the receipt.

Writing off small unpaid balances

Process the payments from A T Haslam and R P Marwood in the same way as the part payments from other customers. There will be unpaid balances of £0.18 and £0.05 respectively. (If you forgot to take a note of these amounts you can find the unpaid balance by searching the list in the Customers window.)

Click on Tools at the top of the screen, then on Write Off, Refund, Return. Choose the Sales Ledger amendments option. From the area list pick Write off Customer Transactions below a value. To be safe a good value to enter is 0.50, although you could put in a higher amount – say 1 (£1.00) – if you wish. Select both the accounts by highlighting them and click on Next. Confirm that you are writing off 23p by clicking on Finish.

Bank receipts

The five items of bank receipts from non-credit customers should be entered by using the Receipt button in the Bank Accounts window.

For each transaction, select the correct nominal ledger code (N/C). This should be 4001 for window cleaning, 4002 for domestic services and 4100 for materials sales. Enter the five transactions separately. Just key in the single number 4 and then click on the Finder button (or press F4) if you forget which nominal Sales account is which.

Reports

You should print, preview or display a *Day Books: Customer Receipts* Summary report and a *Day Books: Bank Receipts* Summary report, using the reports button in the Bank window.

The Reports window will allow you to specify the parameters for items to be listed. Specify a Date Range of 12/10/2000 to 12/10/2000.

The total amount for the report is as follows.

	Net £	*Tax* £	*Gross* £
Customer Receipts	10,508.25	0.00	10,508.25
Bank Receipts	352.00	61.60	413.60
Total	10,860.25	61.60	10,921.85

P Leyser refund

Click on Tools (at the top of the screen, then on Write Off, Refund, Return, and choose the Sales Ledger option. Choose Customer Invoice Refund from the list that appears as you click on Next. Scroll down to the LEYSER account and click on Next. The payment will appear in the window. Select it and click on Next again. You are asked which account you want to post the refund to the bank account 1200. Select this and click on Next. If the information given in the next window is correct, click on Finish.

Account balances - nominal ledger

You can establish these using the Activity button in the Nominal window. The balances should be:

Account	*N/C code*	*Debit entries*	*Credit entries*	*Balance*
Bank current account	1200	50,921.85	50,477.20	444.65
Debtors control account	1100	31,517.67	11,568.23	19,949.44

Account balances - sales ledger

Click on the Customers button and scroll down until you find the account ELITEC. You should find that the balance outstanding on this account is £1,497.81.

SOLUTION TO ASSIGNMENT 5: OTHER CASH TRANSACTIONS

Many of the tasks for this assignment are similar to tasks that were set in Assignments 1-4. There are invoices from new and existing suppliers, invoices to new and existing customers, and payments and receipts. In addition, however, some of the tasks relate to petty cash transactions, journal transactions and a bank reconciliation. Assignment 5 is therefore a wide-ranging test of your competence with Sage.

Setting up the petty cash system

The petty cash system is set up by withdrawing £300 in cash from the bank. This bank-cash transaction should be recorded in the nominal ledger as a journal entry. Click on the Journals button in the Nominal Ledger window. The fields should be completed as follows.

(a)   Reference. Use the cheque number as a reference for the transaction. This is 000122.

(b)   Date 13/10/2000.

(c)   The double entry is as follows. (It doesn't matter whether you do the debit or the credit entry first.)

N/C	Details	T/c	Debit £	Credit £
1200	To petty cash	T9		300.00
1230	From bank account	T9	300.00	

Save the transaction, then press Esc or click on Close.

Invoices from suppliers

The invoices from suppliers can be entered using the Invoices button in the Suppliers window. This allows you to enter new supplier details, where appropriate. The transaction date should be the invoice date, not the date on which you are processing the transactions. Some invoices relate to different items of expense, and so different nominal ledger account codes. For example, the invoice from Great North Hotel should be recorded on three lines, for nominal ledger account codes 7402, 7406 and 7502 respectively. All the purchase invoice transactions should have a tax code T1. Your accuracy in entering the transactions is tested by a later task in the assignment. If you cannot remember how to process supplier invoices, refer back to Chapter 4.

Customer invoices

You should now be familiar with the procedure for entering invoices. Ensure you assign each sales item to the appropriate nominal ledger account code - 4000 for contract cleaning, 4001 for window cleaning, 4002 for domestic services and 4100 for materials sales. All transactions should have a T1 tax code, and a date of 16/10/2000.

Payments to suppliers

To record the payments to suppliers, Click on Bank and then on the Supplier button. Look up the supplier account reference codes if you need to, using the Finder button or the F4 function key to display the supplier accounts on screen.

For the Ace Telephone Answering and ANS Newspaper Group invoices, *key in* the amount paid in the Amount box, then Tab to the Payment box and click on Pay in Full. With the ANS Newspaper Group payment, confirm that the payment on account should be posted.

Before you record the payment from Wells Business Systems you should post the credit note. Use the Calc Net option to allocate the amount correctly.

Receipts from customers

Click on the Customer button in the Bank Accounts window. The receipts from the three customers can be processed in a similar way to the payments to suppliers. Don't forget that there *must* be a reference number. Use the number of the invoice being paid.

V J Richardson cheque

This transaction can be posted as a journal entry. Click on the Journals button in the Nominal Ledger window. The entries in the main part of the screen should be:

N/C	Details	T/c	Debit £	Credit £
1200	Loan - V J Richardson	T9	10000.00	
2300	To bank account	T9		10000.00

Alternatively, you can post the transaction as a bank receipt, using the Receipt button in the Bank Accounts window. The N/C code for the receipt should be 2300, the net amount 10000 and the tax code T9.

Petty cash transactions

Click on the Bank button and then select account 1230 Petty Cash.

To post the payments out of petty cash, just click on the Payments button and a window that will be familiar by now will appear.

To post the receipt into petty cash the N/C code 4001 should be used (for window cleaning sales). Enter 72 as the Net amount, then click on the Calc Net button to calculate the VAT automatically. The final entry should be for a net cash receipt of £61.28 and VAT of £10.72.

To produce reports of Cash Payments (or Receipts), click on the Reports button in the Bank window and scroll down until you find the appropriate option. Select the date range 13/10/2000 to 16/10/2000. Print the listing if you have access to a printer. Otherwise, display the listing on screen. An extract from the listing follows.

Blitz Limited

Cash Payments (Summary)

Date from: 13/10/2000

Date to 16/10/2000

99999999

Bank From:

Bank To:

Transaction from: 1

Transaction To: 235

No.	Tp	A/C	Date	Refn	Details	Net	VAT	Total
223	CP	7501	13102000	PC001	POSTAGE STAMPS	24.00	0.00	24.00
224	CP	8205	13102000	PC002	BISCUITS, COFFEE	32.49	0.00	32.49
225	CP	8205	13102000	PC003	MILK	15.20	0.00	15.20
226	CP	7400	13102000	PC004	TAXIS	25.00	0.00	25.00
227	CP	7400	14102000	PC005	TRAIN FARES	9.20	0.00	9.20
228	CP	8205	14102000	PC006	WASHING UP LIQUID	1.75	0.00	1.75
229	CP	7500	14102000	PC007	PHOTOCOPYING	24.00	4.20	28.20
230	CP	7504	15102000	PC008	STATIONERY	37.24	6.52	43.76
231	CP	7400	15102000	PC009	TAXIS	15.00	0.00	15.00
232	CP	8205	16102000	PC010	SANDWICHES, CAKES	38.26	0.00	38.26
233	CP	7304	16102000	PC011	PARKING	7.00	0.00	7.00
234	CP	7400	16102000	PC012	TRAIN FARES	8.40	0.00	8.40
					Totals	237.54	10.72	248.26

Topping up petty cash

Check the balance on the Petty Cash account (N/C 1230) by looking at the list of accounts in and balances in the main Nominal Ledger window. This should show a balance of £123.74.

A cheque for £176.26 cash (£300 - £123.74) must be drawn to top up the petty cash balance to £300.

To post this entry, click on the Journals button in the Nominal Ledger window. The main part of the entry is as follows:

N/C	Details	T/c	Debit £	Credit £
1200	To petty cash	T9		176.26
1230	From bank account	T9	176.26	

Check that the balance on the petty cash account (N/C 1230) is now £300 (look again at the list in the Nominal Ledger window).

Wages and salaries

These transactions can be entered in the nominal ledger accounts as a single journal entry. Click on Journals in the Nominal Ledger window. Key in the date 16/10/2000 and (as instructed) reference J04. The remaining entries should be as follows:

BPP PUBLISHING

N/C	Description	T/c	Debit £	Credit £
1200	Cash for wages	T9		4133.04
2210	PAYE, 16 Oct	T9		2217.96
2211	Nat Ins, 16 Oct	T9		975.20
7001	Directors salaries	T9	1350.80	
7003	Staff salaries	T9	475.75	
6000	Wages	T9	4859.65	
7006	Employers NI	T9	640.00	

The total debits equal the total credits, therefore you can post these transactions as a single journal entry.

Account balances

You can just scroll through the Nominal Ledger window to search for the account balances required by your supervisor. Check that you have the following balances.

N/C		Debit £	Credit £
1100	Debtors control account	25486.83	
1200	Bank – current account	4642.09	
2100	Creditors control account		7677.28
7003	Staff salaries	951.50	
7400	Travelling	301.50	
7700	Equipment hire	503.75	
4000	Sales – contract cleaning		27167.80
4001	Sales – window cleaning		3060.68
4002	Sales – domestic services		1103.90
4100	Sales – materials		1243.74
1230	Petty cash	300.00	
4009	Discounts allowed	101.66	
5009	Discounts taken		258.95

Bank reconciliation

Doing a bank reconciliation can seem a fairly complex task, and you need to be thorough. Your source document is the bank statement itself. You must match every item on the bank statement against a corresponding entry in the nominal ledger bank account.

If you have access to a printer, print out a listing of activity on the Bank Account (1200). Ensure all Sage Windows except the main menu are closed, and select **Settings, Change Program Date** from the menu. Key in the date of the bank statement 16/10/2000.

Now click on the Bank and Reconcile. A listing of transactions in the nominal ledger bank account will appear on screen. It is probably best to *maximise* the window for this sort of detailed screen work: click on the upward-pointing triangle in the top right hand corner of the Bank Reconciliation window. Key in the bank statement end balance in the box provided.

The matching process can now begin. When you match a transaction in the nominal ledger bank account with an item on the statement sent by the bank, you must note the match. Do this by clicking on the transaction on screen. The matched transaction will be highlighted in a different colour. Use the Page Down and Page Up keys, the ↑ and ↓ cursor keys, or the scroll bar to search through the list of transactions on screen.

You should be able to match nearly every item on the bank's statement against a transaction in the nominal ledger account. In this exercise, there is an additional item on the bank statement for bank charges. You should post this item to the nominal ledger (N/C code 7901 for bank charges) and you can do this by:

(a)   Clicking on the Adjustment button.
(b)   Completing the relevant fields in the window that pops up.

When you have matched *every* transaction on the bank's statement against the nominal ledger transactions on screen and you have also entered the bank charges details, you are nearing the end of the bank reconciliation exercise.

Check the balance in the Reconcile Balance field on the screen. This should equal the balance on the bank statement itself (13,381.53). If you have achieved this reconciliation, click on Save.

You can now display or print out a list of reconciled and unreconciled transactions. Click on Reports in the Bank window and obtain reports of Unreconciled Payments and Unreconciled Receipts. Extracts from these are shown below.

Blitz Limited

Unreconciled Payments

Date From: 01/01/2000   Bank From:
Date To: 31/12/2000   Bank To: 99999999

Tp	Date	Refn.	Details	Amount
PP	09102000	000117	Purchase Payment	3192.48
PP	16102000	000123	Purchase Payment	250.00
PP	16102000	000124	Purchase Payment	881.25
PA	16102000	000124	Payment on Account	318.75
PP	16102000	000125	Purchase Payment	1516.50
JC	16102000	000126	TO PETTY CASH	176.26
JC	16102000	J04	CASH FOR WAGES	4133.04
				10468.28

Unreconciled Receipts

Tp	Date	Refn.	Details	Receipts
SR	15102000	10004	Sales Receipt	1000.00
SR	16102000	10046	Sales Receipt	703.24
				1703.24

Overall the position is as follows.

	£
Statement balance	13,381.53
Unpresented payments	(10,468.28)
Unpresented receipts	1,703.24
Trial balance	4,616.49

The trial balance figure is different (by £25.60) from the account balance figure you gave your supervisor earlier. This is because you have now posted the bank charges.

If you load up Assignment 6 you will be able to view the completed reconciliation. (Ensure you change the Program Date to 16/10/2000 or later.)

SOLUTION TO ASSIGNMENT 6: OTHER CREDIT TRANSACTIONS

Posting credit sales transactions

Remember to code each item for the correct sales account in the nominal ledger, and use tax code T1 for every transaction. Whenever a customer exceeds the existing credit limit, make a note of the name, but continue to process the transaction.

The customers who have exceeded their existing credit limit are:

> GHH Commercial Bank
> The Keith Group
> Norris Hydraulics Ltd
> School of Dance
> R I Tepper Ltd

Their credit limit should be increased by £1,000 in each case. To do this, after receiving the 'exceeding credit limit' warning and proceeding with the transaction, without closing the Customers Invoice window click on the Customers button, select the relevant customer account and click on Record. The customer details will then appear on screen. Move to the credit limit field (on the Credit Control tab) and key in a new credit limit (overwriting the old limit) by adding 1000 to the limit. Then click on Save and press Esc twice - you will be back in the Service Invoice Window.

Alternatively, you can post all the invoices first and then alter the credit limits of the Customers later.

Cash sales

The cheques received should be posted as Receipts in the Bank Accounts window. Enter each transaction in turn selecting the correct N/C code. The four entries should be as follows, if the tax code is entered as T1.

Deposit

No.	N/C	Date	Amount	Description	Amount and tax code
500005	4002	21102000	–	Domestic services	51.7 then Calc Net button
500006	4002	21102000	–	Domestic services	44 then Calc Net
500007	4100	21102000	–	Materials sales	37.6 then Calc Net
500008	4100	23102000	–	Materials sales	52.88 then Calc Net

Save each transaction when you have entered the details. You then get a blank window for the next transaction.

The cash receipts should be posted in account 1230 as Petty Cash Receipts. The two entries should be:

Ref	Date	N/C	Details	Net and Tax
PCR002	22102000	4100	Materials sales	25.38 then Calc Net
PCR003	23102000	4002	Domestic services	35.25 then Calc Net

Invoices received from suppliers

Click on the Service button in the Invoicing window. Enter the three transactions, setting up new supplier accounts where appropriate. The tax code is T1 for all three transactions.

Receipts from customers

Click on the Customer button in the Bank Accounts window. Post the seven transactions. Check the instructions in Chapter 7 if you have forgotten how to do this.

Tab through the main Amount box if you can see at a glance which invoice(s) are being settled. Just click on Pay in Full when you get to the relevant Receipt box (Plus2: Paid box). If it is not clear how the payment should be allocated, *type in* the amount received in the main Amount box and then click on Pay in Full in each of the Receipt boxes. When there is no more money to allocate, click on Save.

You should type in the amounts for S T Chanas, Elite Caterers, and Meakin Media.

Contra entries

The accounts of Elite Caterers and Meakin Media can now be settled by contra entries. Take each customer/supplier in turn.

Click on Tools, then on Contra Entries.

(a)   For Elite Caterers, enter both the Sales Ledger A/C and the Purchase Ledger A/C as ELITEC. The screen will display the unpaid invoice balances in the customer account (left-hand side) and the supplier account (right-hand side) for Elite Caterers. Click on each transaction in the sales account and then click on the supplier account transaction. The totals should be the same, and can therefore be set off in full against each other, so just click on OK to post the contra entry.

(b)   For Meakin Media, repeat the procedure. The A/C code is MEAKIN for both the Customers Ledger account and the Suppliers Ledger account. The *first* entry in the customer account and the entry in the supplier account should be selected.

ANS Newspaper Group

Click your way into the Contra Entries window again. Start to post a contra entry transaction, by entering ANSNEW as the Sales Ledger A/C and Purchase Ledger A/C codes. The window should then display unpaid invoices as follows:

	£
In the customer account for ANSNEW	176.25
In the supplier account for ANSNEW	553.75
Difference	377.50

The difference in amounts owing is £377.50, and a cheque should be drawn up for this amount.

Click on Bank, then on Supplier. Post a payment to ANSNEW for £377.50, dated 22 October 2000, cheque number 000127. Key the amount 377.50 into the £ sign box, then tab down to the *invoice* for advertising (amount £553.75) and click on Pay in Full. Then Save this transaction.

Return to the Contra Entries window. You can now process a contra entry for ANS Newspaper Group, in the same way as for Elite Catering and Meakin Media.

Writing off small unpaid balances

Click on Tools, then on Write Off, Refund, Return and opt for the Sales Ledger. Choose Write Off Customer transaction below a value.

Enter a value of 1.01 (£1.01). The screen will display two unpaid balances.

> CAMPBE   1.00
> CHANAS   0.63

Click on both of these and then click on Next. Use a date of 31/10/2000, click Next and confirm the write offs when asked to do so. The total amount written off is £1.63.

Writing off accounts

Look at the Customers window to find the balances on the accounts ADAMSE and HAYNES. You should do this to establish that E T Adams currently owes nothing to Blitz.

With L Haynes & Co, however, there is an unpaid balance on the account. This must be written off as a bad debt.

To write off the bad debt for L Haynes & Co, click on Tools then on Write Off, Refund, Return, and choose the Sales Ledger. This time select the Write off Customer Accounts option. Choose the account reference HAYNES. Two lines are shown, but both relate to the same invoice. Click Next, enter the date of the write-off and click next again. The amount and date of the write-off will show, if these are correct click Finish.

Credit note

The sales credit note to Owen of London should be posted using the SrvCredit button in the Invoicing window. The entry should be:

A/C	Date	Ref	N/C	Description	Amount	T/c
OWENLO	22102000	004	4000	Credit note	150.00	T1

Correcting the N/C code

A correction to an account code is an accounting error. You must first find the transaction reference number. Open the Suppliers window and select the account AA1MIN. Click on Activity. The transaction history of the account will show the October invoice for £158.27. (This includes VAT.) The transaction number is 186.

Click on File, then on Maintenance then on Corrections. In the window that appears scroll to transaction number 186, highlight it and click on Edit.

Activate the *Splits* tab, Click on Edit again and alter the N/C code. Then click on Close, then on Save and confirm that you wish to post the changes. If you scroll down to the end of the list you can see that the correction has been posted.

Newlite Cleaning Fluids

Check the Activity for NEWLIT in the Suppliers window. You should take a note of the transaction number (17) and the details of the invoice that has been posted incorrectly. Then use File ... Maintenance to correct the transaction as just explained.

The details should be:

A/C	NEWLIT
Date	12092000
Inv No	26115
N/C	5000
Details	Cleaning materials
Net Amount	403.00
T/c	T1

The corrected invoice figure is £403.00 net plus VAT of £70.53 giving a total invoice amount of £473.53.

Current balances

To find the current balances on the nominal ledger accounts, simply call up the Nominal Ledger window. Scroll through each account in turn and copy down the balances shown. These should be as follows.

	Code	Balance £	
Bank current account	1200	6754.28	(debit)
Debtors control account	1100	28369.34	(debit)
Creditors control account	2100	7676.90	(credit)
Bad debt write off account	8100	151.32	(debit)
Advertising account	6201	3421.28	(debit)
Sales - contract cleaning	4000	31017.80	(credit)
Sales - window cleaning	4001	4084.68	(credit)
Sales - domestic services	4002	1430.35	(credit)
Sales - materials	4100	1417.34	(credit)

Spreadsheet exercise - Aged Debtors Analysis

The customers owing the five largest amounts are:

A/C	Balance
GHHCOM	3,436.88
OGDENK	3,278.25
KEITHG	3,243.00
NORRIS	2,775.47
ROYALP	1,762.50

You could have found this information out in Line 50 simply by clicking on the word Balance in the main Customers window. This re-sorts the data (smallest balance first), clicking on Balance again will sort in the opposite order (largest balance first).

Customers with a balance of over £1,000 that has been outstanding for more than 30 days are as follows.

A/C	Balance	Current	30 days
OGDENK	3,278.25	564.00	2,714.25
ROYALP	1,762.50	−352.50	2,115.00
GHHCOM	3,436.88	1,703.75	1,733.13
HARVEY	1,715.50	0.00	1,715.50
NORRIS	2,775.47	1,687.77	1,087.70

BPP PUBLISHING

Part F
Appendices

APPENDIX 1: THE BLITZ NOMINAL LEDGER - ACCOUNTS AND CODES

The following is a list of the accounts in the nominal ledger of Blitz Limited.

Fixed assets

0010	FREEHOLD PROPERTY
0011	LEASEHOLD PROPERTY
0020	PLANT AND MACHINERY
0021	PLANT AND MACHINERY DEPRECIATION
0030	OFFICE EQUIPMENT
0031	OFFICE EQUIPMENT DEPRECIATION
0040	FURNITURE AND FIXTURES
0041	FURNITURE AND FIXTURES DEPRECIATION
0050	MOTOR VEHICLES
0051	MOTOR VEHICLES DEPRECIATION

Current assets

1001	STOCK
1002	WORK IN PROGRESS
1003	FINISHED GOODS
1100	DEBTORS CONTROL ACCOUNT
1101	SUNDRY DEBTORS
1102	OTHER DEBTORS
1103	PREPAYMENTS
1200	BANK CURRENT ACCOUNT
1210	BANK DEPOSIT ACCOUNT
1220	BUILDING SOCIETY ACCOUNT
1230	PETTY CASH
1240	COMPANY CREDIT CARD
1250	CREDIT CARD RECEIPTS

Current liabilities

2100	CREDITORS CONTROL ACCOUNT
2101	SUNDRY CREDITORS
2102	OTHER CREDITORS
2109	ACCRUALS
2200	SALES TAX CONTROL ACCOUNT
2201	PURCHASE TAX CONTROL LIABILITY
2210	PAYE
2211	NATIONAL INSURANCE
2230	PENSION FUND
2300	LOANS
2310	HIRE PURCHASE
2320	CORPORATION TAX
2330	MORTGAGES

Financed by

3000	ORDINARY SHARES
3001	PREFERENCE SHARES
3100	RESERVES
3101	UNDISTRIBUTED RESERVES
3200	PROFIT AND LOSS ACCOUNT

BPP
PUBLISHING

Sales

4000	SALES - CONTRACT CLEANING
4001	SALES - WINDOW CLEANING
4002	SALES - DOMESTIC SERVICES
4009	DISCOUNTS ALLOWED
4100	SALES MATERIALS
4101	SALES TYPE E
4200	SALES OF ASSETS
4400	CREDIT CHARGES (LATE PAYMENTS)
4900	MISCELLANEOUS INCOME
4901	ROYALTIES RECEIVED
4902	COMMISSIONS RECEIVED
4903	INSURANCE CLAIMS
4904	RENT INCOME
4905	DISTRIBUTION AND CARRIAGE

Purchases

5000	MATERIALS PURCHASED
5001	MATERIALS IMPORTED
5002	MISCELLANEOUS PURCHASES
5003	PACKAGING
5009	DISCOUNTS TAKEN
5100	CARRIAGE
5101	DUTY
5102	TRANSPORT INSURANCE
5200	OPENING STOCK
5201	CLOSING STOCK

Direct expenses

6000	PRODUCTIVE LABOUR
6001	COST OF SALES LABOUR
6002	SUB-CONTRACTORS
6100	SALES COMMISSIONS
6200	SALES PROMOTIONS
6201	ADVERTISING
6202	GIFTS AND SAMPLES
6203	PUBLIC RELATIONS (LIT & BROCHURES)
6900	MISCELLANEOUS EXPENSES

Overheads

7001	DIRECTORS SALARIES
7002	DIRECTORS REMUNERATION
7003	STAFF SALARIES
7004	WAGES - REGULAR
7005	WAGES - CASUAL TEMPORARY STAFF
7006	EMPLOYERS NI
7007	EMPLOYERS PENSIONS
7008	RECRUITMENT EXPENSES
7100	RENT
7102	WATER RATES
7103	GENERAL RATES
7104	PREMISES INSURANCE
7200	ELECTRICITY
7201	GAS
7202	OIL
7203	OTHER HEATING COSTS

Overheads
(continued)

7300	FUEL AND OIL
7301	REPAIRS AND SERVICING
7302	LICENCES
7303	VEHICLE INSURANCE
7304	MISCELLANEOUS MOTOR EXPENSES
7400	TRAVELLING
7401	CAR HIRE
7402	HOTELS
7403	UK ENTERTAINMENT
7404	OVERSEAS ENTERTAINMENT
7405	OVERSEAS TRAVELLING
7406	SUBSISTENCE
7500	PRINTING
7501	POSTAGE AND CARRIAGE
7502	TELEPHONE
7503	TELEX/TELEGRAM/FACSIMILE
7504	OFFICE STATIONERY
7505	BOOKS ETC
7600	LEGAL FEES
7601	AUDIT & ACCOUNTANCY FEES
7602	CONSULTANCY FEES
7603	PROFESSIONAL FEES
7700	EQUIPMENT HIRE
7701	OFFICE MACHINE MAINTENANCE
7800	REPAIRS AND RENEWALS
7801	CLEANING
7802	LAUNDRY
7803	PREMISES EXPENSES (MISC)
7900	BANK INTEREST PAID
7901	BANK CHARGES
7902	CURRENCY CHARGES
7903	LOAN INTEREST PAID
7904	HP INTEREST
7905	CREDIT CHARGES

Miscellaneous

8000	DEPRECIATION
8001	PLANT & MACHINERY DEPRECIATION
8002	FURNITURE/FIX/FITTINGS DEPRECIATION
8003	VEHICLE DEPRECIATION
8004	OFFICE EQUIPMENT DEPRECIATION
8100	BAD DEBT WRITE OFF
8102	BAD DEBT PROVISION
8200	DONATIONS
8201	SUBSCRIPTIONS
8202	CLOTHING COSTS
8203	TRAINING COSTS
8204	INSURANCE
8205	REFRESHMENTS
9998	SUSPENSE ACCOUNT
9999	MISPOSTINGS ACCOUNT

APPENDIX 2: SHORTCUT KEYS

The table below shows the various functions assigned in Sage to the F keys along the top of the keyboard. You can view this key from within Sage 50 by selecting **Help, Shortcut Keys** from the pull-down menu.

BPP PUBLISHING

APPENDIX 3: MANAGING THE BLITZ DATA AND SAGE

This appendix contains some general advice on running the BPP Blitz case study and Sage. If you will be using the case study data on a network, please consult the IT department of your organisation. (The contents of the CD could be copied to a network location and acccsscd from there.) **For information on loading the Blitz data refer to Chapter 2, section 7.**

Topics covered here are as follows.

- Setting up Sage Line 50 or Sage Instant Accounting
- Company defaults
- Backing up and restoring data using Sage

Setting up Sage

Follow the instructions in the Sage manuals for installing the software. If you are installing Sage Line 50 or Sage Instant Accounting for the first time choose the following options:

- Create a **new** company or a new set of data files

- General Business – **Standard** chart of accounts

- The **Company Details** you enter does not matter, as when you load one of the Assignments the correct Blitz company details and chart of accounts will overwrite any existing data. But, for the record, the Blitz Company details are shown below.

Blitz Limited
25 Apple Road
London
N12 3PP

- **Financial Year** – starts in August 2000

- All other options can be ignored (ie by clicking on **Next** or on **Finish**)

Backing up and restoring data using Sage

Backing up

The Sage package offers you the chance to back up your data onto a floppy disk or into another directory whenever you exit the program. You can also do this at other times by clicking on the word **File** at the top of the main window and choosing the **Backup** option. It is not a difficult procedure: it is very similar to the Save and Save As options in any other Windows program.

*If you want to keep a copy of, say, your finished versions of Assignments 1 and 2 in back up form, save the individual backup files in separate **directories** on your floppy disk.*

A single 1.44 MB floppy disk is large enough to store backups of all six Sage assignments in this book.

Restoring data

You restore data by clicking on **File** in the main window and choosing the **Restore** option.

Index

BPP
PUBLISHING

See overleaf for information on other
BPP products and how to order

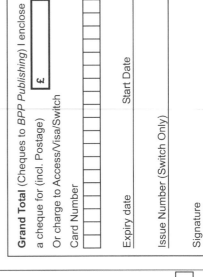

AAT Order

To BPP Publishing Ltd, Aldine Place, London W12 8AW
Tel: 020 8740 2211. Fax: 020 8740 1184
E-mail: Publishing@bpp.com Web:www.bpp.com

Mr/Mrs/Ms (Full name) _____
Daytime delivery address _____
_____ Postcode _____
Daytime Tel _____ E-mail _____

	5/01 Texts	6/01 Kits	Special offer	5/01 Passcards	Tapes
FOUNDATION (ALL £9.95)					
Unit 1 Recording Income and Receipts	☐	☐	All	☐	
Unit 2 Making and Recording Payments	☐	☐	Foundation		
Unit 3 Ledger Balances and Initial Trial Balance	☐	☐	Texts and	£4.95 ☐	£10.00 ☐
Unit 4 Supplying Information for Mgmt Control	☐	☐	Kits		
Unit 20 Working with Information Technology	☐	☐	(£80)		
Unit 22/23 Healthy Workplace & Personal Effectiveness	☐		☐		
INTERMEDIATE (ALL £9.95)		8/01 Kits			
Unit 5 Financial Records and Accounts	☐	☐	All	£4.95 ☐	£10.00 ☐
Unit 6 Cost Information	☐	☐	Inter'te Texts	£4.95 ☐	£10.00 ☐
Unit 7 Reports and Returns	☐	☐	and Kits (£65)		
Unit 21 Using Information Technology	☐	☐	☐		
TECHNICIAN (ALL £9.95)					
Unit 8/9 Core Managing Costs and Allocating Resources	☐	☐	Set of 12	£4.95 ☐	£10.00 ☐
Unit 10 Core Managing Accounting Systems	☐	☐	Technician		
Unit 11 Option Financial Statements (A/c Practice)	☐	☐	Texts/Kits	£4.95 ☐	£10.00 ☐
Unit 12 Option Financial Statements (Central Govnmt)	☐	☐	(Please		
Unit 15 Option Cash Management and Credit Control	☐	☐	specify titles		
Unit 16 Option Evaluating Activities	☐	☐	required)		
Unit 17 Option Implementing Auditing Procedures	☐	☐	(£100)		
Unit 18 Option Business Tax (FA01)(8/01 Text)	☐	☐	☐		
Unit 19 Option Personal Tax (FA 01)(8/01 Text)	☐	☐			
TECHNICIAN 2000 (ALL £9.95)					
Unit 18 Option Business Tax FA00 (8/00 Text & Kit)	☐	☐			
Unit 19 Option Personal Tax FA00 (8/00 Text & Kit)	☐	☐			
SUBTOTAL	£	£	£	£	£

TOTAL FOR PRODUCTS £ ☐

POSTAGE & PACKING

Texts/Kits

	First	Each extra	
UK (max £10)	£2.00	£2.00	£ ☐
Europe*	£4.00	£2.00	£ ☐
Rest of world	£20.00	£10.00	£ ☐

Passcards/Tapes

	First	Each extra	
UK	£2.00	£1.00	£ ☐
Europe*	£2.50	£1.00	£ ☐
Rest of world	£15.00	£8.00	£ ☐

Grand Total (Cheques to *BPP Publishing*) I enclose

a cheque for (incl. Postage) £ ☐

Or charge to Access/Visa/Switch

Card Number ☐☐☐☐☐☐☐☐☐☐☐☐☐☐☐☐

Expiry date _____ Start Date _____

Issue Number (Switch Only) _____

Signature _____

We aim to deliver to all UK addresses inside 5 working days; a signature will be required. Orders to all EU addresses should be delivered within 6 working days. All other orders to overseas addresses should be delivered within 8 working days. * Europe includes the Republic of Ireland and the Channel Islands.

REVIEW FORM & FREE PRIZE DRAW

All original review forms from the entire BPP range, completed with genuine comments, will be entered into one of two draws on 31 January 2002 and 31 July 2002. The names on the first four forms picked out on each occasion will be sent a cheque for £50.

Name: _____ **Address:** _____

_____

_____

How have you used this Interactive Text?
(Tick one box only)

☐ Home study (book only)

☐ On a course: college _____

☐ With 'correspondence' package

☐ Other _____

Why did you decide to purchase this Interactive Text? *(Tick one box only)*

☐ Have used BPP Texts in the past

☐ Recommendation by friend/colleague

☐ Recommendation by a lecturer at college

☐ Saw advertising

☐ Other _____

During the past six months do you recall seeing/receiving any of the following?
(Tick as many boxes as are relevant)

☐ Our advertisement in *Accounting Technician* magazine

☐ Our advertisement in *Pass*

☐ Our brochure with a letter through the post

Which (if any) aspects of our advertising do you find useful?
(Tick as many boxes as are relevant)

☐ Prices and publication dates of new editions

☐ Information on Interactive Text content

☐ Facility to order books off-the-page

☐ None of the above

Have you used the companion Assessment Kit for this subject? ☐ **Yes** ☐ **No**

Your ratings, comments and suggestions would be appreciated on the following areas

	Very useful	Useful	Not useful
Introductory section (How to use this Interactive Text etc)	☐	☐	☐
Chapter topic lists	☐	☐	☐
Chapter learning objectives	☐	☐	☐
Key terms	☐	☐	☐
Assessment alerts	☐	☐	☐
Examples	☐	☐	☐
Activities and answers	☐	☐	☐
Key learning points	☐	☐	☐
Quick quizzes and answers	☐	☐	☐
List of key terms and index	☐	☐	☐
Icons	☐	☐	☐

	Excellent	Good	Adequate	Poor
Overall opinion of this Text	☐	☐	☐	☐

Do you intend to continue using BPP Interactive Texts/Assessment Kits? ☐ Yes ☐ No

Please note any further comments and suggestions/errors on the reverse of this page.

Please return to: Nick Weller, BPP Publishing Ltd, FREEPOST, London, W12 8BR

REVIEW FORM & FREE PRIZE DRAW (continued)

Please note any further comments and suggestions/errors below

FREE PRIZE DRAW RULES

1   Closing date for 31 January 2002 draw is 31 December 2001. Closing date for 31 July 2002 draw is 30 June 2002.

2   Restricted to entries with UK and Eire addresses only. BPP employees, their families and business associates are excluded.

3   No purchase necessary. Entry forms are available upon request from BPP Publishing. No more than one entry per title, per person. Draw restricted to persons aged 16 and over.

4   Winners will be notified by post and receive their cheques not later than 6 weeks after the relevant draw date.

5   The decision of the promoter in all matters is final and binding. No correspondence will be entered into.